MW01106128

Outsourcing R&D in the Pharmaceutical Industry

Outsourcing R&D in the Pharmaceutical Industry

From Conceptualisation to Implementation of the Strategic Sourcing Process

Dr. Bianca Piachaud

First published 2004 by
PALGRAVE MACMILLAN
Houndmills, Basingstoke, Hampshire RG21 6XS and
175 Fifth Avenue, New York, N.Y. 10010
Companies and representatives throughout the world.

PALGRAVE MACMILLAN is the global academic imprint of the Palgrave Macmillan division of St. Martin's Press, LLC and of Palgrave Macmillan Ltd. Macmillan® is a registered trademark in the United States, United Kingdom and other countries. Palgrave is a registered trademark in the European Union and other countries.

ISBN 1–4039–3729–X hardback

This book is printed on paper suitable for recycling and made from fully managed and sustained forest sources.

A catalogue record for this book is available from the British Library.

Library of Congress Cataloging-in-Publication Data
Piachaud, Bianca, 1973–
    Outsourcing R&D in the pharmaceutical industry : from conceptualization to implementation of the strategic sourcing process / Bianca Piachaud.
        p. cm.
    Includes bibliographical references and index.
    ISBN 1–4039–3729–X
        1. Pharmaceutical industry – Research – European Union countries. 2. Drugs – Research – European Union countries. 3. Contracting out – European Union countries. 4. Research, Industrial – European Union countries – Management. 5. Cooperative industrial research – European Union countries. 6. Research and development partnership – European Union countries. I. Title : Outsourcing R & D in the pharmaceutical industry. II. Title.

HD9666.A2P53 2004
615'.1'0685—dc22   2004050111

10 9 8 7 6 5 4 3 2 1
13 12 11 10 09 08 07 06 05 04

Printed and bound in Great Britain by
Antony Rowe Ltd, Chippenham and Eastbourne.

Contents

List of Tables

List of Figures

List of Abbreviations

AIDS	Acquired Immune Deficiency Syndrome
CRO	Clinical Research Organisation
DNA	Deoxyribonucleic Acid
ECU	European Currency Unit
EU	European Union
FDA	Food and Drug Administration
GCP	Good Clinical Practice
GDP	Gross Domestic Product
GLP	Good Laboratory Practice
GMP	Good Manufacturing Practice
GNP	Gross National Product
HGP	Human Genome Project
HMO	Health Maintenance Organisation
NCE	New Chemical Entity
NDA	New Drug Application
NHS	National Health Service
OECD	Organisation for Economic Co-operation and Development
OTC	Over-the-Counter
PBM	Pharmaceutical Benefit Manager
PD	Pharmacodynamic
PEDC	Pharmaceutical Economic Development Council
PK	Pharmacokynetic
PLA	Product Licence Application
POM	Prescription-only-Medicine
PPRS	Pharmaceutical Price Regulation Scheme
R&D	Research & Development
RCT	Randomised Clinical Trial
SLA	Service Level Agreement
UK	United Kingdom
UNCTC	United Nations Centre on Transnational Co-operation
USA	United States of America

Acknowledgements

I would like to express my deep gratitude to Professor Mahendra Raj and Dr. Matthew Lynas of the Aberdeen Business School, the Robert Gordon University and to Professor Colin Carnall of Warwick Business School, Warwick University for their constructive guidance and invaluable support in providing me with critical commentaries on sourcing strategy in relation to the firm. Without their contribution, this book would not be possible.

I would also like to sincerely thank the personnel at GlaxoWellcome Research and Development, Greenford, for acting in the capacity of industry collaborator. Sincere thanks are also extended to all the other pharmaceutical companies that participated in this study and for providing me with key insights into the workings of the pharmaceutical industry. Without the contribution and participation of the personnel involved, this book would not have been feasible.

Particular thanks to my friends and colleagues for their encouragement and support, and for providing a lively discourse on the research topic. Very special thanks are extended to Dr. Fotios Moustakis for his continuous support and kindness. Thank you for providing me with the strength of spirit and the encouragement needed to complete this book and bring it to fruition.

Finally, I would like to extend my deepest gratitude to my parents Christopher and Cynthia for their love and support, and for providing me with the means to undertake this research. This book is dedicated to them with my deepest appreciation.

Preface

The pharmaceutical industry is passing through a very challenging period in its evolution with the traditional approaches to conducting pharmaceutical research and development being increasingly challenged. Successful pharmaceutical organisations have recognised the need to effectively leverage resources and so have come to rely on the wealth of expertise provided by specialist external suppliers. This practice of contracting to external organisations the services and tasks normally performed by internal departments has now become commonplace across the pharmaceutical sector. Essentially, the two most important motives for outsourcing R&D is the need to access sources of innovation in pharmaceutical research, and to reduce the excessive costs of conducting the many activities associated with the R&D process. Yet despite its growing occurrence, the outsourcing phenomenon represents a radical departure from the traditionally held philosophy of the large pharmaceutical firms, which were established with a view to maintaining superiority in as many areas of the R&D process as possible. However, this book demonstrates that if pharmaceutical firms are to successfully reap the benefits of a strategic sourcing partnership, then a fundamental change to traditional ways of thinking must also take place if it is to complement the changes that are made to how R&D is managed.

Although much of existing literature on collaborative R&D has focussed on the dynamics of alliances, joint ventures and licensing agreements between large and small firms, the academic community has failed to examine the nature of outsourcing in relation to the pharmaceutical firm. This book therefore examines the strategic aspects of outsourcing in relation to the pharmaceutical firm. Through this analysis, a 'Strategic Sourcing Model' is developed with the aim of providing a holistic view to external sourcing, from conceptualisation through to implementation and management of the outsourcing arrangement.

Introduction

Background and purpose of the book

During the past century, the pharmaceutical industry has experienced a series of dramatic changes as a result of developments in science and technology, which have spawned new opportunities for innovation. Of these transformations, the most recent to have swept the industry is what has now come to be known as the biotechnology revolution. This has served to transform the possibilities and capabilities of the traditional pharmaceutical company, and its research and development environment.

Traditionally, the R&D activities of large pharmaceutical firms were kept within the boundaries of the organisation, with various forms of collaborative agreements seen as second best to the strategic option of conducting these activities alone. More recently however, the external contribution from the standpoint of the firm to the creation and successful application of technology has steadily increased, and the innovation process has become much more interactive. When taken from the standpoint of the pharmaceutical firm, the reasons for this change in behaviour are the increasing speed and the mounting cost of innovation, the shortening of product life cycles, together with a simultaneous and systematic rise in the costs of successfully launching a new product on the market. These factors have contributed greatly to the reshaping of the pharmaceutical industry, especially with regard to the strategies employed by individual firms. The vast proliferation of technologies and approaches to research combined with increasing financial pressures has made complete self-reliance in the pharmaceutical manufacturing process impossible. This has led to a strategic change towards a high level of R&D partnership activity within the industry.

What is clear is that the pharmaceutical industry has undergone a technological paradigm shift which has allowed it to think differently about drug research and design. Today, the innovator is no longer the individual company but rather a group of agents with complementary as well as heterogeneous skills and assets that are connected with one another through an elaborate and often complex, network arrangement. Consequently, pharmaceutical innovation is no longer exclusively contained within the domain of in-house research but is to be found in a network of R&D partnerships and alliances, which the industry has embraced in all its various forms – licensing, joint ventures, mergers, alliances of both an academic and industrial nature, and outsourcing. Yet despite its growing occurrence, the outsourcing phenomenon represents a radical departure from the traditionally held philosophy of the large pharmaceutical firms, which were established with a view to maintaining superiority in as many areas of the R&D process as possible. This book therefore demonstrates that if pharmaceutical firms are to successfully reap the benefits of a strategic sourcing partnership, then a fundamental change to traditional ways of thinking must also take place if it is to complement the changes that are made to how R&D is managed.

Although much of existing literature on collaborative R&D has focussed on the dynamics of alliances, joint ventures and licensing agreements between large and small firms, the academic community has failed to examine the nature of outsourcing in relation to the pharmaceutical firm. While most authors have identified the rationale for outsourcing, its advantages and disadvantages, as well as the critical success factors required for implementing a successful sourcing strategy, very few studies have examined the effects of outsourcing on organisational processes. In terms of the pharmaceutical industry, an academic study pertaining to the impact of outsourcing on R&D organisation has yet to be identified. Accordingly, the principal aim of this book is to examine the nature of outsourcing, its effect on managerial policies, and to identify the critical success factors required for effective implementation.

Objectives of the book

The book examines the strategic aspects of outsourcing in relation to the firm, and presents a theory on the concept of outsourcing with reference to the particular needs of the pharmaceutical sector. Therefore the desired outcome is to provide a fresh insight into effectively managing the buyer–supplier relationship. Through this analysis, a 'Strategic Sourcing Model' is developed with the aim of providing a holistic view to external sourcing, from conceptualisation through to implementation and management of the outsourcing arrangement.

More specifically, the objectives of the book are to:

- *Examine* the operating environment of the pharmaceutical industry;
- *Assess* the role of outsourcing within the pharmaceutical product development process;
- *Identify* the critical success factors required for effective partnership management;
- *Determine* the impact that outsourcing has had on conventional R&D organisation;
- *Propose* solutions in the form of the Strategic Sourcing Model.

Organisation of the book

The book is composed of six chapters whose content and structure are as follows:

Chapter 1 serves as an introduction to the pharmaceutical industry, and provides a general understanding of the dynamics of the global pharmaceutical market. The chapter identifies some of the defining characteristics of the industry, and provides an overview of the three most important markets for pharmaceutical products: the United States, the United Kingdom and the European Union.

Chapter 2 examines the competitive environment of the pharmaceutical industry in relation to internal and external influences. The aim is to assess the importance of those parameters that are most likely to determine the future strategic direction of the firm. The ensuing implications for business are also discussed.

Chapter 3 examines the strategies employed by pharmaceutical companies in response to the competitive pressures faced by the industry. It explores how the biotechnology revolution provided the catalyst for collaborative R&D, and in particular, examines the rationale and motives for collaboration between pharmaceutical firms and external agents. The chapter also examines some of the implications of collaboration and how it affects the dynamics of the firm.

Chapter 4 provides a framework for appraising the 'make-or-buy' decision through a discussion of core competency theory in relation to R&D. An overview of the pharmaceutical research and development process is presented, while various modes of collaboration are also discussed.

Chapter 5 examines the nature of outsourcing and its application to the pharmaceutical product development process. The chapter provides a general overview of the rationale for outsourcing as well as the potential costs and benefits of sourcing external supply. Some of the implications of outsourcing are also discussed.

Chapter 6 examines the effect of outsourcing on the conventional R&D practices of the pharmaceutical firm. The chapter also discusses the 'Strategic Sourcing Model' which is aimed at providing a systematic framework for facilitating a coherent and holistic approach to implementing and managing the buyer–supplier relationship. To this end, a number of critical success factors are identified.

The discussion is followed by the conclusion which incorporates a short overview of the findings. Recommendations for future research are also made.

1
An Overview of the Global Pharmaceutical Industry

The global pharmaceutical industry is a dynamic industry, one which has evolved rapidly over the last century, and is one that is still undergoing considerable transformation through advances in science and technology. It is therefore appropriate that any analysis of the industry must begin by providing an overview of the workings of the pharmaceutical industry in general rather than to provide a snapshot of the industry at a particular point in time. In this way, the most salient features of the industry may be highlighted.

1.1 Foundations of the modern pharmaceutical industry

The non-commercial aspect of compounding and dispensing new drugs far predates the modern pharmaceutical industry. Pharmacopoeia that provided systematic listings of numerous drugs for various illnesses, including associated compounding and dosage requirements existed in ancient Greece and Egypt. These medicines were resurrected in Europe in the Middle Ages and became the foundation for streams of research and medical practice throughout the nineteenth century. In many ways these treatments had the characteristics of today's pharmaceutical offerings: each was part of a whole line of cures, they were administered by specialists, the dosages were indicated by the symptoms and debates existed among the experts of the day as to the correct drug and dose for a particular condition.[1]

Until the mid-nineteenth century however, the marketplace did not influence the actions of incumbents and drug development was not a business. What would be called research was instead tied to religious, academic and professional organisations and was often motivated by professional and academic goals. These broad trajectories produced streams of medical research in Germany, France and the United Kingdom (UK) through the eighteenth and nineteenth centuries, reflecting different national philosophies of medicines, research and commerce.[2]

The groundbreaking theoretical work of Pasteur on the causes of infection, including the subsequent practical development of the theory by himself and Lister, marked one of two watersheds of the modern pharmaceutical industry in the late nineteenth century. The other stemmed from earlier attempts by William Perkins who succeeded in producing the first artificial dye, called 'Aniline Purple'. German and Swiss companies, that were quick to take advantage of this discovery, began to synthesise a wide range of dyes as well as a range of compounds that were considered therapeutically useful. A striking example of such research was Aspirin, which was developed in 1899 by the German company Bayer.[3] Another German company named Hoechst, actively supported Paul Elrich's work in developing his concept of the 'magic bullet'. This involved using synthetic dyes, which were able to stain animal tissues differently, as a delivery system to carry medicines to particular parts or organs of the body.[4]

While Elrich's work stimulated further drug research both at home and abroad, very few drugs were discovered in the next twenty-five years. The advent of the Second World War however provided the stimulus for the development of Penicillin, the first antibiotic to be manufactured on a commercial scale. Flemming had discovered its anti-microbial properties in 1928, but it was a further nine years before Florey and Chain developed it as a potentially useful therapeutic agent.[5]

By this time, many of the current industry leaders were now active in the manufacture of pharmaceuticals. Some of these companies included Bayer and Hoechst of Germany, the Swiss firms Roche and Ciba-Geigy, and American firms Pfizer, Eli Lilly, Merck and Abbot Laboratories. Those in the UK included Glaxo, Beecham and the Wellcome Foundation. The competitive positions that these firms occupied in 1948 were a function of both the traits they possessed prior to the war, as well as the opportunities that were made available to them by the war itself.[6] The latter point is particularly important in the light of the serious economic distortions that existed after the war. In effect, the American pharmaceutical industry dominated a global market in which it had been second level at best, just five years previously.

Those American firms that had participated in the development of deep tank fermentation techniques had acquired large reservoirs of knowledge and an understanding about antibiotics in general, which subsequently became an important source of new drugs.[7] In addition, American firms also controlled the physical resources needed to mass-produce new antibiotics. Even if European firms could have acquired the necessary capital investment, as well as other resources, they would still have lagged in the Research & Development (R&D) competencies and manufacturing experience required to develop new antibiotics. Only the UK had relatively comparable R&D skills for developing such antibiotics and this was made possible through the ongoing research programmes conducted at Oxford University.[8] As a result, the economic potential that antibiotics represented as the dominant force of the post-war industry was largely controlled by American firms. Yet despite the 'imbalance' of resources between the Americans and the Europeans, the post-war era did witness a wave of fresh discoveries as the search for new pharmaceuticals intensified.

In 1943, Dr. Selman Waksman of Rutgers University discovered the anti-tuberculosis agent Streptomycin. This was followed by a rising tide of new products, beginning with chloramphenicol, the first broad spectrum antibiotic discovered in 1947. The tetracycline range of products were later discovered in early 1948; followed by the development of corticosteroids, oral contraceptives, antihistamines, antidepressants, diuretics, semi-synthetic penicillin and many more during the 1950s, all of which were soon patented.[9] Thus within a space of about twenty-five years, the pharmaceutical industry had been transformed from a commodity business, where each company manufactured a full range of medicines, into a research and marketing intensive conglomerate. Through the growth of synthetic organic chemistry in the 1940s, it was therefore possible to synthesise molecules previously unknown in nature and this led to the appearance of a new form of business: the research intensive pharmaceutical industry.

Developments in legislation in relation to product patent also played a major role in the evolution of the pharmaceutical industry. Such changes in legislation also enabled companies to perform particular activities that would not have been possible some years previously. For example, changes in French legislation in the mid-1940s allowed chemical companies with expertise in fermentation techniques to diversify into the pharmaceutical arena.[10] Similarly, the antibiotic era of the 1960s and early 1970s saw several smaller firms in the United States of America (USA) transformed into global industry leaders via the development of synthetic antibiotics. Eli Lilly, Abbot Laboratories, Squibb and Pfizer were all firms that grew significantly during the 1960s with product lines dominated by these drugs.[11] However, antibiotics constituted a single therapeutic class of remedy, and this focus therefore meant that firms were largely competing with similar products that were used for similar indications. As a foundation for the long-term stability of the pharmaceutical firm, the narrow product base that it provided was offset by the strength of the global demand for antibiotics. Only a few of these firms had established strong prescription drug products in therapeutic classes other than antibiotics. Consequently by the end of the 1950s, the domination of patented antibiotics by American firms had been greatly reduced by new products from firms such as Beecham, Glaxo and Wellcome within the UK.[12] Competition and technological competence had now become more widely dispersed.

As for the modern pharmaceutical industry, firms have witnessed the evolution of a new science in the form of biotechnology, in which much of the innovation effort has gone into producing new medicines for human consumption. Many of these biotechnology firms have formed close working relationships, and even financial linkages with the major pharmaceutical companies. By 1984 it was estimated that there were some 200 biotechnology companies worldwide whereas the figure today stands in the order of approximately 1000.[13]

It is clear that the companies which comprise the modern pharmaceutical industry derive from a number of different backgrounds, and operate in diverse sectors of the industry. According to Pradhan (1983) this diversity of operation may be classified into five key groups.[14]

1. Medicinal chemical manufacturers Medicinal chemical manufacturers produce the active ingredients used in pharmaceutical preparations. This component of the industry produce bulk organic and inorganic chemicals and their derivatives, prepare drugs from animal sources, synthesise or isolate products into pure form, and extract active agents from botanical drugs and herbs such as alkaloids.

2. Biological product manufacturers These firms produce vaccines, serums, toxins and analogous products such as allergenic extracts, normal blood serums and blood plasma for human use, as well as products for diagnostic use.

3. Ethical pharmaceutical manufacturers Ethical pharmaceutical manufacturers formulate drugs into suitable dosage forms such as tablets, capsules, injectables, elixirs, syrups and ointments. The products are called 'ethical' because they are promoted to healthcare professionals and are available to individuals through hospitals, pharmacies, chemist shops, and physicians through the provision of written or oral prescriptions.

4. Proprietary product manufacturers These firms produce preparations that are common home remedies used for the relief of minor temporary ailments. Their products are promoted to the general public and can be purchased without prescription.

5. Private formula or Brand manufacturers These companies manufacture products for distributors, or produce generic and home remedies under their own brand name.

1.2 Characteristic features of the pharmaceutical industry

Although the industry's history is comparatively brief, its accomplishments are nonetheless impressive. A flood of lifesaving medicines have emerged from the world's research laboratories over the past half century which have helped combat many fatal diseases whilst eradicating others. To this end, pharmaceutical manufacturers have in essence helped to alter mortality patterns in many parts of the world. However these achievements alone do not make the pharmaceutical industry a worthy subject of study. The performance of these companies, whether measured in terms of product development, prices, safety or efficacy is a vital determinant of health, and therefore merits further investigation.

The first notable characteristic of the pharmaceutical industry is that despite the fact that government regulation varies from one country to the next; all governments intervene extensively to ensure that national standards and requirements are met. The second most prominent feature of the industry is its unique configuration. At one end there exist teams of organic chemists, biochemists, biophysicists and pharmacologists, while at the other there are complex and competitive networks for distribution and promotion, which operate in highly regulated markets. Contained between these two critical components of the industry is the production of pharmaceuticals. Another equally important aspect of the industry is the extent of internationalisation and diversity that exists. Although much of the industry's research and production occurs in only a very few countries, the market for pharmaceuticals is a global one. Similarly, the types of firms that comprise the pharmaceutical industry are just as varied and diverse as their markets. Although a small number of companies dominate every phase of the pharmaceutical manufacturing process, the membership of the industry is actually very large. In addition to the multinationals and their subsidiaries, the industry also includes many small- and medium-sized firms, niche producers and other specialists defined by their research and marketing strengths, or by the specific types of drugs they produce. Nevertheless, the characteristics, and in particular the elements of structure and morphology which so clearly differentiate the ethical drug industry from any other are much more wide ranging and diverse. It is therefore important to highlight those characteristics that give the industry its unique features.

1. The scale of the industry   One of the most obvious features of the pharmaceutical industry is that it is characterised by a very large number of small- to medium-sized manufacturers, and a small number of large multinationals that are international in operation. These large firms are concentrated in the highly industrialised OECD (Organisation for Economic Co-operation and Development) nations.

Table 1.1 provides a typology of the global pharmaceutical industry. Group A contains those countries that have the largest and most sophisticated pharmaceutical and scientific base. All types of firm exist in each of these countries but it is the large, integrated corporations that dominate in every case. In the field of research, unlike that of the development and distribution of pharmaceutical products, research centres have not migrated to other parts of the world. As a result, this component of the industry is highly centralised being located either in the country where the firm has its headquarters, or in another country with comparable research capabilities and an advanced scientific base. It is estimated that more than 90 per cent of the new drugs that have been marketed by the industry since 1960 were discovered and developed in one of the countries contained in this group (see Table 1.2).[15] Within Group B however; the industry consists of only innovative and reproductive firms. Here research, production and distribution capabilities are modest in comparison with the industry leaders.

Table 1.1   Typology of the global pharmaceutical industry

Group A		Group B	
Countries with a significant research base		Countries with innovative capabilities	
Belgium	Switzerland	Australia	India
France	United Kingdom	Austria	Ireland
Germany	United States	Canada	Israel
Italy		China	Portugal
Japan		Denmark	Republic of Korea
Netherlands		Finland	Spain
Sweden		Hungary	Russia

Table 1.2   Top 20 pharmaceutical companies in 2002

Rank	Company	Country	Sales Revenue ($ million)
1	Pfizer	USA	28 288
2	GlaxoSmithKline	UK	27 060
3	Merck & Company	USA	20 130
4	AstraZeneca	Sweden/UK	17 841
5	Johnson & Johnson	USA	17 151
6	Aventis Pharma	France/Germany	16 639
7	Bristol-Myers Squibb	USA	14 705
8	Novartis	Swiss	13 547
9	Pharmacia & Upjohn	Sweden/USA	12 037
10	Wyeth	USA	10 899
11	Eli Lilly & Company	USA	10 385
12	Abbot Laboratories	USA	9 700
13	Roche	Swiss	9 355
14	Schering-Plough	USA	8 745
15	Sanofi-Synthelabo	France	7 045
16	Takeda	Japan	7 031
17	Boehringer-Ingelheim	Germany	5 369
18	Bayer AG	Germany	4 509
19	Schering AG	Germany	3 074
20	Sankyo	Japan	2 845
	Total sales for 2002		246 355

Source: Data taken from the European Federation of Pharmaceutical Industries (EFPIA) Website: *http://www.efpia.org*, the Association of the British Pharmaceutical Industry (ABPI) Website: *http://www.abpi.org.uk* and the Pharmaceutical Research and Manufacturers of America (PhRMA) Website: *http//www.phrma.org*

Table constructed by author.

2. Innovation   The pharmaceutical industry is critically reliant on continuing flows of new products, which are the results of R&D. The profitability and ultimately the survival of the major firms in the industry depend on the maintenance of competitive position, which in turn is determined by the rate of innovation. As the importance of innovation has increased, so have the costs of the innovative effort. In 1981 the industry spent just over $5 billion on research and development activities, while in 1998 the research intensive drug companies spent $40 billion, with the biotechnology sector spending a further $9 billion on human healthcare.[16] In 2002, the industry average rose to approximately $45 billion (see Table 1.3).

The average R&D intensities in the pharmaceutical industry have been rising steadily, resulting in a squeeze on profits in an industry that

Table 1.3   R&D expenditure of the top 20 pharmaceutical companies in 2002

Rank	Company	Country	R&D Expenses ($ million)
1	Pfizer	USA	5176
2	GlaxoSmithKline	UK	4108
3	Johnson & Johnson	USA	3957
4	Aventis Pharma	France/Germany	3235
5	AstraZeneca	Sweden/UK	3069
6	Novartis	Swiss	2799
7	Roche	Swiss	2746
8	Merck & Company	USA	2677
9	Pharmacia & Upjohn	Sweden/USA	2359
10	Bristol-Myers Squibb	USA	2218
11	Eli Lilly & Company	USA	2149
12	Wyeth	USA	2080
13	Abbot Laboratories	USA	1562
14	Schering-Plough	USA	1425
15	Boehringer-Ingelheim	Germany	1304
16	Sanofi-Synthelabo	France	1152
17	Takeda	Japan	1020
18	Bayer AG	Germany	1014
19	Schering AG	Germany	896
20	Sankyo	Japan	641
	Total R&D for 2002		45587

Source: Data taken from the European Federation of Pharmaceutical Industries (EFPIA) Website: *http://www.efpia.org*, the Association of the British Pharmaceutical Industry (ABPI) Website: *http://www.abpi.org.uk* and the Pharmaceutical Research and Manufacturers of America (PhRMA) Website: *http//www.phrma.org*

Table constructed by author.

has historically enjoyed above average returns. Between the 1970s and the 1990s, average R&D intensities in the main drug producing countries rose from 7–8 per cent to 10–12 per cent.[17] The main causes for this have been an increase in regulatory requirements together with diminishing returns to the drug discovery process, combined with the new directions of the innovative effort itself. Research projects have increasingly been aimed at understanding the cause of a particular disease as well as studying the side effects of drugs on the human body. Furthermore, a greater research effort has been directed towards understanding more complex diseases such as cancer and arthritis for which no easy solutions are forthcoming. Added to this has been the growing complexity and significant cost of the industry's move into the field of biotechnology. Recent estimates suggest that the cost of getting a New

Chemical Entity (NCE) to market stands at approximately $611 million over a twelve-year period.[18] Of this, $441 million is spent on failure, while $170 million is spent on success.

These trends have created turmoil in an industry that has been dominated by approximately 30 firms over the past 50 years. In the early 1990s, these firms were responsible for 75 per cent of total expenditures on R&D in the pharmaceutical sector and 60 per cent of global sales of an estimated total of $200 billion.[19] However despite the considerable and increasing risk associated with pharmaceutical innovation, investments in R&D still continue to grow. Whilst in the late 1970s most large pharmaceutical companies spent on average 10 per cent of their sales revenue on R&D, today that figure stands at more than 15 per cent.[20]

Although the industry witnessed a high rate of growth with regard to patenting activity between 1980 and 1995, this has failed to produce a corresponding increase in the flow of new medicines to market. According to the Centre for Medicines Research International, only 35 NCEs (as opposed to reformulations of existing products), were launched on the world market in 1998, making it the lowest total since 1979.[21] Studies conducted by Alexander *et al.* (1995)[22] and Drews *et al.* (1996)[23] also support the case of an 'innovation deficit' within the pharmaceutical industry (see Table 1.4). This phenomenon may however reflect the existence of a 'plateau' in the life cycle of the industry.

3. *Pharmaceutical products* Pharmaceutical products can be divided into three broad categories. The first consists of pharmaceuticals that are available to the public only on prescription. Known as 'prescription only' medicines or POMs, these products are dispensed by an authorised dispensing unit. The second consists of those products that are only

Table 1.4 Global NCE introductions 1961–92

Period	Germany	UK	Switzerland	USA	Japan
1961–70	112	45	66	202	80
1971–80	91	29	48	154	74
1981–90	67	28	48	142	129
1990	3	5	4	10	7
1991	3	4	4	13	12
1992	2	5	2	10	14
Total	278	116	172	531	316

Source: Data taken from the Centre for Medicines Research International (CMR) Website: *http://www.cmr.org*

Table constructed by author.

available through a pharmacist; while the third group consists of those products for which no prescription is required. These are referred to as 'over-the-counter' medicines or OTCs. A further distinction can also be made between patented and non-patented pharmaceuticals, and between branded, commodity and corporate products. Branded products refer to those sold under a brand name, while commodity products refer to those sold under the generic name of the basic active chemical ingredient. In the case of corporate products, these are the ones where the company name or an abbreviation of it plays a conspicuous part in the identification of the product.

Pharmaceutical products also possess unique characteristics: (1) the demand for pharmaceuticals is a derived demand. Due to the demand for healthcare, pharmaceutical products are also demanded; (2) the task of choosing a particular product is usually made by a prescribing physician and not the consumer; (3) few patients have to pay the full cost of the consumption of medicines; and (4) all pharmaceutical products require marketing approval before they are released into the healthcare market.

4. The distribution of pharmaceutical products   Although the distribution of pharmaceutical products begins with the manufacturer, it is later dispersed amongst one or more different types of outlets comprising wholesalers, dispensing pharmacists, dispensing physicians, health shops, mail order companies (in the case of the USA) and hospitals. It is from one of these outlets that the consumer then receives the product. However, the supply of pharmaceuticals from manufacturer to outlet is sometimes varied since the scale of trade along each path differs. For example, in the UK around a half of hospital supplies are obtained directly from industry, with the other half from pharmacies. Conversely in the case of Ireland, France and Germany over 80 per cent of hospital supplies come via pharmacies that procure for industry and wholesalers.[24]

5. The patent System   According to the United Nations Centre on Transnational Corporations (UNCTC) there are four forms of patent protection applicable to the pharmaceutical industry. These include (1) patents on the composition of matter; (2) product patents which are granted for a specific product; (3) process patents that relate to production process rather than to the finished product; and (4) application or process patents.[25] Product and process patents are by far the most widely used by incumbents and it is the product patent system that is generally recognised to be more effective in protecting the innovator from competition. This system of patent protection is currently employed in the UK, Belgium, Germany, France, Italy, Japan, Switzerland, Ireland and the USA. However, these countries also allow the use of process patents.[26]

Studies conducted by Walker (1971) suggest that pharmaceutical patents are a highly significant resource control, and thus a very important source of market power for the drug firms holding them.[27] However, recent studies suggest that this source of market power is being eroded through the reduction of 'effective patent life' (which refers to the patent life remaining after the drug has been introduced to the market), brought about by changes in government regulation pertaining to new drugs.

In most developed countries nominal patent life, which is the period from patent grant to the end of patent life, is in excess of 15 years. Nevertheless, studies conducted by Schwartzman (1976) have indicated that the effective life from product introduction to the end of patent protection is actually declining. This raises significant problems for pharmaceutical companies since the 'pay-back' period of a new drug is even shorter than the effective patent life.[28] Since product patent ensures monopoly profits until the time the drug is superseded by a new discovery, innovating firms cannot rely on the effective patent life to recoup the full costs of developing and marketing the product.

6. *Pharmaceutical pricing policies*   The pricing of pharmaceutical products is one of the more controversial issues associated with the pharmaceutical industry. Because of this, price controls are one of the most prevalent forms of government intervention. Almost all governments regulate product prices, though a few choose to limit profits or to influence prices through more direct means. For example, in some European countries the price of a product is intrinsically linked to the governing authority's approval for marketing a drug. If there is no agreement on price between the company and the regulatory body, marketing approval will therefore not be granted.

Although the actual methods of price control differ, most countries choose to regulate both retail and wholesale prices. Price-fixing procedures also vary, depending on whether the drug is a new entrant to the domestic market or an established product for which a price increase is requested. In some instances governments merely stipulate the maximum price, while others set the actual price and apply different pricing policies for locally produced products and imports.[29] Therefore when examining the basic principles of pharmaceutical pricing, a number of factors become pertinent to its consideration. These include the existence of reimbursement lists (lists of products for which the health insurance system will or will not pay a contribution to), the incidence of conditions treated, the number of dispensing pharmacists and physicians per capita, and the incentives and intensity to prescribe.

7. Government regulation of the industry   Public policy initiatives to contain escalating healthcare costs has redefined the boundaries and economics of medical care across most OECD economies. Although the specifics of the reforms differ from country to country, their underlying thrust requires healthcare systems to come to grips with essential market realities and the need to justify medical interventions on the grounds of efficacy and efficiency. Although medicinal purchases rarely account for more than 15 per cent of total healthcare spending, the pharmaceutical industry is an obvious target for reform.[30] For one, pharmaceuticals are among the few easily identifiable commodity inputs in an otherwise far less transparent and politically complex process. There is also the widely held view that pharmaceutical prices are excessively high, and that average pre-R&D operating profit margins of 40 per cent are neither necessary to recoup companies' research investments nor are conducive to bringing truly innovative therapies to market.[31] As a result, little policy resistance exists to containing costs through pharmaceutical price controls, reference pricing, generic substitution and selective prescriptions. Whether OECD countries will evoke more market reforms depends on the range of available policy alternatives and the reactions of market participants to them.

1.3   The pharmaceutical industry in the European Union

The removal of trade barriers in the European Union (EU) has allowed firms to have access to an integrated population of more than 350 million, making it the largest consumer market in the world.[32] While a market of this size provides tremendous opportunities for many companies, the removal of trade barriers also threatens many firms by allowing new competition to enter their markets. As of December 2003, there were 15 national markets within the EU, each with its own approval and registration procedures, as well as individual pricing structures. Accordingly, the impact of changes in EU legislation has been particularly important for a regulated industry such as pharmaceuticals.

The pharmaceutical industry in Europe consists of over 2000 companies. It is the largest trade bloc in the world with individual countries having considerable individual market shares (France 20 per cent, Germany 19 per cent, the UK 16 per cent and Italy 11 per cent). In 2002, the total production of pharmaceuticals amounted to (Euro) €160 billion, while exports totalled €130 billion, and imports €90 billion.[33] This is illustrated in Table 1.5.

Table 1.5 EU pharmaceutical industry overview 1990–2002

Industry	1990 (€ million)	2000 (€ million)	2001 (€ million)	2002 (€ million)
Production	63 142	130 060	149 792	160 000
Exports	23 180	89 065	114 182	130 000
Imports	16 113	63 863	80 353	90 000
Trade Balance	7 067	25 202	33 829	40 000
R&D Expenditures	7 941	17 202	18 869	19 800
Employment (units)	500 762	559 410	582 341	582 500

Source: Data taken from the European Federation of Pharmaceutical Industries (EFPIA) Website: *http//www.efpia.org*

Table constructed by author.

1.3.1 The role of Member Governments

The objective of controlling the admission of new pharmaceutical products to national markets is to make sure that products are safe, effective and of good quality. It is up to the applicant to satisfy the regulatory authority, whose purpose is to evaluate the evidence and to come to a decision. Thus, the objectives of healthcare regulators operating in the EU are threefold.[34] The first is to make sure that pharmaceuticals are effective and safe to use. Accordingly, the admission of new products to national markets is strictly controlled since proof of safety, efficacy and quality is universally required. This process of registration applies not only to genuinely novel products but also to those based on existing ingredients, although the requirements for these are generally less stringent. The second objective is to limit pharmaceutical expenditure. In all Member States, each country is strongly committed to the provision of healthcare, whether directly or indirectly through national insurance agencies. Expenditure for this purpose has greatly increased over the past twenty-five years and economy measures have therefore become necessary. The third objective is to encourage the development of the local pharmaceutical industry for strategic reasons, not only as a source of income and employment, but to also economise on foreign exchange. Measures employed for this purpose may be either positive or negative, with positive measures relating to subsidies and tax concessions, while negative measures include tariffs and restrictions on imports.

1.3.2 Healthcare expenditure

In 2000, European countries spent from 6 per cent (Luxembourg) to 10.6 per cent (Germany) of their Gross Domestic Product (GDP) on

Table 1.6 Total spending on healthcare as a percentage of GDP 1970–2000

Country	1970 (% GDP)	1980 (% GDP)	1990 (% GDP)	2000 (% GDP)
Austria	5.3	7.6	7.1	8.0
Belgium	4.0	6.4	7.4	8.7
Denmark	–	9.1	8.5	8.3
Finland	5.6	6.4	7.9	6.6
France	–	–	8.6	9.5
Germany	6.3	8.8	8.7	10.6
Greece	6.1	6.6	7.5	8.3
Ireland	5.1	8.4	6.6	6.7
Italy	–	–	8.0	8.1
Luxembourg	3.6	5.9	6.1	6.0
Netherlands	–	7.5	8.0	8.1
Norway	4.4	7.0	7.8	7.8
Portugal	2.6	5.6	6.2	8.2
Spain	3.6	5.4	6.6	7.7
Sweden	6.9	9.1	8.5	7.9
United Kingdom	4.5	5.6	6.0	7.3
Europe	4.9	7.1	7.5	8.1

Source: Data taken from the European Federation of Pharmaceutical Industries (EFPIA) Website: *http//www.efpia.org*

Table constructed by author.

healthcare. The rate of increase of expenditure over 1990–94 (30 per cent) has been almost halved since 1985–90. As a share of healthcare expenditure, pharmaceuticals represent approximately 15 per cent of GDP across Europe, a figure that has remained somewhat consistent since 1980. In 1996, investment in the 12 leading European countries totalled (European Currency Unit) ECU10.5 billion, a fivefold increase over 1980. Since then, the pace of growth has slowed markedly to 3 per cent, per annum. In 2001, the countries with the highest expenditure on healthcare were Germany (€21 355 million), France (€16 309 million), UK (€10 502 million), and Italy (€11 608 million).[35] This is evident in Table 1.6.

1.3.3   Pricing and reimbursement

National governments are the principal customers of the pharmaceutical industry and it is they who bear the major cost of the total healthcare bill. Yet despite the common approach to healthcare provision, Member States all employ differing policies with regard to the pricing of pharmaceutical products. In Italy for example, the stipulated price is very much based on a multiple of direct production costs, which include the costs of raw materials and labour. In France, the price is determined by an assessment of the R&D effort, the therapeutic advantage offered and the novelty of a new drug. In Britain, a key determinant is the use of profit controls which limits the return on investment the pharmaceutical company can make on its sales to the National Health Service (NHS). Each year firms negotiate with the Department of Health a global return on capital based on sales incurred to the NHS during the course of the previous year. The rate of return is fixed on an individual basis, taking into consideration the scale and nature of the company's relevant investments and activities, and associated long-term risks.[36] Provided that the rate is not systematically exceeded, firms are then free to set the prices of new products as they see fit.

Several Member States however, do not fix the prices of individual drugs. The Netherlands for example operates a free market, relying on other means to control total pharmaceutical expenditure. Denmark in effect does the same. Germany, formerly the European example of free pricing, now restricts reimbursement under the national health insurance system to a fixed sum for multi-source products with identical active ingredients. This divergence in prices is therefore the result of a combination of factors caused by: (1) deferring price control and reimbursement schemes among the Member States; (2) the volume of drug consumption; (3) manufacturing costs; (4) transfer pricing; (5) product patent status; (6) the profit margins of wholesalers and pharmacists; (7) value-added tax rates and (8) varying packaging sizes.[37] In addition to controlling the prices of ethical drugs, all Member States employ further control mechanisms in the form of 'positive' and 'negative' lists of drugs.

1.3.4 Demand characteristics

Traditionally, prescription medicines have represented about 80 per cent of the total value of the EU pharmaceutical market, with the remaining 20 per cent accounted for by OTC treatments. Because the majority of consumers are insured against the cost of prescription drugs, there is only a modest concern with price. Instead, greater concern is placed upon the effectiveness and usefulness of the drug. To this end, patients must rely on the prescribing doctor (who is also principally interested in the drug's effectiveness and therapeutic value), for guidance. Thus, the physician and the general practitioner play an important role in influencing the scale and nature of pharmaceutical consumption.

Within the EU there exist vast differences in the propensity to consume drugs, with southern Europeans generally consuming more drugs per capita than northern Europeans.[38] Allied with these different consumption patterns are also variations in price, with the highest consumers having lower prices than those that consume less. This would suggest that there is an element of price elasticity in relation to the demand for pharmaceutical products. An additional factor is the existence of differing medical traditions and sociological factors between northern and southern Europe which also plays an influencing role in determining consumption patterns across Europe. Thus it is evident that the EU pharmaceutical market is not only divided by wide variations in wealth, but also by attitudes towards the use of medicines. Since such attitudes are not only embodied in the training and behaviour of doctors but also in the expectations of patients, it is likely that such variations will remain in the years to come.

1.3.5   Supply characteristics

Taking the EU as a whole, 43 per cent of sales are by indigenous companies to their own national markets. In every Member State the locally owned industry has a disproportional large share of the local market, with the exception of France and Germany where market share exceeds 50 per cent. As a result, the supply of pharmaceuticals to the Member States of the EU is highly internationalised. Supplies from companies based in other EU countries make up a further 23 per cent of total supply with German, British and French firms comprising the most important sources. Nevertheless, the very strong international orientation of Belgium, Danish and Dutch companies is also apparent. In addition, approximately 34 per cent of supplies come from firms based outside of the EU, with American firms accounting for 23 per cent of the total market and Swiss firms 11 per cent.[39]

With regard to the actual supply of pharmaceutical products, companies employ two principle sources. One is by trade and the other is through local manufacture. Local production by affiliates of foreign multinationals is mostly common in the larger countries, especially where restrictive attitudes towards imports formally existed. Countries such as France, Italy and Spain fall into this category. Among the smaller countries of the EU, Greece and Portugal have encouraged the development of local production facilities through a variety of means. Although foreign companies dominate their local markets, most of the products consumed are made locally.

1.3.6   Future opportunities and threats

The pharmaceutical industry in the EU is unique in nature and therefore possesses significant differences to those of other markets. The differences that do exist are largely due to the advanced stage of market development that has taken place, as well as the multi-country nature of the overall market structure. To this end, the opportunities and threats facing the EU pharmaceutical industry are:

Opportunities for EU firms (1) the emergence of the Eastern European markets; (2) mutual and harmonised approval of drugs, leading to swifter market entry and possibly to longer patent protection; (3) an increase in the elderly population, which will enable continuous growth for pharmaceuticals in established therapeutic segments; and (4) standardisation of delivery systems, leading to economies of scale in production.

Threats facing EU firms (1) greater bargaining power of buyers, especially by member governments; (2) efforts to encourage the consumption of generic drugs in order to reduce the cost of healthcare; (3) increasing rivalry within the industry brought about by consolidation; and (4) an increase in parallel importing.

1.4 The British pharmaceutical industry

In a report published by the Pharmaceutical Economic Development Council (PEDC) in 1986, particular attention was placed upon the importance of the British pharmaceutical industry to the economy as a whole. Essentially, this was because growth within the industry has been very satisfactory over a long period, innovative companies have continued to remain profitable, and the industry's high rate of internationalisation has led to a substantial balance of trade surplus.[40] This robust development of the nationally based pharmaceutical industry has led to considerable benefits in employment and investment, and has contributed greatly to enhancing the nation's technological capacity. For the PEDC, the industry therefore typifies the type of sector that must be sustained and developed if international competitiveness is to be ensured.

1.4.1 Market size

The British pharmaceutical industry is large and has grown rapidly since the interwar years. Over the past decade, output of pharmaceutical products rose by 92 per cent in the ten years upto 1992, double the 46 per cent increase by the whole of the chemical industry, including that of pharmaceuticals. The comparable figure for the whole of the UK manufacturing sector was 16 per cent, while for all UK production output the figure stood at 22 per cent. Yet despite this enviable growth (which has made pharmaceuticals one of the top four industries along

Table 1.7 UK pharmaceutical sales 1980–2002

Year	NHS sales (£ million)	OTC sales (£ million)	Total (£ million)
1980	826	246	1 246
1990	2 533	855	3 388
2000	7 073	1 658	8 731
2001	7 753	1 711	9 464
2002	8 601	1 734	10 335

Source: Data taken from the Association of the British Pharmaceutical Industry (ABPI) Website: *http//www.abpi.org.uk*

Table constructed by author.

with aerospace, defence and electronics), the industry is small when compared with world output and accounts for no more than 6 per cent of total production.[41]

In the United Kingdom there are approximately 400 individual manufacturers of both national and international origin, which together comprise one of the largest pharmaceutical markets in the world. Essentially, the British pharmaceutical industry comprises two sectors: that of prescribed pharmaceuticals and OTC medicines (see Table 1.7). While the OTC market is very much reliant on the domestic sector, prescribed pharmaceuticals encompasses a global dimension. The industry also enjoys an outstanding record of innovation with five of the ten most prescribed medicines having their origins in the UK. British pharmaceutical companies conduct nearly a quarter of all industrial research and development in the UK and spend more than a fifth of their turnover on R&D. To this end, the industry invested £3.2 billion in researching and developing new medicines in 2002. Pharmaceutical export sales have also grown rapidly, with exports for 2002 estimated at £10.33 billion, thereby creating a record trade surplus of £2.6 billion, while exports per employee accounted for nearly £150 000.[42] The country therefore enjoys the third largest trade surplus in pharmaceuticals, behind that of Switzerland and Germany.

1.4.2 The regulatory regime

There is a common perception within the industry that it has been subjected to severe restrictions on its commercial operations, through the imposition of government controls on the prescribing of drugs in addition to further restrictions on profitability, prices and promotion. In the UK, ethical pharmaceutical prices are controlled via the Pharmaceutical Price

Regulation Scheme (PPRS) which was first introduced in 1957 by the Department of Health to counter the monopoly position conferred by the patent system.[43] The objective of this scheme was to control the cost of healthcare for the government while at the same time, allowing for a satisfactory but restricted return on capital. To further increase its influence in this area, the government also introduced a 'limited list', which was further divided into a 'white list' and a 'black list'. The 'white list' contained the medicines that the doctors could prescribe under the NHS regime, while the 'black list' contained those drugs for which the NHS would not reimburse the prescription charges. The 'limited list' was first introduced in 1985 and initially covered seven pharmaceutical categories. These included analgesics for mild to moderate pain, benzodia zapine sedatives and tranquillisers, cough and cold remedies and, tonics and vitamins.[44]

Additionally, the pharmaceutical industry's profit on sales to the NHS (which is its largest customer) is also effectively controlled by the PPRS. Under this scheme, each firm is allocated a target rate of return on capital by the regulatory authority. Other restrictions include profit regulation through prices. For example, if the 'Annual Financial Returns Forecast' for a forthcoming year highlights a deficit on the profitability target, the government would then grant an increase in price. However if the profitability target is exceeded, the company would then be required to pay the excess to the government, or accept a year without further price increases.

1.4.3 Prescribed pharmaceuticals

Prescribed pharmaceuticals play a dominant role in the British pharmaceutical industry (see Table 1.8). Much of the development that has taken place within this area of pharmaceuticals is derived from the offshoots of conglomerate chemical companies that had the personnel and the research facilities to sustain a pharmaceutical industry. GlaxoSmith Kline is an example of a company grown out of healthcare, while Medeva is a modern company focussed on further developing research originally carried out by other companies. The most recent sector to have emerged is that of biotechnology, which specialises in the development of novel biopharmaceutical products.

Due to the diversity of its incumbents, the British pharmaceutical industry is able to successfully cover all therapeutic groups. However the four most important categories consist of the following:

1. *Gastrointestinal system*   Although not the largest therapeutic group in terms of net ingredient cost or the number of prescription items it

Table 1.8   Top 20 UK pharmaceutical products in 2002

Rank	Product	Manufacturer	Total sales (£ million)
1	Zocor	Merk Sharp & Dhome	310.67
2	Lipitor	Pfizer	237.70
3	Zoton	Wyeth	229.03
4	Istin	Pfizer	170.23
5	Losec	AstraZeneca	162.77
6	Zyprexa	Eli Lilly & Company	121.07
7	Seretide	GlaxoSmithKline	115.54
8	Lipostat	Bristol-Myers Squibb	109.86
9	Tritace	Aventis Pharma	104.33
10	Sereven	GlaxoSmithKline	101.91
11	Efexor	Wyeth	100.22
12	Seroxat	GlaxoSmithKline	96.15
13	Zestril	AstraZeneca	81.17
14	Cardura	Pfizer	79.49
15	Flixotide	GlaxoSmithKline	76.15
16	Omeprazole	Generic	75.78
17	Cipramil	Lundbeck	75.37
18	Plavix	Sanofi/Bristol-Myers Squibbb	72.87
19	Zoladex	AstraZeneca	67.89
20	Vioxx	Merk Sharp & Dhome	64.77

Source: Data taken from the Association of the British Pharmaceutical Industry (ABPI) Website: *http//www. abpi.org.uk*

Table constructed by author.

contains, the gastrointestinal system has been the most successful therapeutic group particularly because of ulcer healing drugs such as Zantac and Tagamet.

2. Cardiovascular   The second largest category is the cardiovascular group of therapies. Although it is the second largest in terms of the number of prescription items, it is the largest group in terms of healthcare expenditure. This is because disease of the circulatory system is cited as the main cause of mortality in Britain. Nevertheless, the growth of this segment has begun to slow in recent years.

3. Respiratory system   This category continues to attract strong growth with healthcare spending escalating at a rate in excess of 10 per cent per annum. Since 1980, the value of the market for respiratory medicines has increased fourfold.

4. Central nervous system   This is the fourth of the major therapies. As measured by the cost of prescription, it is the cheapest of the four therapies to treat. In 1980, it attracted over 80 million prescriptions.

1.4.4   OTC pharmaceuticals

This comprises a much smaller segment than prescribed pharmaceuticals, but is one that is growing rapidly. In Britain, growth has been achieved in the OTC market through the movement of drugs from ethical to OTC status. Growth has also been further stimulated by a receptive public who has been willing to accept self-medication as a viable alternative to a doctor's prescription. This sector has also been boosted by the move to OTC status by two of the world's leading drugs which include Zantac and Tagamet, and by several other pharmaceutical products. The OTC sector is also supported by household brand names such as 'Disprin' and 'Paracetamol' contained in the analgesics group, as well as by a multitude of cough and cold remedies. Many of these products are sold at a small price, and are therefore cheaper than the prescribed alternative. The expansion of the OTC sector has also been helped by recent rises in prescription charges. Accordingly, the top three categories of OTC medicines are analgesics (pain killers), cough and cold remedies and treatments for stomach and digestive disorders. Although these products have for a long period of time been the mainstays of the OTC industry, other categories of product have also grown in importance. These include remedies for hay fever and vitamin supplements, as well as anti-smoking therapies all of which have come into prominence through the release of medicines formally restricted by prescription. These movements infer opportunities for further expansion into the OTC sector.

1.4.5   Future opportunities and threats

The British pharmaceutical industry is one that possesses a national comparative advantage both technologically and in the balance of overseas trade. The companies that comprise this sector do form a recognisable industry, competing among themselves in the field of high technology healthcare. Official policies of actively encouraging the technological leaders, both foreign as well as domestic, at the expense of less ambitious followers, has allowed for particular comparative advantages to be built up.[45] As a result, the pharmaceutical industry in Britain has progressed at a rate, and in directions that could not have previously been foreseen. In assessing its future, the opportunities and threats facing the British pharmaceutical industry are:

Opportunities for British firms   (1) the highly internationalised nature of the British pharmaceutical industry indicates that particular opportunities will emerge as the world economy develops and trade is further liberalised. The most notable of these opportunities is the emergence of the Eastern European and Chinese markets; (2) the prospect of increased patent protection to 20 years in Europe will be particularly beneficial to UK pharmaceutical manufacturers with an international presence; (3) regulatory and market changes will encourage significant growth in the OTC and generic sectors. This will be particularly beneficial to flexible, fast moving multinationals, and to the overall UK pharmaceuticals market.

Threats facing British firms   (1) the pressure on costs and the harmonisation of standards will lead to a significant rationalisation of European operations, with low cost countries tending to benefit at the expense of higher cost centres like that of the UK; (2) the growth in the OTC and generic sectors as previously indicated will be a particular threat to those firms whose product line is weak, and (or) which may have many off patent products.

1.5   The American pharmaceutical industry

The regulatory system in the United States is one of the more unusual amongst the industrialised countries. This is because American pharmaceutical companies operate in an essentially free market where the government pays only a small proportion of overall healthcare costs. This absence of price controls has spawned a number of indirect methods for limiting consumption charges, and as a result, many cost conscious health plans have emerged to satisfy the growing demand for cheaper medicines. One such example is the emergence of the Health Maintenance Organisation (HMO), which provides a list of medical services and drugs that are paid for by a flat monthly fee. A policy of generic substitution is also aggressively pursued, together with a number of other measures.

The USA currently devotes a higher percentage of its GDP to healthcare than any other major industrialised country. However its expenditure on pharmaceuticals (12 per cent) meets the average for any industrialised country. In 2002, total domestic sales of ethical pharmaceuticals were estimated at $145 billion, making it the largest pharmaceutical market in the world (see Table 1.9). In 1996, the export of pharmaceutical products exceeded imports by $173 million (2.4 per cent of 7.33 billion), with more than half of that sum going to Europe. Despite the pressures faced by the research intensive pharmaceutical industry, American-based companies invested approximately $32 billion in research and development activities in 2002. This represented a 7.7 per cent increase over expenditures in 2001, and is more than triple the investment made in 1990 (see Table 1.10). Of the total investment, $26.4 billion was spent within the

Table 1.9   US domestic sales and overseas sales 1970–2002

Year	Domestic sales ($ million)	Overseas sales ($ million)	Total ($ million)	Annual change (%)
2002	145 213	51 464	196 677	10.1
2001	130 715	47 886	178 602	10.9
2000	115 881	45 199	161 081	10.4
1990	38 486	19 838	58 325	17.8
1980	11 788	10 515	22 304	17.8
1970	4 552	2 084	6 636	–

Source: Data taken from the Pharmaceutical Research and Manufacturers of America (PhRMA) Website: *http//www.phrma.org*

Table constructed by author.

Table 1.10   US domestic R&D and overseas R&D expenditures 1970–2002

Year	Domestic R&D ($ million)	Overseas R&D ($ million)	Total ($ million)	Annual change (%)
2002	26 384	5 667	32 051	7.7
2001	23 502	6 220	29 772	14.4
2000	21 363	4 667	26 030	14.7
1990	6 802	1 617	8 420	14.9
1980	1 549	427	1 976	21.5
1970	566	52	618	–

Source: Data taken from the Pharmaceutical Research and Manufacturers of America (PhRMA) Website: *http//www.phrma.org*

Table constructed by author.

USA with $5.6 billion spent abroad. American companies also spent 18.2 per cent of domestic sales on R&D inside the USA, which made it the highest percentage of any major US industry.[46]

1.5.1   The retail market

In the United States, the economics of selling pharmaceuticals through retailers was determined to a greater extent by the Federal Food, Drug and Cosmetics Act of 1938.[47] Regulations promulgated under this act effectively required that a drug be dispensed through a doctor's prescription whenever the Food and Drug Administration (FDA) determined that the drug could not be labelled in such a way that consumers could use it safely.[48] Because of this prescription only limitation on pharmaceutical sales, the physician performed a gate keeping function, as it was he who selected the drug that was to be purchased by the patient. Prior to the 1950s, the law in most US states actually allowed the pharmacist to select any manufacturer's chemicals or compounds in compliance with a doctor's order. During the 1950s however, all state governments enacted laws requiring pharmacists to use a specific manufacturer's products if the physician wrote the prescription using the firm's brand name, rather than the drug's chemical name. Today unless specifically forbidden by the physician, the pharmacist can once again use a generic equivalent even when a brand name is used in writing the prescription. Such flexibility was achieved in 1984 through further amendments to the legislation governing pharmaceuticals, which helped to hasten the entry of multi-source products into the market following patent expiration.[49]

In 1984, the US Congress passed the Drug Price Competition and Patent Term Restoration Act (also known as the Waxman-Hatch Act) which simplified the requirements for FDA approval of generic substitutes.[50] This Act was designed to encourage competition, but it did not independently generate wide spread declines in the profitability of pharmaceutical companies for several reasons. First, the habits of doctors and pharmacists were apparently difficult to break. Although state laws allowed a pharmacist to substitute a generic equivalent for a branded drug, unless the prescription indicated otherwise, this form of substitution was uncommon. Second, the credibility of independent companies specialising in the production of generics was undermined by a scandal in 1989, which reinforced the reluctance of physicians and pharmacists to substitute generic equivalents for branded drugs. By the early 1990s however, several major pharmaceutical companies entered the generics market by establishing their own divisions specialised in generics, or by obtaining interests in companies that sold generic substitutes. Third, the Waxman-Hatch Act did not diminish pharmaceutical profitability because purchasers of pharmaceutical products had just begun to develop the institutional structure necessary for comparing the prices of therapeutic alternatives. Therefore, by simplifying the requirements for FDA approval on generics, Waxman-Hatch on the whole greatly reduced the research necessary for entry into some therapeutic segments. With the subsequent growth of managed care, the demand for generics increased dramatically. By the middle of 1994, generic drugs accounted for approximately 37 per cent of all pharmaceutical prescriptions.[51]

1.5.2 Managed care and Health Maintenance Organisations

The 1980s also witnessed new forms of retailing that took advantage of the newly established changes to selling practice. Many of these new forms of retailing were tied to the rise of HMOs and other similar managed care insurance plans which were used as a method of controlling healthcare costs in the United States. Such payment plans were especially important for covering the cost of hospital and physician services. The concept of 'managed care' refers to systems in which responsibility for payment is linked more tightly to decision making about the provision of healthcare services than it is in traditional indemnity insurance plans.[52] Although managed care takes a variety of contractual forms, it typically provides members with medical insurance and basic healthcare services, using volume and long-term contracts to negotiate discounts with healthcare providers.

Managed care organisations monitor the prescription and usage of drugs through a variety of means. For instance, HMOs often use formularies, or lists of drugs that are compiled by committees of pharmacists and physicians who compare the prices and therapeutic value of various products. Member physicians are therefore encouraged to specify drugs from the formulary when prescribing. The existence of such formularies has therefore increased awareness among physicians about pharmaceutical prices and has helped create a process through which administrators could align incentives. Logically then, the next step towards lowering healthcare costs was to impose greater restriction in formulary management. To this end, an organisation with an 'actively managed' formulary relied on a relatively short list of acceptable drugs that favoured generics.

This use of formulary substitution allowed pharmacists to go beyond generic equivalents and to use near substitutes, a practice previously found only in the clinical environment, unless expressly forbidden. As a result, patent protected manufacturers were brought into much closer competition with one another. Furthermore, such measures also helped to shift the power of retail transactions towards the payer. In this environment, only truly unique new drugs have the potential to sustain high profit margins due to a lack of substitute rivals. With or without government mandates it was estimated that by 1997 close to 80 per cent of insured Americans would be enrolled in managed care programmes, an increase of approximately 20 per cent since 1982.[53]

1.5.3 The clinical market

In contrast to retail sales, sales to hospitals and government institutions provide a more competitive setting due to the use of formularies and bulk purchasing. Since the formulary represents the products that the hospital can use for certain indications, pharmaceutical companies are therefore obliged to bid to have their products included. In most instances hospitals select a shortlist of choices from which physicians working in the hospital can make a selection. By the 1960s, American hospitals had determined that such a list could satisfy over 99 per cent of their medical needs. Pharmaceutical firms therefore discovered the hospital market to be far more cost conscious than the retail sector since the cost of a drug is initially borne by the hospital. Although these costs are included in the patient's hospital bill, hospitals can improve margins and cut total spending by controlling product acquisition costs. For example, a drug that needs to be administered twice a day rather than four times daily could reduce nursing and pharmacy expenditures by up to 50 per cent.[54] It could then be argued that because the drug offers an effective selling point, it could in fact justify a higher price. However in reality, clinical revenues are in fact much lower, with some branded products sold at only 20 to 30 per cent of their wholesale price. Since insurance reimbursement for particular services from both public and private sources were set at fixed levels in the 1990s, hospitals and similar clinical purchasers have therefore become increasingly sensitive to price.[55]

1.5.4   Future opportunities and threats

Although for much of the past century, Europe has been the leader in pharmaceutical innovation, in 1997, the United States overtook Europe for the first time in terms of both innovative effort (level of R&D investment) and in the output of its innovative activity (the number of NCEs discovered). The American pharmaceutical market has grown twice as fast as its European counterpart over the past decade. In 1990, the major European research-based companies spent 73 per cent of their worldwide R&D expenditures in EU territory, whereas in 1999, these same companies spent just 59 per cent.[56] Of this transfer of R&D investment, the United States was the principal beneficiary. The American pharmaceutical industry is therefore both the largest and best-developed market within the global pharmaceutical industry and as such, it has considerable opportunities to exploit over the next few years. Nevertheless, there are also some formidable problems that the industry will have to contend with in the short to medium term.

Opportunities for American firms   (1) within established markets the demand for pharmaceutical products will continue to grow; (2) the ageing populations in most OECD countries will create demand in a number of therapeutic areas, some of which remain underdeveloped; (3) advances in biotechnology will provide a principle source of many new drugs; and (4) the OTC market is expanding and is expected to grow significantly in the future.

Threats facing American firms   (1) the desire of major drug purchasers such as HMOs and other managed care organisations to reduce expenditure on medicines will result in downward pressure on prices; (2) the rise of generic drug companies will continue to present a significant threat to the industry; (3) increased government regulation will further exacerbate the drug approval process, particularly in the case of 'me-too drugs'; (4) industry consolidation will create ever larger rivals of roughly equal size, leading to increased competition; and (5) changing social attitudes could have a number of spill-over effects any of which could affect ethical drug consumption and the type of treatment people seek.

Notes

1. W. Bogner and H. Thomas, *Drugs to Market: Creating Value and Advantage in the Pharmaceutical Industry* (Oxford: Pergamon, 1996).
2. Ibid., Bogner *et al*. (1996).
3. J. Taggart, *The World Pharmaceutical Industry* (London: Routledge, 1993).
4. Ibid., Taggart (1993).
5. Ibid., Taggart (1993).
6. W. Bogner and H. Thomas, *Drugs to Market: Creating Value and Advantage in the Pharmaceutical Industry* (Oxford: Pergamon, 1996).
7. Ibid., Bogner *et al*. (1996).
8. Ibid., Bogner *et al*. (1996).
9. J. Taggart, *The World Pharmaceutical Industry* (London: Routledge, 1993).
10. A. Earl-Slater, 'Pharmaceuticals', in P. Johnson (ed.), *European Industries: Structure, Conduct and Performance* (London: Edward Elgar, 1993), pp. 75–100.
11. W. Bogner and H. Thomas, *Drugs to Market: Creating Value and Advantage in the Pharmaceutical Industry* (Oxford: Pergamon, 1996).
12. Ibid., Bogner *et al*. (1996).
13. L. Galambos and J.L. Sturchio, 'Pharmaceutical Firms and the Transition to Biotechnology: A Study in Strategic Innovation', *Business History Review*, 72, Issue 2 (1998), pp. 250–78.
14. S. Pradhan, *International Pharmaceutical Marketing* (Westport: Quorum Books, 1983).
15. R. Ballance, J. Pogany and H. Forstner, *The World's Pharmaceutical Industries* (London: Edward Elgar, 1992).
16. 'Consolidation Enters a More Frantic Phase: Pharmaceutical Companies Face Increasing Pressures to Merge', *Financial Times*, 15 March 1999.
17. M. Sharp and P. Patel, 'Europe's Pharmaceutical Industry: An Innovation Profile', in A. Arundel and R. Garrelfs (eds), *Innovation Measurement and Policies*, Conference Papers, Luxembourg (1996), pp. 163–8.

18. T. Jones, *The Chances of Market Success in Pharmaceutical Research and Development* (London: Office of Health Economics, 1999), pp. 29–38.
19. M. Sharp and P. Patel, 'Europe's Pharmaceutical Industry: An Innovation Profile', in A. Arundel and R. Garrelfs (eds), *Innovation Measurement and Policies*, Conference Papers, Luxembourg (1996), pp. 163–8.
20. P. Ramirez and A. Tylecote, 'Technological Change in the Pharmaceutical Industry: A Literature Review from the Point of View of Corporate Governance', *Unpublished Papers*, Sheffield University Management School, University of Sheffield, Sheffield (1999), pp. 1–35.
21. Ibid., pp. 1–35.
22. D.L. Alexander, J.E. Flynn and L.A. Linkins, 'Innovation, R&D Productivity and Global Market Share in the Pharmaceutical Industry', *Review of Industrial Organisation*, 10 (1995), pp. 197–207.
23. J. Drews and S. Ryser, 'Innovation Deficit in the Pharmaceutical Industry', *Drug Information Journal*, 30, Issue 1 (1996), pp. 97–108.
24. A. Earl-Slater, 'Pharmaceuticals', in P. Johnson (ed.), *European Industries: Structure, Conduct and Performance* (London: Edward Elgar, 1993), pp. 75–100.
25. United Nations Centre on Transnational Corporations (UNCTC), *Transnational Corporations and the Pharmaceutical Industry: Introduction and Summary of Findings* (New York: United Nations, 1979), pp. 1–163.
26. Ibid., pp. 1–163.
27. H. Walker, *Market Power and Price Levels in the Ethical Drugs Industry* (Indianapolis: Indiana University Press, 1971).
28. D. Schwartzmann, *Innovation in the Pharmaceutical Industry* (Baltimore: John Hopkins University Press, 1976).
29. R. Ballance, J. Pogany and H. Forstner, *The World's Pharmaceutical Industries* (London: Edward Elgar, 1992).
30. R. Boscheck, 'Healthcare Reform and the Restructuring of the Pharmaceutical Industry', *International Journal of Strategic Management: Long Range Planning*, 29, Issue 5 (1996), pp. 629–42.
31. Ibid., pp. 629–42.
32. P. Chaudhry, P. Dacin and J.P. Peter, 'The Pharmaceutical Industry and European Community Integration', *European Management Journal*, 12, Issue 4 (1994), pp. 442–53.
33. European Federation of Pharmaceutical Industries and Associations (EFPIA), 'The Pharmaceutical Industry in Figures: 2003 Update' (Brussels: EFPIA, 2003), *http://www.efpia.org/6_publ/Infigures2003.pdf*
34. M.L. Burstall, *Research on the Costs of Non-Europe: Basic Findings* (Brussels: Economists Advisory Group, 1992), pp. 21–48.
35. European Federation of Pharmaceutical Industries and Associations (EFPIA), 'The Pharmaceutical Industry in Figures: 2003 Update' (Brussels: EFPIA, 2003), *http://www.efpia.org/6_publ/Infigures2003.pdf*
36. M.L. Burstall, *1992 and the Regulation of the Pharmaceutical Industry* (London: The IEA Health and Welfare Unit, 1990), pp. 23–42.
37. P. Chaudhry, P. Dacin and J.P. Peter, 'The Pharmaceutical Industry and European Community Integration', *European Management Journal*, 12, Issue 4 (1994), pp. 442–53.
38. M.L. Burstall, *Research on the Costs of Non-Europe: Basic Findings* (Brussels: Economists Advisory Group, 1992), pp. 21–48.

39. Ibid., pp. 21–48.
40. J. Taggart, *The World Pharmaceutical Industry* (London: Routledge, 1993).
41. R. Caines (ed.), *Keynote Market Review: The UK Pharmaceutical Industry*, Second Edition (London, 1995), pp. 7–15.
42. Association of the British Pharmaceutical Industry (ABPI), 'Facts and Statistics from the Pharmaceutical Industry: Pharmaceuticals and the UK Economy' (London: ABPI, 2003), *http://www.abpi.org.uk/statistics/section.asp? sect = 2*
43. J. Taggart, *The World Pharmaceutical Industry* (London: Routledge, 1993).
44. R. Caines (ed.), *Keynote Market Review: The UK Pharmaceutical Industry*, Second Edition (London, 1995), pp. 7–15.
45. T. Corley, 'The British Pharmaceutical Industry Since 1851', *Discussion Paper*, XII, Series A, Centre for International Business History, University of Reading, Reading (2000), pp. 1–33.
46. Pharmaceutical Research and Manufacturers of America (PhRMA), 'Pharmaceutical Industry Profile 2003' (Washington, DC: PhRMA, 2003). *http://www.phrma.org/publications/publications/profile02/index.cfm*
47. W. Bogner and H. Thomas, *Drugs to Market: Creating Value and Advantage in the Pharmaceutical Industry* (Oxford: Pergamon, 1996).
48. Ibid., Bogner *et al.* (1996).
49. C. Tarabusi and G. Vickery, 'Globalisation in the Pharmaceutical Industry, Part II', *International Journal of Health Services*, 28, Issue 2 (1998), pp. 281–303.
50. National Institute for Health Care Management (NIHCM), *A Primer: Generic Drugs, Patents and the Pharmaceutical Industry* (Washington DC: NICHAM, 2002).
51. Ibid., pp. 1–28.
52. A. McGahan, 'Industry Structure and Competitive Advantage', *Harvard Business Review*, 72, Issue 6 (1994), pp. 115–24.
53. W. Bogner and H. Thomas, *Drugs to Market: Creating Value and Advantage in the Pharmaceutical Industry* (Oxford: Pergamon, 1996).
54. Ibid., Bogner *et al.* (1996).
55. A. McGahan, 'Industry Structure and Competitive Advantage', *Harvard Business Review*, 72, Issue 6 (1994), pp. 115–24.
56. European Federation of Pharmaceutical Industries and Associations (EFPIA), 'The Pharmaceutical Industry in Figures: 2003 Update' (Brussels: EFPIA, 2003), *http://www.efpia.org/6_publ/Infigures2003.pdf*

2
Competition in the Pharmaceutical Industry

The pharmaceutical industry is influenced by, and reacts to, the external environment within which it operates. The strategies adopted by firms within the industry are chosen on the basis that they may provide the most effective defence against a number of external pressures as well as internal determinants. In examining the competitive environment of the pharmaceutical industry it is therefore important to assess those parameters that are most likely to determine future strategy. To this end, a structural analysis of competition which focuses on both the operating and remote environments of the pharmaceutical industry is required.

2.1 The operating environment of the pharmaceutical industry

The purpose of formulating competitive strategy is to associate a company with its operating environment. Although the external environment is wide ranging, encompassing social as well as economic forces, the key aspect of a firm's external environment is the industry in which it operates. Industry structure can greatly influence and determine the competitive forces at play, as well as the strategies available to the firm. Forces outside of the industry are also significant as they are capable of affecting all firms within the industry. Therefore what is important is the capacity of firms to effectively deal with these external forces. Since the intensity of competition in an industry is rooted in its underlying economic structure, the degree of competition that exists goes well beyond the behaviour of current competitors. Competition in an industry instead depends on five basic competitive forces, whose collective strength determines the ultimate profit potential of the industry.

In an analysis of the competitive strategy of industries and competitors, Porter (1980) proposed a model for effectively conducting a structural analysis of competition within a given industry. Although the underlying structure of an industry is reflected in the strength of the five competitive forces, these must be distinguished from the many short-term factors that can affect competition and industry profitability in a transient way. For example, fluctuations in economic conditions over the business cycle can influence the short-term profitability potential of all firms within an industry. Factors such as material shortages, industrial action and sudden increases in demand can also play an influencing role. Although such factors may have tactical significance, the focus of any analysis must be to identify the basic, underlying characteristics that provide the parameters in which competitive strategy can be set. Given that each firm within an industry possesses a unique set of strengths and weaknesses for effectively coping with the structure of the industry even though industry structure can, and does, shift gradually over time; an understanding of the structure of an industry must always be the starting point for any subsequent strategic analysis. To this end, each of the five competitive forces will be examined in relation to the pharmaceutical industry.

2.1.1 Barriers to entry in the pharmaceutical industry

New entrants to an industry bring new capacity, the desire to gain market share as well as substantial resources. The threat of entry into an industry depends on the barriers to entry that are present, together with the reaction of existing competitors to the new entrant. If the barriers to entry are high and the potential entrant can expect sharp retaliation from established incumbents, then the actual threat of entry into the industry will be low. For the pharmaceutical industry, such barriers to entry are closely related to the nature of the specialised product. Owing to the degree of sophistication, differentiation, technical expertise, reliability, safety and the level of R&D investment required (combined with the lengthy period of innovation, government regulation and stringent quality control measures), acceptable products are in themselves difficult to produce without any guarantee of commercial success.[1] For these reasons, the barriers to enter the pharmaceutical industry are indeed high.

1. Economies of scale   Economies of scale refer to a decline in the unit cost of a product (or function that goes into producing a product) as the absolute volume per period increases. Such scale economies deter entry by forcing the potential entrant to enter on a large scale, thereby risking severe retaliation from existing firms or from entering on a small scale, thereby accepting a cost disadvantage – both of which are undesirable options. Since the pharmaceutical industry is a highly research intensive sector, it is characterised by a small number of innovative firms all of which have considerable resources in R&D, and which encompass highly developed economies of scale. As such, a considerable increase in the size and economic potential of the firm is required before any significant effect can be made on the industry.

2. *Product differentiation* Product differentiation occurs when established firms achieve brand identification and secure customer loyalty through the efforts of past advertising, customer service, product differentiation, or simply by being the first to enter the market. Differentiation creates barriers to entry by forcing potential entrants to spend considerable resources in order to overcome established customer loyalties. Since this carries with it the potential of considerable start-up losses, product differentiation can therefore act as a significant deterrent to entry. In the case of the pharmaceuticals, this is a very important feature of the industry and one that represents a substantial entry barrier. Given the cost and the scale to which R&D is required to produce a new product offering, most innovative firms keep within the boundaries of a select number of therapeutic areas in which they are expert. Even the largest pharmaceutical manufacturers do not cover more than a few therapeutic segments at any given time.[2] Accordingly, a very high degree of product differentiation exists within the industry.

3. *Capital requirements* The need to invest considerable financial resources in order to compete creates a significant barrier to entry, especially when the capital required is for investments in R&D, acquiring new technology and the development of appropriate infrastructure facilities. When applied to the pharmaceutical sector, this barrier to entry is almost insuperable given the degree to which capital and financial resources are required. This together with the inherent risks involved with innovative research makes this a formidable barrier to entry.

4. *Government regulation* Another significant barrier to entry is government policy. Governments have the power to limit or even foreclose entry into an industry through a variety of means. Such measures can include the enforcement of licensing requirements and the imposing of restrictions on the access to raw materials. Given the nature of its output, the pharmaceutical industry is one of the most highly regulated industries in the world. Since all governments agree that pharmaceuticals must meet the universally required standards of safety, efficacy and efficiency before a product is permitted on to the market, a number of

stringent clinical trials must be completed before a drug is approved. Regulations in the form of manufacturing guidelines also exist to ensure product quality, not only in areas of manufacturing, processing and the packaging of pharmaceutical preparations, but also for medicinal chemicals as well. This requires that those therapeutic ingredients both medicinal as well as chemical, together with other raw materials must be of a consistently high quality. Production facilities must also be constructed and operated in accordance with predetermined standards and employees are required to receive special training, while an elaborate system of records on operating procedures must also be maintained. Government policy also plays a pivotal role in the issue of licenses and patents. As such, the stipulations imposed through government regulation therefore present a very high entry barrier.

2.1.2   Bargaining power of buyers in the pharmaceutical industry

Buyers compete with an industry by forcing down prices, bargaining for better quality and by bringing competitors into competition with each other. Customer groups can vary in size and form as they may be large, small, single, grouped, consumers, commercial, industrial or institutional, the nature of which influences their position within the market and hence their bargaining power.[3] Thus the power of each of the most important buyer groups depends on the position of the buyer within the market and on the relative importance of its purchases from the particular industry. In the pharmaceutical industry the demand for medicines is a derived demand and depends on the incidence of disease and the need to prevent certain types of illnesses. The information required to diagnose an ailment and to determine a suitable course of treatment is held by an intermediary, usually a specialist in healthcare. Therefore in most instances product choice is not determined by the buyer but by the specialist instead, given the commonly held view that the 'doctor knows best'. This delegation of choice makes these medical practitioners a strong purchasing group with considerable buying power. Buyers within the pharmaceutical industry are also composed of a third party, which in most industrialised nations is the purchaser of national healthcare or national governments. Therefore when applied to the context of prescription pharmaceuticals, buyers to the pharmaceutical industry are composed of a three-tier-group: namely healthcare specialists (doctors), consumers (general public) and healthcare purchasers (national governments).[4] When taken either collectively or as a component of the group, these customers are able to exert considerable buying power through bargaining leverage and price sensitivity. However, such reactions are counter balanced because of the buyer's dependency on the industry for novel treatments and products.

1. Buyer concentration   If a single or group of buyers purchases a large volume of industry output, the profitability of that industry will be highly dependent on retaining the custom of this purchasing group. In the case of the pharmaceutical industry, the degree of concentration amongst buyers is demonstrated through the purchasing patterns of hospitals. Due to budgetary constraints faced by many hospitals today, many become increasingly cost conscious consumers. This has forced many to form buying groups in order to obtain quantity discounts on their pharmaceutical purchases. Furthermore, hospitals have also turned to buying cheaper generic versions of medicines whenever possible. These changes in practice have placed these institutions in a very strong negotiating position *vis-à-vis* the industry.

2. Switching costs   It is possible for a buyer to face few switching costs if such costs have the capacity to restrict the buyer to a particular seller. However if switching costs are low, the bargaining power of the buyer will therefore be higher. For the pharmaceutical industry, such costs are present and can play an important role in certain segments of the market. An area in which this is particularly potent is the institutional sector where the switching costs incurred in changing from one medical device manufacturer to another is often so expensive that it can act as a significant entry barrier. Switching costs can also manifest itself in the form of information and is applicable in instances where a doctor becomes accustomed to prescribing a particular drug, produced by a specific manufacturer, for a particular illness. Because of this deep confidence in the drug, considerable persuasion is required on the part of a competitor's sales representative to convince the doctor to switch to an alternative product.

3. Threat of backward integration   If buyers are either partially integrated or pose a threat of backward integration, they are in a strong position to demand bargaining concessions from their customers. When applied to the pharmaceutical industry, the ability to integrate backwards is of little consequence given that firms are able to capitalise on this collusion by raising the price of a new product in a particular therapeutic segment. Such increases in price can be justified for two reasons. The first is to recover investments in R&D and second to take advantage of the dependency of the buyer upon the pharmaceutical product. Through this, buyers are placed in a vulnerable position in relation to the manufacturers.

4. Full information Where the buyer is well informed about the pattern of demand, actual market prices, and even supplier costs; the buyer can achieve greater bargaining leverage than in instances where such information is limited. When taken in the context of the pharmaceutical industry, buyers can exert much of their bargaining power through the search for information. Nevertheless, this form of bargaining power cannot be exerted in isolation given that buyers need the support of strong infrastructure in the form of political stability as well as government legislation. Since both these features are found in all industrialised nations there is comprehensive legislation governing pharmaceutical manufacture, which is rigorously enforced.

2.1.3 Threat of substitute products in the pharmaceutical industry

A substitute product may be defined as a product that can perform the same function as a branded product.[5] Substitutes limit the potential returns of a manufacturer by placing a ceiling on the prices that firms can potentially charge for a product. The more attractive the price alternative offered by the substitute, the greater the effect on industry profits. Given that the number of substitute products available will vary widely from one industry to the next, each product will differ in how it replaces the branded product and the extent to which it represents a threat.

Although the threat of substitute products within the pharmaceutical industry has historically been weak, changes in socio-economic trends indicate changes to established practices. Therefore if the definition of a substitute product is to be limited to alternative medicines such as anthropomorphic medications and homeopathic remedies, then the threat of such alternatives within markets of the developed countries is far from serious.[6] However if the term 'substitute' is taken to include generic products, then its effect is significantly different.

Given that there are no significant R&D costs involved, the manufacture of generics is considerably less expensive than those of branded products. This of course provides an immediate cost advantage, especially when taken in the context of institutional buying. Since the risk of product failure is also minimised as all relevant testing is initially conducted by the pioneering firm, production costs are significantly reduced and hence, product prices. Although it can be argued that without the inclusion of generic products, the threat of substitutes is very weak, when generics are included, the threat of competition changes immediately. Porter (1980) therefore suggests that the substitute products that deserve the most attention should ideally be those products that:

a. are subject to trends which improve their price performance trade-off with the industry's product;
b. are produced by industries earning high profits;
c. can rapidly come into play if some development increases competition in the industry and causes a price reduction or an improvement in performance.[7]

When applied to the pharmaceutical industry it is clear that it adheres to all the specified criteria. (1) Those generic products that do not involve any innovative cost have an obvious advantage in terms of price. (2) The pharmaceutical industry has always been associated with above average profits. (3) The removal of patent protection supports increased competition.

However, it must be pointed out that not all governments choose to adopt a generic drug policy despite the significant price advantages offered and the reduced element of risk. This is because the buyer segment of the pharmaceutical industry which comprises doctors, hospitals and national governments may not always be in mutual agreement regarding the usage of generic products. Therefore it can be argued that on the whole, the threat of substitutes (excluding generics) is still weak. However this is a feature that cannot be disregarded given the socioeconomic changes taking place, which influence the ways in which generics are viewed. The threat of generics therefore has the potential to develop into a much more potent force in the future.

2.1.4   Bargaining power of suppliers in the pharmaceutical industry

Suppliers can exert bargaining power over participants in an industry by threatening to raise prices or to reduce the quality of purchased goods and services. Such measures can affect the total profitability of an industry by making it unable to recover cost increases through its own pricing systems. The pharmaceutical industry consists of many groups of suppliers who vary in size, as well as in the types of products supplied to the industry. Examples include raw chemicals, bulk pharmaceuticals, biological products, packaging and laboratory equipment, as well as production machinery. However, the products supplied do not include tangible commodities alone since the pharmaceutical industry also purchases a number of services from outside suppliers. Such services include quality control, clinical testing, provision of industrial information and certain R&D activities. Taken within this context, suppliers to the pharmaceutical industry can be grouped into three categories, each of which highlights a different aspect of supplier bargaining power.

1. *Classification according to the firms served* The pharmaceutical industry is highly fragmented, consisting of a very small number of large multinationals and a very large number of small to medium sized domestic firms which produce branded and generic products. Each type of firm employs different approaches and negotiation strategies in relation to its suppliers. Thus, the methods employed are based upon the purchasing power of the firm and its dependence upon the supplier's products. In the context of the large multinationals, firms tend to produce their own complex active ingredients and easy to synthesise products in-house, not merely in the interests of security, but also to ensure an efficient, reliable and cheap source of supply. Despite the move towards more tapered integration (producing some of their needs for a given product in-house, while purchasing the rest from outside suppliers), owing to the sheer size and nature of these multinational corporations, these companies are placed in a strong position to achieve the quality and level of service they would demand and expect from outside suppliers at reasonable industry prices.[8]

2. *Classification according to the products supplied* This is especially important when applied to supplies of raw chemicals, bulk pharmaceuticals and biological products, since the concentration of suppliers is higher than the concentration of buyers in the pharmaceutical industry. Due to this feature, those firms with the greatest purchasing capacity, or those with a better buying relationship with their suppliers are placed in a stronger bargaining position than those without.

3. *Classification according to the regulations and national drug policies of the buyer's country* The legislation governing the country in which the buyer is located is important because it has a direct impact upon the legislative demands made upon the pharmaceutical industry. Therefore the more developed the country's national healthcare policy, the greater the legislation governing the industry itself. Such legislation not only affects domestic pharmaceutical manufacturers, but national and multinational subsidiaries as well. It is therefore inevitable that the same legislation will extend to the suppliers of chemical and biological products since these products form the basic ingredients of pharmaceutical output. Accordingly, suppliers to the pharmaceutical industry are also subject to the same quality control standards as those applied to the final product. Each supplier is therefore controlled and vetted by the

buyer prior to being accepted as an official supplier. Consequently suppliers must meet the same rigorous standards of quality, as do their pharmaceutical buyers. This implies that the bargaining power of suppliers *vis-à-vis* the industry is somewhat evenly balanced on the whole.

2.1.5   Intensity of rivalry in the pharmaceutical industry

The degree of rivalry within an industry can be active or passive, intense or moderate. It exists as a driving force between firms within an industry as they compete for the best positions in the market place. Rivalry occurs because one or more competitors foresee an opportunity to improve market position and share. Therefore competitive manoeuvres by one firm will have an effect on all competitors within an industry, and can provoke counteractive measures by incumbents. Such behaviour therefore implies that firms are mutually dependent. When examined in the context of the pharmaceutical industry, rivalry tends to be concentrated in five key areas.

1. The number of competitors   Where there are equally balanced competitors, the outcome of rivalry is a much more evenly distributed market share. This invokes an urgent need to protect existing market share, and often results in in-fighting and retaliation amongst competitors. However in instances where the industry is concentrated or dominated by a few firms, the leader(s) can impose discipline, as well as play a co-ordinating role within the industry by enforcing price leadership strategies. In the case of the pharmaceutical industry the concentration of research-based pharmaceutical firms is very high, with the top one hundred firms accounting for about 80 per cent of pharmaceutical sales worldwide.[9] Due to this high level of concentration, combined with the semi-oligopolistic nature of the therapeutic markets, the level of rivalry that exists within the pharmaceutical industry is very high.

2. Lack of differentiation or switching costs   Where the product or service is a commodity, the choice exercised by the buyer is to a great extent influenced by the price of the product and the level of service provided. This leads to fierce competition amongst competitors and thereby, a volatile environment. With regard to product differentiation, this provides a degree of insulation against competitive rivalry through customer loyalty and the preferences attached to particular products. In the case of the pharmaceutical industry, switching costs are substantial, while product differentiation remains high due to the singularity of therapeutic sectors and the specificity of modern drugs. This is often further exacerbated if the active ingredient makes different formulations and drug administrations pharmaceutically difficult to achieve, or too expensive to replicate. Such differences rest in the bioavailability of the active substance (a factor which is not visibly obvious), thus creating a need for specialised and expensive personal to promote the product to the appropriate buyer segment.[10] For this reason, it is not uncommon for the firm that is first to enter the market with a new formulation to generally retain the largest proportion of market share for a given therapeutic segment. Under these circumstances, the intensity of rivalry is greatly reduced.

3. *Diverse competitors*   Competitors with diverse strategies, origins, cultures, values and relationships employ different approaches to competing in the market place. Such firms will interpret market signals very differently, making it hard to establish a set of rules for competing within a particular industry given that strategic choices agreeable to one competitor will not be suitable to another. Foreign competitors also add diversity to an industry while the same is true of small, domestic firms. In the pharmaceutical industry, the companies that comprise this sector are diverse because they derive from a number of different backgrounds and operate in different therapeutic segments. This leads to greater competition between the different players.

4. *High strategic stakes*   Rivalry can become more intense if a number of firms have a high strategic stake within the industry. In such instances, the ambitions of these firms may often prove to be destabilising because of the competitive strategies employed. This is because aims are often expansionary in nature, accompanied with a willingness to sacrifice profitability in the short-term. In the case of the pharmaceutical industry, the long innovation time required, combined with a low probability of discovering a truly novel NCE often results in fierce competition for proprietary products amongst pharmaceutical manufacturers. In an industry where the ability to be first on the market with a new product is synonymous with market leadership, the intensity of rivalry is very high.

5. *High exit barriers*   Exit barriers include economic and strategic motivations that keep companies competing in business even though they may be earning low or negative returns on their investments. The major sources of exit barriers as identified by Porter (1980) are:

a. Specialised assets that are particular to the business or location. These either have low liquidation values, or have high transfer or conversion costs;

b. Fixed costs of exit that includes labour agreements and resettlement costs;

c. Strategic inter-relationships which are the inter-relationships between the principal business unit and other components of the company that relate to image, marketing ability, access to financial markets and shared facilities;

d. Emotional barriers arising from a deep connection to a particular business, loyalty to employees, fear for one's own career and pride, all of which contribute to management's unwillingness to make economically justified exit decisions;

e. Government and social restrictions that result from government dissuasion to exit the industry based upon concerns for job losses and the effect on the regional economy.[11]

If any one of the factors that affect the intensity of competition within an industry changes, there will also be a corresponding change to the degree of rivalry amongst competitors. To illustrate this point, such transformations could relate to (1) changes in technology, which can change the level of fixed costs; (2) new corporate cultures brought about by merger and acquisition activity within an industry; or (3) through changes brought about by industry growth.[12] When applied to the pharmaceutical industry, the high financial investments needed to become a viable competitor translates into extremely high exit barriers for any firm wishing to leave the industry. This factor helps to maintain the intensity of rivalry amongst firms over the long term.

2.2   The remote environment of the pharmaceutical industry

Competition in the remote environment of the pharmaceutical industry consists of four key factors and can be examined using Political, Economic, Social and Technological (PEST) analysis. These four elements affect all companies in every sector of the pharmaceutical market and drive the high levels of R&D expenditure by the industry.

2.2.1   Political Forces

1. Regulatory requirements   The pharmaceutical industry is governed by legislation that is both rigorous and complex. Each new product is required to undergo comprehensive clinical testing prior to being marketed. Since all regulatory bodies demand independent evidence pertaining to a drug's efficacy, safety and quality, vast amounts of data are required. In the case of the FDA for instance, the required data can sometimes exceed more than one hundred thousand pages.[13] The purpose of this exercise is to establish the intended use of the drug, the dosing regime, the contra-indications that can occur, its interactions with other prescription medications and to identify the 'Adverse Event' patterns associated with the drug. Such information is later used for labelling and in compiling user guides.[14] In some countries, evidence to justify the intended price of the product must also be produced.

2. Price and profit controls   Nearly 80 per cent of all pharmaceutical sales occur in the USA, Japan and the EU. Although there continues to be mounting pressure on pharmaceutical prices in all of the three major markets, the American pharmaceutical industry has yet to experience central government interference on pharmaceutical pricing. Despite the fact that the industry has enjoyed annual growth rates of approximately 10 per cent per annum over the past ten years, pressure on pharmaceutical prices have instead come from the providers of health insurance and HMOs. [15] This has occurred directly and indirectly via organisations such as Pharmaceutical Benefit Managers (PBMs) whose role is to negotiate prices and then provide the drugs to HMOs. An important outcome of this has been the development of formularies, which has served to limit the prescription potential of doctors in the United States. As for the EU, the price of a drug may vary by as much as 250 per cent amongst Member States where the price of a pharmaceutical product is fixed in each country using a different set of criteria.[16] As a step to overcoming such pricing differentials, the 'Pricing Transparency Directive' of 1986, was established to reduce such variations in price, as well as to counteract national favouritism.

3. Decrease in effective patent life   The effective patent life (or the length of time between marketing a drug and the expiry date of its product patent) has consistently declined over the past thirty years in many of the Western economies.[17] As a counteractive measure, pharmaceutical firms have attempted to lobby authorities into recognising that pharmaceuticals should be awarded special patent status due to the lengthy period of clinical development required. In 1992 the EU introduced legislation which thereby made it possible to extend the protection afforded by patents for pharmaceutical and herbicidal products for a maximum period of five years. Known as 'Supplementary Protection Certificates' this change in regulation allows the extension of product patent to a maximum of 15 years.[18] However, it is only applicable to drugs that have had an unusually lengthy period of development. Despite the new extension periods, research-based pharmaceutical companies still face the problem of recovering the increasingly high costs of their R&D efforts over a shortening product life-cycle.

2.2.2   Economic forces

1. Rising cost of Research & Development   According to Hughes (1999), innovative pharmaceutical R&D has become progressively more expensive due to a number of factors. For example, (1) Global clinical development has become more complex as companies aim to achieve simultaneous submission in all the major markets; (2) The cost per patient has risen because of Good Clinical Practice (GCP) requirements, the cost of using investigators and due to the increased number of investigative procedures undertaken on each patient; (3) Greater priority is given to research on chronic diseases, for which clinical testing is more complex, time consuming and costly; (4) Therapeutic targets have also become more complex, and with it, the development programmes themselves have become more complex and expensive to administer.[19] These changes imply that in the long term, only the large, multinational pharmaceutical companies will be able to engage in the traditional approach to drug discovery. Compared to the 1970s when pharmaceutical firms would have had active R&D programmes in virtually all of the therapeutic areas, most firms today are involved in researching less than ten therapeutic segments.

2. Product risk   The pharmaceutical industry is characterised by an unusual risk profile in that the large investments required to bring a new product to market does not imply any guarantees of return. The reasons for this are numerous. New products can be commercially disappointing due to adverse drug reactions, market forces or obsolescence. The product may also be unsuited to the medical condition it was initially designed to treat and therefore failed to reach the final stages of clinical testing. As a result, companies have become much more selective about the type of candidates that should proceed to the next stage of development and have accordingly streamlined their R&D pipelines.

3. Greater generic competition   Without patent protection, generic drugs would pose an even greater threat to novel therapies since it costs the pharmaceutical manufacturer far less to develop a generic product than to bring an original discovery to market. Although many pharmaceutical companies have successfully defended their products against generic competition, it has been found that after the first year of patent expiration as many as 20 generic copies can enter the market. In the USA, penetration rates by generics rapidly approach 50 per cent within the first year of patent expiry, while after five years, this figure has been known to approach 80 per cent.[20]

2.2.3   Social forces

1. Changing demographics   Over the past century, the level of life expectancy in the developed world has increased considerably. On average, the life expectancy of the populations of the wealthier OECD nations is rising steadily, partially because of falling birth rates and partially because of improved healthcare for the elderly. From an average of 9 per cent in 1990, it is forecast that 15.3 per cent of the population will be over 65 years of age in 2010 and over 22 per cent in 2040.[21] This presents the pharmaceutical industry with a significant opportunity for developing medicines that will target this particular age group.

2. Closer scrutiny of pharmaceutical prices   Healthcare expenditure as a percentage of Gross National Product (GNP) has risen steadily over the years in most of the developed nations where national governments are the industry's largest consumer. For national governments the issue of controlling drug expenditure is of vital importance, and as a result, a number of policies have been implemented. Evaluations to assess cost minimisation, cost effectiveness, cost benefit, cost utility and quality of life are just a few measures now insisted on by the purchasers of healthcare.

3. The emergence of alternative medicines   In a landmark study on the frequency and distribution of alternative therapy use in the United States, Dr. David Eisenberg identified a substantial increase in the use of at least one 'alternative' treatment by the American population (figures rose from 33.8 per cent in 1990 to 46.3 per cent in 1997).[22] Both the 1990 and 1997 surveys showed that alternative or complementary therapies were used most frequently for chronic conditions, including back problems and other skeleto-muscular and degenerative conditions, anxiety, depression and headache, all of which were consistent with their growing incidence in modern society and the associated limitations of orthodox medications. More significantly, visits by the US population to alternative medicine practitioners, extrapolated to be 629 million in 1997, far exceeded visits made to primary care physicians, which amounted to just 386 million.[23] This substantial increase in alternative and complementary medicine usage not only reflected the increased number of visits made to such practitioners, but also to the growing proportion of the population that sought these alternative therapies. These findings together with similar trends witnessed in other developed countries are indicative of the changes in socio-demographic factors that are currently taking place and therefore hold significant implications for the pharmaceutical industry.

2.2.4   Technological forces

1. The emergence of biotechnology   Drug discovery has recently enjoyed a number of technological breakthroughs, which have allowed for a focussed approach to the identification of effective therapies for specific diseases. One such breakthrough has been the emergence of biotechnology. This new science encompasses a range of established and developing laboratory skills such as molecular biology, transgenic skills, bacterial and viral technologies, and accelerated methods of drug synthesis and screening.[24] One of the main advantages of biotechnology is that it can potentially reduce the time taken to discover a drug. First generation biotechnology has also been associated with producing safer and more effective medicines, particularly through the production of endogenous molecules and their analogues. Regulatory authorities in the USA have approved the process of bio-pharmaceuticals in a shorter period of time than chemical entities simply because bio-pharmaceuticals have had a much better safety profile by being endogenous and because they have the potential to treat life threatening diseases.[25]

2. Impact of genomics   The Human Genome Sequencing Project has stimulated the field of pharmaco-genomics as a molecular extension of pharmaco-genetics. Because of these advances, the sequences of genes that are implicated in many inherited diseases are becoming known. The benefit of this branch of science is that it presents the possibility of designing and prescribing drugs for specific diseases based on the genome of the patient to be treated and thus presents a tremendous opportunity for enhancing pharmaceutical discovery efforts.

2.3   Implications for business

The pharmaceutical industry is faced with the challenge of surviving and succeeding in an environment that has become more complex and uncertain, and one that is characterised by rapid developments in technology and organisational dynamics. Rather than being producer driven, the market for pharmaceuticals today is essentially customer-led. The price of a product has become a key indicator of the extent to which the market truly values the products that are discovered, marketed and sold. Therefore the price that a company charges for its product is the culmination of every decision made along the production chain from discovery through to marketing. If companies are to survive this challenging environment, firms can no longer permit internal processes to determine price levels, as this has now become the privilege of the customer. In an era of customer-led demand for low cost and high quality products, a fundamental re-think of the firm's very essence is therefore fundamental. To this end, companies need to re-examine every aspect of how strategy is implemented and business conducted. Undoubtedly this will give rise to a number of important issues that question the long held and accepted ways of managing pharmaceuticals, particularly in relation to five key areas.

1. Innovation   The discovery, development and marketing of new pharmaceutical products, is the essence of the research based pharmaceutical industry. As a result of the transformation towards a customer-led marketplace, important issues have been raised which present a number of challenges to pharmaceutical firms. Of greater significance is the issue of cost. The total cost of bringing a new product to market from discovery through to launch, including the cost of capital with a risk premium and the cost associated with failures, is estimated to be approximately $500 million incurred over a twelve to thirteen year period.[26] Of this total, approximately 30 per cent of the costs are concentrated in exploratory research while the remaining 70 per cent are invested in subsequent phases of clinical development. At the same time, the percentage of sales spent on innovation has been rising steadily from approximately 6 per cent in the 1960s to approximately 20 per cent by the late 1990s.[27] However, this rise in cost and the growing quantity of resources invested in pharmaceutical innovation are due to a combination of factors other than inflation. Traditionally, the growth rate of the firm has been linked to new product introductions since it was believed that a rise in investment for innovation would guarantee more novel products. In addition, the shift from acute to chronic therapy has also increased the complexity of the research process, while the demands for regulatory data have almost doubled since the mid-1980s, both of which have served to lengthen the time it takes to get a product to market. Furthermore, companies with low levels of product innovation have also spent vast amounts of capital in an effort to secure future sources of revenue. As a result therefore, pharmaceutical companies face the immediate prospect of lower margins and almost no price flexibility for existing products in the world's largest markets.

2. Productivity   Two important features have emerged in relation to the level of research productivity within pharmaceutical firms. As research moves up the technology curve it not only becomes more expensive and complex, but the level of output also begins to decline. Furthermore as size and complexity increase, so do organisational inefficiencies. This mix of technological complexity, rise in cost, the effect of diminishing returns, as well as greater levels of bureaucracy have led to growing levels of inefficiency within the pharmaceutical innovation process.[28] The implication of this long-term decline in innovative productivity therefore suggests that companies are not as successful as they used to be at innovation.

3. *Quality*   A growing number of new products that reach the market are perceived to be derivatives, or those that offer a low level of therapeutic benefit, safety advantages or cost savings over already existing products. The adoption of class and therapeutic substitution are customer responses to what is perceived to be poor value. Pharmaceutical companies therefore need to customise innovative output to more closely match the needs of its sophisticated, cost-conscious and value-driven customer base.

4. *Focus*   Historically, research-intensive pharmaceutical companies have achieved a significant proportion of their sales through developing 'annuity drugs' that treat long-term chronic diseases within the largest number of patients. Because of this, the real strength of all of the major pharmaceutical companies is found in the various therapeutic groups that are served. Since many of these therapeutic groups are now mature and already have well satisfied patients, with mature products going off-patent and with no new novel therapies forthcoming, there is the potential for a price ceiling to be placed on many of the leading products that are experiencing the move to generic status. This move towards organised generic, class and therapeutic substitution is a signal that imitative R&D will be less rewarding in the future. Therefore one of the most important issues facing many pharmaceutical companies today is the question of whether they have the capacity to convince customers to pay premium prices (that will provide satisfactory returns) for the future development of more undifferentiated drugs. Many of the diseases that are as yet fully untreatable, such as AIDS (Acquired Immune Deficiency Syndrome), various forms of cancer and multiple sclerosis are some of those that provide the most lucrative business opportunities. At the same time, healthcare providers and insurers within the industrialised nations continue to debate the sensitive issue of whether society can afford the costs of maintaining and extending the quality of life. Consequently, an inherent paradox exists. The implication of this is whether pharmaceutical companies have the capacity to rapidly produce unique products that are truly successful in treating unconquered diseases while at the same time obtaining the high prices that are required to pay for cutting-edge research.

5. *Pharmaco-economics*   According to Piachaud (2002), one of the most significant developments in the move towards customer-led change is

the accelerated search for mechanisms that would establish a sense of 'value-for-money' as perceived by customers. This has led to the creation of pharmaco-economics, which encompasses a set of tools for making more rational decisions about the selection of drugs. Methods include cost-benefit analysis, cost effectiveness, cost minimisation, cost utility, the quality of adjusted life years, and the forecasting of eventual outcomes.[29] Within the pharmaco-economic framework, issues that are of relevance to customers include matters pertaining to price negotiation, reimbursement and co-payment levels, formulary listings, substitution, treatment guidelines and improvements in prescription decision making.[30] For the pharmaceutical industry, the primary use of pharmaco-economics is to demonstrate value in order to support the marketing of products. It is also used when selecting projects for R&D purposes.

If pharmaceutical companies are to be able to reverse the potential decline of their profit margins, it is important that an atmosphere of acceptance is created amongst customers concerning the value of pharmaceutical offerings rather than of cost. If customers are not convinced that healthcare costs can only be reduced through integrated approaches rather than by ingredient cost containment measures, then this effort will surely fail. Therefore unless research based firms can discover a mechanism by which future returns for a successful product can be secured (thereby justifying the significant investment required for high risk, cutting-edge research), there will be a general decline in the number of products offering genuine solutions to healthcare problems. Furthermore, many of the development pipelines are already saturated with chemical class variations of existing products, which will only serve to provide minor improvements to the efficacy and safety of a drug. This is because such substances only have a limited potential to create meaningful differentiation over already existing brands, as well as over cheaper generic and therapeutic substitutes. In addition, the degree of patent protection available no longer provides a safety net over gross profit margins. Therefore the key issue once again focuses on the extent to which customers perceive how much a product is actually worth.

2.4   The changing nature of the pharmaceutical market

1. Product innovation is no longer the only determinant of business success
The market for pharmaceuticals is determined by the degree of innovation success which is a function of how well a product is perceived to offer new or better solutions to a patient's clinical needs. Increasing

demand-side controls on prescribing autonomy, competition between providers and the concentration of buying power, together with the growth of sophisticated product selection criteria have all combined to encourage a radical re-think of traditional R&D strategies. Companies are therefore now obliged to make rationale decisions based on the effective re-allocation of resources. To this end, new and better products must be favoured over those considered marginal since the criteria for selection must be based on those that will provide proven clinical benefits and true value-for-money. Those products deemed mediocre must therefore be abandoned.

2. Physicians are no longer the most influential customers   In the past, the role of the physician was considered crucial in instances where there was complete freedom of choice with regard to prescribing and in instances where there was relatively little concern for cost containment measures, and where payers had only few mechanisms at their disposal to monitor physician compliance. Since the end of the 1980s, fundamental changes have occurred as both public and private sector buyers realised that a policy of cost containment could only truly be effective if 'industry focused' supply-side controls were effectively linked with 'physician and patient focused' demand side-controls.[31] This realisation has resulted in the development of a variety of cost containment measures ranging from formularies to prescribing guidelines, mandatory substitution to cheaper products, as well as practice protocols. Therefore, while the physician remains an important buyer in the pharmaceutical marketplace, the upstream consolidation of buyers together with tighter cost control measures has irreversibly shifted the balance of power.

3. Competition is much more multifaceted   Traditionally competition in the pharmaceutical industry was simply based on a product's features and clinical performance. Today however, competition is much more multifaceted. Customers now have a greater capacity to make more informed decisions that are based on the clinical performance and cost implications of competing products. The expanding range of generic drugs and the growing acceptance of generic substitutability combined with the enhanced therapy provided by recent introductions, have merged to drive down the price of new products. Furthermore, the slow levels of growth experienced in many of the world's pharmaceutical markets has enhanced the need for a greater portion of market share and has thus led to increased rivalry within the marketplace. Because of these changes, competition is now firmly based on the firm's ability to meet the needs of a cost-conscious, powerful and sophisticated customer base in the most effective manner.

4. Operating costs are crucial   In the past, the strong flow of new products at premium prices inferred less scrutiny on operating costs. With the advent of a free market for pharmaceuticals, operating costs have since become a major concern for pharmaceutical producers. As a result, new product pricing strategies based on past practices is now almost impossible. The question of how well a company allocates its resources and assigns its cost structures is of vital importance if growth is to be ensured in a cost conscious marketplace. Pharmaceutical manufacturers must therefore be able to discover, produce and sell products that customers not only want, but are also willing to pay for.

5. Need to satisfy healthcare needs rather than simply sell a product Pharmaceutical companies have recognised the need to reposition the business in two significant ways. First, companies are becoming fully integrated contributors to providing improved healthcare delivery, and they are also becoming fully accredited partners with other members in the healthcare chain.[32] The need for becoming directly involved in achieving the optimal outcome of a product is just as important as overseeing a product from the initial stage of conception to its launch on the marketplace.

It is therefore evident that a number of transformations have occurred, all of which have necessitated change at both the industrial and organisational level. According to Malone (1996)[33] such transformations can be summarised as follows:

1. The need to learn to adapt: How can an organisation effectively cope with constant and multi-dimensional change, and how can the firm boost its capacity for learning and adaptability?
2. Optimal organisational structure: How should a company be structured for maximum responsiveness to continuous and often unpredictable changes in the marketplace, and how should it organise its network of customers and suppliers?
3. Identify essential skills: What leadership qualities are needed to effectively guide an organisation in the future?
4. Support and nurture innovation: How can an organisation create the environment needed to spur continuous streams of innovation?
5. Accurately measure success: As intellectual capital and other intangibles play a greater role in the success of the firm, how can an organisation apply traditional accounting measures to more accurately portray the true assets, liabilities and long-term prospects of the firm?

The implications of these changes are both fundamental and far reaching, involving every aspect of the pharmaceutical business. The traditional market for pharmaceuticals has given way to one that is much more dynamic and customer orientated – a market that is continuously evolving and ever changing. In light of these competitive changes, it is clear that companies need to alter their strategic map and adopt a number of approaches that will meet the requirements of a modern and far more aggressive market. To this end, the industry has witnessed a proliferation of strategies designed to meet the prevailing forces of competition.

Notes

1. J. Taggart, *The World Pharmaceutical Industry* (London: Routledge, 1993), pp. 116–53.
2. Ibid., Taggart (1993).
3. M.E. Porter, *Competitive Strategy: Techniques for Analysing Industries and Competitors* (New York: Free Press, 1980).
4. Ibid., Porter (1980).
5. Ibid., Porter (1980).
6. J. Taggart, *The World Pharmaceutical Industry* (London: Routledge, 1993), pp. 116–53.
7. M.E. Porter, *Competitive Strategy: Techniques for Analysing Industries and Competitors* (New York: Free Press, 1980).
8. N. Bosanquet, 'From Prairie to Garden: Where Next for Pharmaceuticals in Europe?', *European Business Journal*, 6, Issue 4 (1994), pp. 39–49.
9. European Federation of Pharmaceutical Industries and Associations (EFPIA), 'Did You Know That?' (Brussels: EFPIA, 2003), *http://www.efpia.org/2_industdidyouknow2.htm*
10. N. Bosanquet, 'From Prairie to Garden: Where Next for Pharmaceuticals in Europe?', *European Business Journal*, 6, Issue 4 (1994), pp. 39–49.
11. M.E. Porter, *Competitive Strategy: Techniques for Analysing Industries and Competitors* (New York: Free Press, 1980).
12. Ibid., Porter (1980).
13. R. Hughes and C.E. Lumley (eds) *Current Strategies and Future Prospects in Pharmaceutical Outsourcing* (London: Technomark Consulting Services Limited and the Centre for Medicines Research International, 1999), pp. 3–29.
14. Ibid., pp. 3–29.
15. A. Gambardella, *Science and Innovation: The US Pharmaceutical Industry during the 1980s* (Cambridge: Cambridge University Press, 1995).
16. N. Bosanquet, 'From Prairie to Garden: Where Next for Pharmaceuticals in Europe?', *European Business Journal*, 6, Issue 4 (1994), pp. 39–49.
17. International Federation of Pharmaceutical Manufacturers Association (IFPMA), *The Question of Patents: The Key to Medical Progress and Industrial Development* (Geneva, IFPMA, 1998).
18. The European Patent Office, 'Supplementary Protection Certificates in INPADOC', *http://www.european-patent-office.org/news/epidosnews/source/epd_2_01/4_2_01_e.htm*

19. R. Hughes and C.E. Lumley (eds) *Current Strategies and Future Prospects in Pharmaceutical Outsourcing* (London: Technomark Consulting Services Limited and the Centre for Medicines Research International, 1999), pp. 3–29.
20. ——, National Institute for Health Care Management (NIHCM), *A Primer: Generic Drugs, Patents and the Pharmaceutical Industry* (Washington DC: NICHAM, 2002), pp. 1–28.
21. R. Hughes and C.E. Lumley (eds) *Current Strategies and Future Prospects in Pharmaceutical Outsourcing* (London: Technomark Consulting Services Limited and the Centre for Medicines Research International, 1999), pp. 3–29.
22. D.M. Eisenberg, R.B. Davis and S.L. Ettner, 'Trends in Alternative Medicine Use in the United States 1990–1997: Results of a Follow-up National Survey', *Journal of the American Medical Association*, 280, Issue 19 (1998), pp. 1569–75.
23. Ibid., pp. 1569–75.
24. M. Brannback, J. Nasi and M. Renko 'Technological, Structural and Strategic Change in the Global Pharmaceutical Industry: The Finnish Biotechnology Industry', *Unpublished Papers*, Turku School of Economics and Business Administration, Tampere University of Technology and Industrial Management, Tampere (2001), pp. 1–26.
25. R. Hughes and C.E. Lumley (eds) *Current Strategies and Future Prospects in Pharmaceutical Outsourcing* (London: Technomark Consulting Services Limited and the Centre for Medicines Research International, 1999), pp. 3–29.
26. European Federation of Pharmaceutical Industries and Associations (EFPIA), 'Did You Know That?' (Brussels: EFPIA, 2003), *http://www.efpia.org/2_industdidyouknow2.htm*
27. B. Piachaud, 'Challenges Facing the Pharmaceutical Industry: Factors Influencing Drug Choice and Strategy', *Contemporary Review*, 280, Issue 1634 (2002), pp. 152–7.
28. Ibid., pp. 152–7.
29. Ibid., pp. 152–7.
30. Ibid., pp. 152–7.
31. B.G. James, *The Pharmaceutical Industry in 2000: Reinventing the Pharmaceutical Company* (London: The Economic Intelligence Unit, 1994), pp. 10–27.
32. Ibid., pp. 1–27.
33. T.W. Malone, M.S. Scot-Morton and R.R. Halperin, 'Organising for the Twenty-First Century', *Strategy & Leadership*, 24, Issue 4 (1996), pp. 6–11.

3
Strategies for Innovation and Competitive Advantage

For a number of years, pharmaceutical companies have departed from a tradition of strict vertical integration so as to gain access to external sources of technology and expertise for the purpose of product and technological development. It is therefore necessary to examine the strategies employed by pharmaceutical companies at both the firm and industry level. To this end, particular emphasis must be placed on strategies of collaboration and co-operation between pharmaceutical firms and external agents given that a rise in such activity follows the trend of the wider industrial community.

3.1   The structure of the pharmaceutical industry

The structure of the pharmaceutical industry has remained virtually unchanged from the early 1950s through to the early 1990s. While continuous demand for better healthcare created strong market growth; patents, trademarks and escalating regulatory requirements also provided effective barriers to new competition. The result of operating in this fast growing, protected market was that all incumbents were able to prosper, with even the most mediocre of firms capable of producing a performance which was unrivalled in almost any other industry. This was soon to change by the early 1990s as multiple customer-led challenges combined to destabilise the structure of the industry. The concerns voiced by cost-conscious consumers helped to bring about price sensitivity and cost-containment measures by directing demand towards more cost-effective products. At the same time, proactive customer and regulatory policies helped reduce barriers to generics, thereby encouraging new competitors as the costs of competing fell and the costs of entry evaporated. In other words, knowledgeable customers became increasingly aware of the inter-changeability of products, classes of substance and even therapies. These factors combined to escalate the costs associated with marketing pharmaceutical products, while at the same time two other profound changes occurred – the productivity of innovation declined and the costs of research escalated.

Accordingly pharmaceutical companies were required to greatly increase spending on R&D in an attempt to counteract the effects of declining prices, as leading products began to lose patent protection, and to re-capture earnings that were being eroded by generic competitors. The combined prospects of shrinking product life cycles, declining unit prices and increased risk, together with the growing realisation that much of current research may not obtain the necessary prices to cover the future cost of innovation, has led to a secular change in the structure of the pharmaceutical industry. This new industry structure is the result of three drivers for change as identified by James (1994).[1]

1. Desire to access customers   The traditionally large customer base comprising primarily of physicians has evolved into a small and concentrated group of powerful decision makers comprising payers, insurers and intermediaries. This new group has re-structured their demands in three different ways. The first is the demand for a low cost supply of drugs for the treatment of chronic diseases which would meet the medical requirements of large numbers of patients. The second is the need for both clinical and economic justification that would facilitate the making of more informed decisions regarding the use of expensive treatments and new medications. The third is through the sharing of risk with suppliers which would necessitate payment for a drug on a capitated basis.[2]

2. Desire to access technology   Scientific and technical knowledge is now so widely dispersed that it is impossible for any one firm to gain a lasting competitive advantage in all aspects of the R&D process. Advanced research has become inherently more risky with the scale of resources required to finance not just the discovery and development of new drugs, but also the purchase of new technology and expertise.

3. Increased competition   Customer led competition has evolved into areas that are completely new for pharmaceutical companies. The need to demonstrate competitive leverage (which is based on a company's capacity to be a low cost supplier) not only applies to low-priced, low-volume products, but also to more advanced therapies. As such, competitive strength requires that the pharmaceutical firm successfully leverage its customer relationships. This ranges from collaborative risk and information sharing through to forward integration.

From this it is evident that size has become an important factor for the pharmaceutical industry. For the first time, economies of scale in manufacturing and the critical mass necessary to negotiate with buyers and to reduce costs have become decisive factors for success in the low cost supply of a broad range of products. In addition, size in relation to resources is also critical. This is not just relation to financing the skills base required to develop high quality pharmaceutical products, but to also support small innovative companies in order to buy-in product licences that can be added to the product portfolio.

3.2 Firm and industry-based strategies

The reputation of the pharmaceutical industry is partly based on the fiercely independent character of its firms and its self-contained methods of operation. Pharmaceutical companies have proved to be exceptionally profitable and highly innovative, having achieved a high degree of success through avoiding much direct competition, while at the same time relying very little on co-operative alliances. Today however, these practices are no longer the hallmarks of the industry with firms increasingly involved in mergers and acquisitions, and various forms of strategic partnering alliances. Against a background of accelerated change, pharmaceutical companies have responded to the growing need for change in a number of different ways. Thus the industry's transformation is mirrored in the strategic decisions of the firms themselves – the way in which firms choose to compete and collaborate.

3.2.1 Re-engineering strategies

The terms 're-engineering', 'business process redesign' and 'process innovation' have come to symbolise the design and implementation of radical changes in business processes in order to achieve significant improvements in cost, service and time performance. The pharmaceutical industry, with its complex arrangement of management, information, service and support systems (all of which are involved in the discovery, development, manufacture, distribution and the selling of pharmaceutical products), has readily adopted the notion of re-engineering with the expectation of improving overall performance in two key areas.

a. Time to market Efforts to reduce the life cycle of a new product has become a major concern for pharmaceutical companies since the development time of many new products is often longer than the life span of the branded product itself. The time it takes to bring a new product to the market is one of the longest in any industry, taking an average of nine to eleven years, plus a further two years for the regulatory approval phase. This comprises a mean time of 12 years from synthesis to first launch, as is illustrated in Figure 3.1. In addition, new product development cycles put the industry at a distinct disadvantage in terms of its ability to modify products to meet the changing 'value' perceptions of customers as even minor enhancements can take up to a further two years.[3]

With the costs and time required for introducing pharmaceutical products ever increasing, the reduction of development time by two to three years, together with early positioning – either through the capture or maintenance of market share – can help in eliminating up to two or three years off overall time-to-market. Therefore any process that can deliver a product at least two years faster, automatically adds its equivalent to the patent-protected earning power of a leading product.

Although reducing the time it takes to get a product to market can help lower cost and enhance market potential, it is those products that offer substantial clinical and economic value (as perceived by the customer) that will reap any premiums. Efforts to reduce overall time to market will be of little consequence if the customer will not pay for the cost of development. It is important for companies to instead refine product selection methods that will mirror the demands of customers

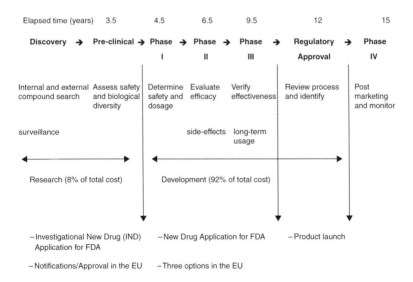

Figure 3.1   New product development times for pharmaceuticals

more accurately prior to reducing product development times and the overall time-to-market.

b. Manufacturing The pharmaceutical industry is marred by significant costs within manufacturing, which are derived from the complex nature of the manufacturing process itself. The need to accommodate a variety of functions that include low-volume batch manufacturing, varying package sizes and formulations, specialised presentations as well as low-volume products have contributed to producing low levels of utilisation, high fixed costs and low levels of productivity within areas of manufacturing.[4] Although significant productivity gains have been made as a result of re-engineering efforts in the manufacturing function, much of this has failed to integrate manufacturing with research in terms of process development. Therefore while re-engineering holds valuable promise, it has failed to significantly improve overall financial or market performance. However in terms of the significant cost, time and productivity improvements that have been made, much of this has occurred primarily within narrow business processes rather than across the whole manufacturing spectrum.

3.2.2 Reshaping strategies

The convergence of two key trends, as identified by James (1994) has led to a radical reshaping of business practices within the pharmaceutical industry. First, the move towards 'managed care' has required that both buyers and providers of healthcare reconsider traditional approaches to the delivery of effective healthcare services. It is widely accepted that the only way to manage costs is to improve effectiveness as well as efficiency, which would force competition into the system and thereby create a new value chain that will encompass all the previously discrete players, thus integrating their activities into one seamless system. However, the implication of this new value chain is that it has diminished the ability of pharmaceutical companies to remain isolated players that maintain control over their own value chain systems.[5]

Second, financial risk has moved away from the purchasers of healthcare towards users and suppliers. Since the early 1960s until the mid-1980s, financial risk was chiefly the concern of the payer who in most cases was represented by government agencies in developed countries. However, by the late 1980s the financial risk involved with healthcare was more widely dispersed due to increases in co-payments and deductibles for patients, the implementation of hospital appraisals, budgets for the purchase of medicines, and a system of penalties and incentives for pharmacists. All these proposals thus combined to shift the burden of payment away from the purchasers of healthcare. By the mid-1990s, pharmaceutical companies were also prepared to share the risk with payers and providers in order to secure a competitive advantage. Moving from the perspective of internal risk (which stems primarily from the ability to find, develop and introduce new products), the degree of financial risk for a pharmaceutical company had shifted externally towards sharing risk with customers and suppliers.

The result of these two convergent forces is a fundamentally new set of strategic decisions, which have the capacity to collectively reshape the pharmaceutical business. As a result, pharmaceutical firms have sought to develop new value propositions that encroach on decision-making in managed care. From this, two new strategies have emerged. They are capitation and disease management. The focus on capitation relates to the full provision of pharmaceutical services over a fixed period at a fixed price, irrespective of utilisation. Disease management on the other hand, encompasses the provision of drugs and other related products together with comprehensive training schemes for patients, physicians, nurses and pharmacists so that these groups may follow approved treatment programmes. Both these strategies are designed with the intention of bringing the pharmaceutical firm closer to the customer through the use of forward integration, as well as by assuming part of the risk of both the payer and provider.

It is evident that both these schemes go beyond the traditional 'value-added' approach to a system of 'shared value'. Such policies generate a new value proposition by looking at the problem of effective healthcare delivery from the perspective of the customer in order to create a positive selling environment over the longer term. In this new era, packaging benefits, outcomes and risk are all seen as major opportunities for creating beneficial, long-term partnerships. The selling of just the physical product is therefore, no longer viewed as being enough.

3.2.3   Strategies for research and development

A research and development strategy is essentially based on the systematic evaluation of various inter-firm relationships. Since firms are not faced with the exclusive selection between strategies, a delicate balance has to be struck on where to place the emphasis.[6] According to Twiss (1992), a company may draw on a number of strategies in order to successfully implement a programme of research and development such as:

1. Offensive strategy   As the name suggests, an offensive strategy is a high risk strategy with potentially high returns. It not only demands considerable skill in technological innovation, including the ability to see new market opportunities relating to technology, but to also have the necessary competence to swiftly translate such opportunities into commercial products. In most cases a strong research orientation together with the application of new technology is required.

2. Defensive strategy   This is essentially a low risk strategy with potentially low returns. Essentially, a defensive strategy is much more appropriate to developmental aspects of the research and development spectrum, because in this instance, new technology is viewed as less important than the ability to exploit an existing technology to the fullest extent.[7]

3. Licensing agreements   Licensing presents many opportunities for commercial exploitation, and can be achieved through purchasing the outcomes of another company's R&D programme. This is viewed as optimal since there is little to gain from rediscovering what can be readily obtained from another source at an economical price. Since even the largest companies cannot afford to explore all technological alternatives or to produce all innovations internally, licensing provides a viable and cost effective alternative.

4. Interstitial strategy   This is normally referred to as a 'niche' strategy. Here a company deliberately attempts to avoid direct confrontation by examining the weaknesses of its competitors and then exploiting potential opportunities when it is feasible to do so.

5. Market creation   Most new products and processes that are discovered and launched, act as substitutes within an existing market. Occasionally however, the prospect of creating an entirely new market is presented when an advancing technology provides the opportunity to develop a product that is completely new.

6. Maverick strategy   This enables a company with expertise in a new technology to launch a new product in a competitor's market with the aim of reducing the size of the total market. However, this may only succeed in the long term if supported by an offensive strategy that facilitates the retention of technological leadership.

7. Acquisition of people or companies   This strategy provides an alternative to purchasing a competitor's technology through a licensing agreement. In this case, a company may acquire some of its competitor's employees, or even a complete project team. Although there are a number of reasons why one company may decide to take-over or merge with another, synergy and the matching of resources play an important part, while gaining access to technology and other resources can also be a critical factor.[8]

3.2.4 Mergers and acquisitions

The composition of the global pharmaceutical industry was remarkably stable from the early 1960s until the end of the 1980s. Although individual firms moved up or down in rank, there were almost no new entrants among the major producers and no single firm claimed more than 3–4 per cent of the global pharmaceutical market.[9] By the end of the 1980s however, this long period of peaceful coexistence was disrupted as the number of mergers and acquisitions reached an all-time high (see Table 3.1). Estimates for the 1988 to 1990 period placed the total value of these transactions at approximately $45 billion.[10] Although the pace has now slowed, the industry has nevertheless entered a new phase where mergers and acquisitions are commonplace.

In assessing the motives for mergers and acquisitions, a number of factors influence managerial decision making. These include economic,

Table 3.1 Mergers and acquisitions in the pharmaceutical industry since 1985

Merged or acquired companies	Year
Monsanto and G.D. Searle	1985
Eastman Kodak and Sterling	1988
Dow & Marion and Merrel	1989
Bristol-Myers and Squibb	1989
American Home Products and A.H. Robins	1989
Novo and Nordisk	1989
Merieux and Connaught	1989
Rhone-Poulence and Rorer	1990
SmithKline and Beecham	1991
American Home Products and Cyanamid	1994
Hofmann La Roche and Syntex	1994
Eli-Lilly and PCS Health	1994
Sandoz and Gerber	1994
Bayer and Sterling	1994
Glaxo and Burroughs Wellcome	1995
Hoechst-Roussel and Marion Merrell Dow	1995
Pharmacia and Upjohn	1995
Rhone-Poulenc Rorer and Fisons	1995
Ciba-Geigy and Sandoz	1996
Nycomed and Amersham	1997
Hoffman-la Roche and Boehringer Mannheim	1997
Astra and Zeneca	1998
Sanofi SI and Syntheolab	1998
Hoechst AG and Rhone-Poulence Rorer	1998
Pfizer and Warner Lambert	1999
GlaxoWellcome and SmithKline Beecham	2000

financial, social and strategic motivations. In terms of existing literature, two broad themes can be identified which contribute towards an understanding of why companies acquire or merge. They are:

a)   Strategic management theory

Much of the literature concerned with strategic management theory points to the overriding rationale behind mergers and acquisitions as the need to achieve expansion and growth, as well as the desire to secure efficiencies in both scale and scope. It is therefore necessary to focus upon the external and contextual factors that drive this type of behaviour as a means to understanding the rationale to consolidate. In seeking to identify these motives, Contractor *et al.* (1988) identify a number of objectives which are not mutually exclusive. These include the need to (1) reduce risk, (2) achieve economies of scale, (3) gain access to technology, (4) co-opt or block competition, (5) facilitate a means to international expansion, (6) link the complimentary contributions of the partners in a value chain and (7) overcome government mandated trade or investment barriers.[11]

Also contained within the strategic management framework is the concept of resource dependency and core competencies. When a firm faces a depletion of resources and competencies that are generally unavailable, it is more likely to enter into a merger or acquisition agreement in order to fulfil the necessary requirements. According to Pfeffer *et al.* (1978) resource scarcity prompts organisations to enter into inter-organisational relationships in an attempt to exert power, influence or control over organisations that have the required resources.[12] From this arises the relationship between the competitive advantage of the firm and its core capabilities. Mergers and acquisitions are often pursued as a means to accessing resources from external sources as opposed to internal development, and as a means of gaining access to core competencies, in which the acquiring company feels itself to be deficient.[13] The expectation is that although both companies may individually lack competitive advantage in their chosen market, when taken together, they would have the means of achieving it. The implication of this 'resource-based' view in relation to resource dependency is therefore the same – one of the strongest incentives to merge or acquire is the lack of critical competencies to achieve a significant competitive advantage.

This desire to focus on core competencies acts as a catalyst for growth since mergers and acquisitions are viewed as a quick route to expansion and further development. The pressure to divest what might be considered secondary or tertiary businesses, together with the need to secure complementary acquisitions in order to further develop core competencies, has led to considerable consolidation activity within many industries. This phenomenon is most clearly evident in the pharmaceutical, defence, media, telecommunications and other high technology industries.[14]

b) An economic perspective

When taken from an economic perspective, Market-Power Theory and Agency Theory play a significant role in explaining the motives for mergers and acquisitions in a given industry. Market-Power Theory is primarily concerned with the ways in which companies can improve their competitive performance through the establishment of stronger positions within the market place. Porter (1980) suggests that the relative position which a firm occupies within an industry determines the generic strategies that are the most feasible and profitable.[15] A merger or acquisition strategy can offer a potentially advantageous method by which a firm can improve its existing market position, and hence, market power. Therefore when applied to the study of corporate activity, the motive for achieving market power is most applicable under two sets of conditions. The first occurs when firms enter into *offensive coalitions* with the intention of improving competitive advantage by reducing a competitor's market share. The second occurs in instances when firms enter into *defensive coalitions* so as to construct entry barriers that are intended to secure their position in the market place.

If viewed from the perspective of Agency Theory, the motives for mergers and acquisitions are primarily concerned with governance mechanisms that serve to limit the agent's self-serving behaviour, and include various control and incentive mechanisms.[16] When discussing the nature of Agency Theory, it is important to point out a number of assumptions about the nature of human behaviour, organisations and information. For example, Eisenhardt (1989) suggests that Agency Theory assumes the notion that human behaviour is self-interested and thereby risk averse. It also assumes that organisations contain a degree of conflict between the goals of its members, and that there is an asymmetry of information between principals and agents. Due to these factors, it is probable that management will engage in self-seeking opportunistic behaviour at the expense of the interests of shareholders. Mergers and acquisitions may therefore be viewed as a route to fulfilling these self-serving objectives.

It is also important to take into account the financial considerations behind the need to merge. Jensen (1989) suggests that those firms with free cash flows which find organic growth difficult may prefer mergers or acquisitions as an alternative to returning stock to shareholders.[17] This provides a variant to the traditional empire building argument for expansion by acquisition. Similarly, acquisitions may be used to diversify risk, or to stabilise seasonal variations in cash flow. This would provide the company with more stable earnings, which if substantial, may lower the cost of borrowing, and thereby increase its credit ratings.[18] Another important consideration is the need to enhance shareholder wealth. As suggested by Amin *et al.* (1995), a merger may only be justified if it is expected to make the profits of the merged firms greater than the sum of the original, thereby leading to an increase in shareholder wealth.[19] Accordingly, the decision to acquire another firm must be based on the principle of any other sound investment decision: if the merger adds more value to the firm than initial cost, the process should be undertaken.[20]

It is evident that the motives to merge or to acquire are indeed varied and multidimensional. The stimulus affecting the decision is dependent on a number of factors and consists of both environmental and situational influences. In the case of the pharmaceutical industry, Piachaud *et al.* (2000)[21] have identified a number of factors that drive the incidence of mergers and acquisitions within the industry. These include:

1. Search for critical mass   The search for critical mass is an important motive for mergers and acquisitions within the pharmaceutical sector, since the market share of even the largest pharmaceutical manufacturers are often considered too small to maintain a strong competitive position. While many of the larger pharmaceutical firms look to consolidation as a means of strengthening market position in a given geographic or therapeutic segment, many of the smaller members see increased size as a means to international status and effective competition in a global market place.[22]

2. Enhance R&D capabilities   The annual R&D budgets of the top-tier pharmaceutical producers are considerable, with spending often exceeding 20 per cent of sales and amounting to approximately $1 billion in absolute terms.[23] This has led to high investor expectations, as shareholders expect companies to have strong product pipelines if they are to generate the same profits as had been delivered in the past. Mergers and acquisitions are therefore seen as a means to relieving the tremendous strain placed on the research and development effort and as a means to enhancing the R&D process.

3. Broaden product range   Mergers and acquisitions are often the fastest route to expanding the product portfolio. Merging with, or acquiring another company can help maintain market leadership in existing or novel therapeutic areas. The merger of Amersham and Nycomed in 1997 for example, placed the new company as world leader in 'in-vivo' diagnostic imaging agents.[24]

4. *Access to new technologies*   Recent changes in technology have dominated and revolutionised the pharmaceutical industry, with the traditional methods of drug development superseded by that of biotechnology. In order to keep abreast with the rapid advances in technology, many pharmaceutical firms have resorted to acquiring new technology start-up companies such as biotechnology ventures, as well as larger rivals in order to gain access to research programmes or gene databases.

5. *Cost savings*   Over the years, the level of competition within the pharmaceutical industry has intensified with firms facing increasing pressure from governments and other healthcare institutions to lower prices. Although globally pharmaceuticals represent approximately 15 per cent of total healthcare expenditure, the pharmaceutical industry is often held responsible for the rising cost of healthcare.[25] As a result, the need to cut costs and to rationalise have become decisive factors for success within the industry.

6. *Focus on core capabilities*   Firms today are viewed as a portfolio of core competencies and value creating disciplines since the merit of focussing on 'what one does best' is commonly recognised as sound strategic thinking. This is especially true when taken in the context of 'virtual organisation' where companies outsource peripheral activities and focus on those areas that add value to the overall business. Mergers and acquisitions have thus provided a means to achieving this end.

A merger or acquisition strategy is not an end in itself, but merely an accelerated route to growth. Since no one pharmaceutical company can have a dominant share of the market, achieving a theoretical or even practical critical mass it does imply the notion of self-sufficiency within the industry. Although re-engineering policies with a view to improving business processes have enabled firms to function more efficiently, without a concerted effort to reshape the product offering to meet the needs of the customer, and without a change in the strategic focus of the business, pharmaceutical companies will simply be a variant of their former selves. Unless companies can address both the form and the substance of the changes taking place in the healthcare market, merely doing the same thing however effectively and efficiently is not enough.

3.3   The biotechnology revolution

Historically, the traditional mode of research for pharmaceutical firms was to first identify a new chemical substance, and then test its properties for possible commercial potential. Hence, the skills of the firm were directed towards the identification and purification of novel substances, and large scale clinical testing. This method therefore facilitated the further development of existing organic-chemistry skills. However with the advent of biotechnology, such modes of research changed significantly. New substances were instead identified through the study of the basic function of cells. This then signalled the shift towards biology as the primary science as opposed to organic chemistry.

Although both sciences share similar roots, in the case of biotechnology, the skills used in drug development are not an incremental step beyond existing chemotherapy skills. Instead, biotechnology represents a different trajectory in that it emerges from the basic life sciences.[26] This implies that while both methods may be employed in the identification of identical medical problems, the key competencies required to develop leading-edge products are in fact fundamentally different. In other words, the technology and skills required to produce innovations are distorted. The competencies required for innovative drug development today are therefore no longer to be found within the exclusive domain of established firms. On the contrary, new developments are also to be found within the biotechnology sector. The outcome of this transformation has manifested itself not only in the creation of a new model for researching compounds, but also in the creation of a new organisational niche.[27] The traditional technology of the pharmaceutical industry – organic chemical synthesis – has been superseded by biotechnology.

When attempting to define the term 'biotechnology', it is important to realise that it does not refer to any single technology in particular. Rather, biotechnology refers to a branch of science that encompasses the novel techniques of genetic engineering and monoclonal antibody technology, as well as an array of new technologies derived from the biosciences.[28] The fundamentals of this new approach rest with scientists' understanding of disease processes at the molecular level, while its aim is to design therapies that will block diseases with enhanced accuracy. For the pharmaceutical sector, such new applications have helped to improve not only the quality and efficacy of existing products, but have made possible the formation of an entirely new therapeutics, diagnostics and drug delivery system.

Sharp (1990) refers to the rise of biotechnology as a shift in the technological paradigm, accompanied by a 'technological trajectory' in which innovation and resulting product development are fuelled by the emergence of new ways of thinking.[29] Whereas in the past, pharmaceutical innovation was based on organic chemistry, biochemistry and chemical engineering; in the case of biotechnology, it involves the synthesis of many disciplines such as biochemistry, cell biology, molecular genetics, protein chemistry, enzymology and computer science: thus giving it a multi-disciplinary approach.[30] Consequently, the scientific and technical developments that have taken place within the core technologies used in biotechnology – DNA synthesising and sequencing, cell fusion methodologies for producing hybridomas – as well as associated technologies represent a major *technological discontinuity* in the evolution of the biological and chemical sciences.[31]

When examining the effects of this paradigm shift on the pharmaceutical industry, Sharp (1989)[32] identifies four important outcomes:

1. A process technology Biotechnology is a process technology which focuses on the techniques for finding and developing new drugs, as much as about the new drugs themselves. It has provided the pharmaceutical industry with an alternative to the rising costs and falling productivity associated with traditional search methodologies.

2. Pervasive uncertainty Because these new techniques were previously untried and entirely experimental, there was genuine uncertainty associated with the biotechnology process. The discontinuity implicit in the paradigm shift therefore meant that past experience counted for very little since it was impossible to assess risks against expected probabilities.[33]

3. Importance of academic science In the case of biotechnology, the accelerated development of the science base necessitated a continued dependence on the academic science base, whereas with other new technologies, the locus of knowledge was contained in the research laboratories of the industrial sector.

4. Access new skills The traditional skill of the pharmaceutical industry was that of the chemist. With the advent of biotechnology, the industry was obliged to construct project teams consisting of protein chemists, micro biologists, molecular geneticists, protein crystallographers, molecular graphics experts and experts in fermentation technology and downstream processing.[34] To some extent these were entirely new skills, and as such, it was not easy to find the right people or to rapidly build up in-house teams that could work well together. As a result, pharmaceutical firms found themselves dependent on outsiders to meet the required skills. The advent of biotechnology has therefore given birth to a new type of relationship, where large organisations whose core competencies were traditionally found in the marketing of a product and the co-ordination of development activities; now contract the services of small, innovative suppliers. More importantly, this 'paradigm shift' has spurred the adoption of outsourcing practices within the innovation environment of the pharmaceutical sector.

The prevailing industrial structure consequently owes much to the rise of biotechnology whose influences have been felt further afield than merely the R&D laboratory. Although biotechnology is just one of the many factors that have influenced the evolutionary process of the pharmaceutical industry, its effects have been more profound than most could have first envisaged. Research in the pharmaceutical industry today has been transformed into a richly innovative synergy between a very few large companies and a host of smaller ones. Piachaud *et al.* (2001) suggest that the embracing of biotechnology as an alternative science has caused a *permanent* shift away from the traditional business practices and philosophies embraced by the pharmaceutical industry for decades.[35] The outsourcing of R&D is therefore a very appropriate example. Given that biotechnology is here to stay, a key challenge then for both small biotechnology firms and large global pharmaceutical manufacturers is

> To learn from collaborations with external parties, and to construct a portfolio of collaborators that provides access to the emerging science and technology, as well as the necessary organisational capabilities.[36] (Powell 1998)

What most pharmaceutical companies face is a much more immediate and pressing problem: that of change. The pace of change is now so fast that it is beginning to outstrip the ability of some companies *to* change. The ability to survive will depend largely on the capacity of the firm to sell its emerging product pipeline to a customer-led market. Consequently, the quest for survival in these turbulent waters has not occurred in isolation. The industry has witnessed an explosion of strategic alliances ranging from horizontal and vertical integration with competitors, to tangential alliances with suppliers. These partnerships have spanned a wide spectrum, ranging from diagnostic manufacturers to delivery system developers to distributors – all of which form part of a mission to discover how best pharmaceutical firms should compete in order to survive.

3.4   Collaboration in the pharmaceutical industry

Co-operative strategy is the attempt to realise specific objectives through co-operation rather than through competition. A strategy of collaboration can offer significant advantages to companies that lack particular competencies or resources since it allows the formation of links with other firms that possess complementary skills or assets.[37] It can also facilitate access to new markets, as well as provide opportunities for mutual synergy and learning. Since competitive strategy is primarily concerned with the question of how a firm can gain a competitive advantage over its competitors, two modes of operating can be identified. The first relates to the pursuit of generic strategies such as cost leadership, product differentiation or a shift in strategic focus. The second refers to the degree of competitive advantage that can be derived from a firm's unique competencies and resources, which when combined, can deliver unique products that are both difficult to acquire or imitate.[38] A strategy of co-operation with one or more firms can therefore enhance efforts to secure a greater competitive advantage.

Child *et al.* (1998) suggest that the study of co-operative strategy falls within the domain of corporate strategy in several ways. First, a co-operative strategy should reflect the mission and objectives that corporate management set for a company. Second, co-operation may be sought as a means of sharing the risk associated with the development of new products. Third, it may be incumbent on the corporate function to superimpose a controlling or co-ordinating framework over the different business segments of the firm. More importantly, the connection between corporate and co-operative strategy should stem from the desire of a firm to seek a global presence and competitive advantage by participating in complex networks of collaborative agreements with other companies.[39] In light of this, co-operative strategy is not an alternative to either competitive or corporate strategies. Rather, it relates to a further domain of policy options whose purpose is to enable firms to compete more effectively.

Accordingly, alliances are regarded as the normal agent for co-operative strategy. They are 'strategic' in that they are formed in direct response to opportunities and/or threats faced by the partnering firms. In seeking an appropriate definition of what constitutes an alliance, there is a general agreement among scholars that alliances involve 'autonomous organisations working together to achieve goals that are related to their strategic plans'.[40] Yet despite this general consensus, several areas of disagreement still exist. These relate to (1) whether or not an alliance must be long term in nature; (2) whether it must involve a change in competitive position for the partnering firms; (3) whether alliances are limited to relationships between firms at the same level of the value chain, and; (4) whether the relationship must be of strategic importance to all partners.[41] Because of this, some partnerships may be classified as an alliance while others may not.

When taken within the context of the pharmaceutical industry, it is generally agreed that what constitutes an alliance are those partnerships in which at least one or more partners come together with the intention of entering a new geographical or therapeutic market, or to gain access to particular skills or resources that are located outside the firm.[42] For the purpose of this book,

> An alliance is a relationship that is strategic or tactical, and which is entered into for mutual benefit by two or more parties having compatible or complementary business interests and goals.[43] (Sergil 1996)

However on further scrutiny, it is clear that the concept 'strategy' and 'tactics' within management literature also need clarification, therefore:

> Strategy is the process of planning and directing operations into the most advantageous position before entering into engagement, while Tactics is the process of organising during engagement.[44] (Sergil 1996)

Strategy therefore presumes a level of thoughtfulness, consideration, concern and forward planning for a changing future. However since tactical manoeuvres are entered into during engagement, there is neither the time, nor the resources that would permit careful thought and planning prior to engaging in a particular activity. Since alliances are simply a means to an end, such partnerships are not always formed with long-term intentions. Yet whatever the underlying motivation for its formation, all alliances require the ability to effectively manage partnership agreements.

3.4.1   Rationale for collaboration

Since the end of the Second World War, the pace of economic and industrial change in the West has evolved in three distinct phases. First, there was the immediate post-war phase of organisational inflexibility inherited from the interwar period, with an urgent need to protect ravaged economies. Then from the 1950s onwards industry witnessed the dramatic growth of the multinational firm, and the rise of the M-form of organisation. In time however, these multinationals grew too large and cumbersome to operate efficiently as internal expansion, and the inevitable creation of hierarchy negatively affected organisational flexibility, speed of response to markets, and the free flow of information, which was so desperately needed to implement effective global strategies.[45] The world economy consequently witnessed its third evolutionary phase which manifested itself in the late 1970s through the growth of the venture-capital funded entrepreneurial firm. This gave rise to substantial outsourcing of non-key processes, causing previously internalised value-chain activities to be returned to the marketplace. These factors provided the impetus for the dramatic growth of strategic alliances and other forms of collaboration, particularly in the area of technology and marketing.

Traditionally, the R&D activities of large firms were kept within the boundaries of the organisation, with various forms of collaboration seen as second best to the option of conducting these activities alone. With the dawn of globalisation in the 1980s, and the ensuing dispersion of production, R&D and resources, companies were forced to acknowledge that they could no longer depend on the domestic market for technology as the sole source of scientific expertise. It was therefore necessary to scan and have access to, key overseas locations that were at the forefront of particular technologies, skills or buying requirements.[46] In the past, the external contribution from the perspective of the firm to the creation and successful application of technology has steadily increased, and the innovation process has become more and more interactive. The increasing speed and the mounting cost of innovation, shorter product life cycles, and the systematic rise in the costs of successfully launching a new product on the market have all played a contributory role.[47]

3.4.2   External challenges and internal needs

From an economic point of view, the main argument for alliances is that they are usually formed as a result of an external stimulus, or change in environmental conditions to which companies respond with a feeling of internal corporate need that is best met by seeking a relationship with another organisation.[48] Dunning (1974) suggests that all alliances are initiated by a change in external trading conditions, and that this change reveals an internal resource inadequacy that needs to be corrected if competitive advantage is to be maintained.[49] An alliance will therefore result if both a company and a proposed partner find themselves having complimentary resources and perceived inadequacies. Therefore whatever the external and internal drivers, one of both is necessary for each potential partner to provide a strong enough motivation for a strategic alliance.

According to Child *et al.* (1998), some of the key external driving forces for alliance formation are (1) turbulence in world markets and high economic uncertainty; (2) the existence of economies of scale as competitive cost reducing agents; (3) the globalisation or regionalisation of a growing number of industries; (4) the globalisation of technology; (5) rapid technological change that leads to ever-increasing investment requirements; and (6) the shortening of product life cycles.[50] However, according to Contractor *et al.* (1988)[51] and Kogut (1988)[52] another key determinant is risk. Collaborative ventures can reduce the degree of risk by (1) spreading the risk of a large project over more than one firm; (2) enabling diversification of the product portfolio; (3) facilitating faster entry into a market; and (4) through cost rationalisation (where the cost to the partnership is less than the cost of the investment undertaken by each firm alone). The risk sharing element of collaboration is especially important in research intensive industries such as pharmaceuticals, where each successive generation of new technology costs more to develop, leaving less time to amortise the costs of development.

A company that is able to successfully adopt new technologies, achieve economies of scale and scope, serve global markets, and change its product range regularly is therefore better placed to gain a competitive advantage over its rivals. Since few companies have the internal resources and competencies to meet all of the requirements, firms have resorted to strategic alliances and other collaborative arrangements to cope with the needs of the new economic order. In this instance, the pharmaceutical industry has proved to be no exception. As with the external challenges identified, Porter *et al.* (1986) put forward several reasons why companies would seek external co-operation, which is directly in response to the needs of internal stimuli. These include the need to (1) achieve economies of scale and learning with one's partner; (2) gain access to the benefits of the other firm's assets – be these technology, or access to markets, capital, production capacity, products or manpower; (3) reduce risk by sharing it, especially in terms of capital requirements, and often in terms of research and development expenditure; and (4) help shape the market – for example, by withdrawing capacity in a mature market.[53] Other internally motivated factors include:

a. Resource dependency   Although companies are motivated to form alliances for a wide variety of reasons, most are formed as a result of perceived resource deficiency. Alliances may be 'defensive' in nature, where collaboration occurs in order to defend domains in the face of an external threat from a common enemy. They may also be 'aggressive' in nature, by taking advantage of the prospect to work with a partner on a global scale. In either case, the motivation for the alliance is resource based. Thus the key internal motivation for alliance formation here is to gain the requisite skills or resources needed to respond to a particular external challenge or opportunity.

b. Learning Powell *et al.* (1996) suggest that sources of innovation do not reside exclusively inside firms; instead they are commonly found in the interstices between firms, universities, research laboratories, suppliers and customers.[54] For firms involved in such innovation, the primary objective is to become part of a community in which new discoveries are made, and the learning process is facilitated. In industries that are complex and expanding, and where the sources of expertise are widely dispersed, innovation is found mostly in networks rather than in individual firms.[55]

c. Speed to market Alliances are the fastest means to achieving market presence, so long as the partners each have substantial resources and robust competencies, which when taken alone are insufficient to achieve critical mass. In this instance, internal development would take much longer, while acquisition has the disadvantage of the high level of investment required.

d. Cost minimisation Williamson (1975) suggests that an alliance will be formed only if the partners consider the transaction and other associated costs to be less than what would be incurred by alternative strategic actions.[56] This may however be difficult to substantiate, primarily because transaction costs involve unquantifiable expenditures, which include the loss of proprietary expertise and knowledge that cannot be easily computed as opposed to the costs of production.

In the case of strategic alliances, it could be argued that co-operation needs for its initial stimulus a challenge from a changing external environment. If an organisation develops a particular resource deficiency in relation to an external challenge, or if it wishes to lower risk, or requires speedy access to a market – and it believes that the transaction costs of an alliance would be less than those incurred from internal development or acquisition – then the motivation to collaborate exists. In the case of the pharmaceutical industry, the rationale behind the need to collaborate is evident and is summarised by Sharp (1989) as the (1) international nature of the industry, and the continued fragmentation of markets which make *access to markets* of crucial concern; (2) rapidly increasing cost of research and development and the uncertainty associated with developments in biotechnology argue in favour of *sharing costs and risks*; and (3) very wide range of skills required with the new biotechnology that makes *access to skills and knowledge* an important factor in competitiveness.[57]

3.4.3   Forms of collaborative agreements

Interest in external sources of technology has led the R&D management community to experiment with many different forms of business relationships with 'source' organisations. A wide variety of organisational modes have been utilised in order to access external sources of technology. Since alliance forms can take a number of different configurations, they are defined in different ways by different researchers. Accordingly Table 3.2 synthesises the most common terms used in the literature to define the different types of co-operative agreements currently employed within industry.

When attempting to group the different modes of collaboration, it is possible to categorise these partnerships in terms of their level of integration. Hence, the level of integration may be defined as the extent to which the accessed activities and resources involved in collaboration are integrated or internalised within the firm's own activities and resources.[58] Therefore it is important to point out that in acquisitions (and similarly in mergers), the level of integration is high, since a firm totally integrates the accessed resources and activities. With regard to outsourcing, this requires no integration, since a firm completely externalises technological activities. Under this framework, R&D contracts, research funding and licensing can also be viewed as forms of outsourcing. In the case of joint ventures and minority equity partnerships, each partner partially integrates the accessed activities and resources, with the equity involvement implying a medium to high level of integration. Alliances therefore represent a weakly integrated organisational solution, where each partner gives its own contribution to common activities, with no equity involvement.[59]

3.4.4   Characteristics of the different forms of collaboration

The characteristic features of different organisational forms of collaboration can be examined in relation to five different variables. According to Chiesa *et al.* (1998) these factors include the impact on the firm, time scale, degree of control, elements of time and cost and flexibility.

1. *Differing modes of collaboration and its impact on the firm* in terms of:
   a. *The organisational structure of the collaborating companies*   Given the nature of the specific mode of collaboration, outsourcing does not significantly impact on the structure of the organisation. Acquisitions radically modify the firm's organisational structure since the whole of the acquired company (or a part of it) is internalised into the acquiring firm. This implies that acquired

Table 3.2   Organisational modes of technological collaboration

Acquisition	a company acquires another company in order to access a technology (or technological competence) of interest
Merger	a company merges with a company that has a technology (or technological competence) of interest, and a new company emerges
Licensing agreements	a company acquires a license for a specific technology
Minority equity investment	a company buys an equity in the source organisation in which a technology (or technological competence) of interest is embedded, but does not have management control
Joint venture	a company establishes a formal joint venture with equity involvement and a third entity is created, with a definitive objective of technological innovation
Joint R&D programme	a company agrees with another to jointly carry out research and development on a definitive technology (or technological discipline), with no equity involvement
R&D contract	a company agrees to fund the cost of R&D at a research institute, or university, or small innovative firm, for a definite technology
Research funding	a company funds exploratory research at a research institute, or university, or small innovative firm to pursue opportunities and ideas for innovation
Alliance	a company shares technological resources with other companies in order to achieve a common objective of technological innovation (without equity involvement)
Consortium	several companies and public institutions combine efforts in order to achieve a common objective of technological innovation (without equity involvement)
Networks	a company establishes a network of relationships, in order to remain at the forefront of a technological discipline and to capture technological opportunities and evolutionary trends
Outsourcing agreements	a company externalises technological activities and then, simply acquires the relative output

Source: V. Chiesa and R. Manzini, 'Organising for Technological Collaborations: A Managerial Perspective', *R&D Management* (1998). Copyright Blackwell Publishing.* Reproduced with permission.

* Journal Homepage www.blackwell-synergy.com

resources and activities have to be integrated and co-ordinated within the existing firm, while the roles and responsibilities of the employees often need to be re-defined.

b. *The firm's assets* This refers to both tangible and intangible resources. A strategy of mergers and acquisitions suggests that the assets and liabilities of the acquired firm must be internalised. Outsourcing impacts on the firm's assets only when a patent or a license is acquired. Even in this case, the effect may be limited.

c. *Human resources*   Acquiring a firm suggests that human resources must be integrated within the existing organisation, which often causes difficulty in creating a common corporate culture, and a shared set of principles and values. To a lesser extent, the same could be said for joint ventures.

2. Time scale   This refers to the duration of the collaboration. Outsourcing has a definite time scale; while licensing agreements, funding programmes and research contracts also comprise a well defined time period, after which a new contract must be established if the collaboration is to continue further.

3. Degree of control   This involves control over people, activities and assets. The outsourcing of an activity entails little control, since the company will have an *ex ante* assessment of the partner's resources and an *ex post* evaluation of the output produced. With regard to acquisitions, this involves taking control over a company's activities and resources.

4. Associated time and cost   This is what essentially defines a partnership. Equity modes of collaboration, particularly acquisitions require well-formalised analysis. This involves considerable time and resources with the final decision taken by senior management.

5. Flexibility   This refers to the extent to which the characteristics of the collaboration can be modified. Outsourcing contracts and alliances are somewhat flexible since changing the characteristics of the partnership requires a lesser time and fewer costs than is the case for acquisitions and joint ventures.

3.5   Strategies of collaboration: implications for the industry

1. Re-organise research to improve scientific creativity   Arrow (1983) suggests that scientific creativity is not always correlated with scale laboratories, but rather with flexible and informal organisations that are conducive to the production of ideas of great originality.[60] This suggests that companies need to pay considerable attention to the organisation of research so as to stimulate the research effort. Since pharmaceutical companies cannot wholly abandon systematic experiments in pre-clinical research, routine laboratory work still remains an important part of the discovery process. Thus, it was necessary for pharmaceutical companies to organise their 'upstream' research activities around a small group of talented scientists with limited control exercised on the part of senior management. Within these areas, scientists were accorded greater independence in choosing specific lines of research, since it is they that had the superior technical competencies to pinpoint domains that provided the best opportunities for technological and even commercial success.[61]

2. *Greater 'openness' of research* This form of organisation with minimal hierarchical controls and greater autonomy, implied that pharmaceutical firms had to accept greater 'openness' in research. Basic research and the computerised design of drugs meant that companies had to employ more people with a strong academic background (individuals possessing Doctorates, and academic researchers) who would have internalised, at least in part, the values of the scientific community.[62] Such individuals would therefore be inclined to publish, participate in conferences, and communicate with their colleagues.

Arora *et al.* (1992) note that there are considerable benefits associated with a greater openness of research, and highlight the importance of in-house scientific research as a means of monitoring and absorbing external scientific knowledge. First, company scientists are able to assimilate external scientific knowledge more effectively if they perform similar research themselves; and second, academic scientists are more inclined to exchange ideas with people that they deem to be part of the same 'club'.[63] However, one of the most significant drawbacks of a policy of openness is that firms lose control of internal information. However even if internal information is circulated outside of the firm, competitors would be unable to exploit it effectively unless they have similar tacit capabilities to take advantage of the available knowledge and information. The ability of firms to move quickly into promising new areas of research will once again, depend on the capacity to effectively monitor the wealth of external information, and to capture opportunities that are created largely outside the organisation.[64]

3. *Division of labour in pharmaceutical research* The adoption of more scientific methods in pharmaceutical research and innovation has important implications for market structure and the division of labour within the industry.[65] The principle reason for this lies in the nature of scientific knowledge itself. First, the underlying knowledge base can be broken down into component form, which can later be 'reassembled' into larger pieces of knowledge. Della Valle *et al.* (1993) provide a clear illustration of this phenomenon.

A company or scientific institution can establish the structure of a family of receptors in the human body. Another party clarifies the biological activity of the receptors. A third entity can determine the molecular action of a family of compounds that fit the receptor sites. Finally, the entire set of information could be brought to a fourth party who has the resources to carry out the long and costly clinical trials and to market the product.[66] (Della Valle *et al.* 1993)

Second, scientific knowledge is generic in nature and could therefore be presented in a language that is common across different organisations. This then provides a shared context amongst different firms and research institutions, wherein scientific information can be evaluated and interpreted.[67] These two features when combined encourage a division of labour amongst agents specialised in different segments of the innovation cycle, or in different research areas or market niches.[68]

Traditionally, large bureaucratic organisations were considered the optimal organisational forum for conducting both clinical trials and discovery, and the marketing of new products. With the move towards specialisation amongst firms it is now common that different firms have different comparative advantages. The larger firms have therefore come to recognise the need to be 'flexible' organisations, while smaller, research-intensive firms have recognised the value of selling their research output to larger firms with downstream capabilities. As a result, the benefits of specialisation and a division of labour in innovation are now technically possible because different pieces of knowledge can eventually be reconstructed so that it can be joined with downstream resources as well.[69]

4. The formation of networks   Technology-based industries have traditionally fallen into two categories in terms of the way companies acquire new technology: the 'assemblers' and the 'producers'.[70] Assemblers refer to those firms that construct the product using components that have been invented, developed and manufactured outside the firm. The producers on the other hand, rely on their own internally generated innovations. Until recently, the latter encompassed many of the large pharmaceutical manufacturers who served as the primary innovators in the industry. However with the emergence of biotechnology, such distinctions have become increasingly blurred as new products and processes now require the integration of several technologies and disciplines. Due to the particular constraints and opportunities surrounding commercial biotechnology, companies have been compelled to form an elaborate web of formal alliances and this has led to a rapid increase in inter-firm collaboration worldwide.[71] Therefore, the fact that pharmaceutical firms are engaging in ever-increasing numbers of R&D partnerships suggests that these firms seek to obtain more than just specialist technical expertise. The aim is to encapsulate within the firm novel ways of thinking, rather than just the technical skills that have long been held as the source of innovative success.[72] Whatever the motive for collaboration, it is clear that the innovator is no longer an individual company but a group of agents with both complementary as well as heterogeneous skills and assets that are connected with one another through an elaborate, and often complex, network arrangement.[73] Pharmaceutical innovation is therefore no longer exclusively contained within the domain of in-house research.

The 'biotechnology revolution' has irreversibly altered the composition and the direction of the pharmaceutical industry, with external research organisations taking on the role of suppliers of innovative activity. This has resulted in a new type of supplier relationship, in which large enterprises, whose core expertise is in marketing and in the co-ordination of development, contract the services of small R&D suppliers. Consequently, large pharmaceutical companies can no longer view themselves as the primary innovators in the industry.[74] In effect, large pharmaceutical companies have externalised their position at the forefront of technology. Thus, it appears that a new business strategy towards innovation has evolved – one of management and integration, rather than the execution of certain R&D activities.[75]

> The key for success is to specialise in selected fields, and to rely on partners for complimentary research and specialised technical expertise … individual competitiveness will be replaced by competition amongst networks of firms based on trust, credibility and openness of research … The industry will polarise around two fundamental agents: giant multinational corporations with considerable abilities to manage large and complex organisations, and small to medium sized firms with sophisticated scientific expertise in selected areas, which will act as suppliers of ideas, product opportunities and new technologies.[76] (Drews 1992)

The proliferation of R&D alliances with external source organisations is *not* a temporary phenomenon. Rather, a strategic change towards a high level of R&D partnership activity has taken place. The pharmaceutical industry has undergone a technological paradigm shift that has allowed it to think differently about drug development and design. Because of this, large pharmaceutical firms will continue to rely on small companies and other external agents for the supply of innovative capabilities in order to remain on the cutting-edge of scientific knowledge and research.

Notes

1. B.G. James, *The Pharmaceutical Industry in 2000: Reinventing the Pharmaceutical Company* (London: The Economist Intelligence Unit, 1994), pp. 42–62.
2. Ibid., pp. 42–62.
3. Ibid., pp. 42–62.
4. Ibid., pp. 42–62.
5. Ibid., pp. 42–62.
6. H. Buhariwala and J. Hassard, 'Strategic Research and Development: Towards Co-operative Agreements in the Pharmaceutical Industry', *Working Paper No: 91–21*, Department of Economics and Management Science, University of Keel, Staffordshire (1991), pp. 1–23.
7. B. Twiss, *Managing Technological Innovation*, Fourth Edition (London: Pitman Publishers, 1992).
8. Ibid., Twiss (1992).
9. R. Ballance, J. Pogany, and H. Forstner, *The World's Pharmaceutical Industries: An International Perspective on Innovation, Competition and Policy* (London: Edward Elgar, 1992).
10. Ibid., Balance *et al.* (1992).
11. F.J. Contractor and P. Lorange, 'Why should Firms Co-operate? The Strategy and Economic Basis for Co-operative Ventures', in F.J. Contractor and P. Lorange (eds), *Co-operative Strategies in International Business* (New York: Lexington Books, 1988), pp. 3–27.
12. J. Pfeffer and G.R. Salancik, *The External Control of Organisations: A Resource Dependence Perspective* (New York: Harper and Row, 1978).
13. C. Bowman and D. Faulkner, *Competitive and Corporate Strategy* (London: Irwin, 1997).
14. 'Why the Tough need Acquisitions to Keep Going', *Mergers & Acquisitions*, 28, Issue 6 (1994), pp. 11–19.
15. M.E. Porter, *Competitive Strategy: Techniques for Analysing Industries and Competitors* (New York: Free Press, 1980).
16. K.M. Eisenhardt, 'Agency Theory: An Assessment and Review', *Academy of Management Review*, 14, Issue 1 (1989), pp. 57–74.
17. M.C. Jensen, 'Eclipse of the Public Corporation', *Harvard Business Review*, 67, Issue 5 (1989), pp. 61–74.
18. C. Bowman and D. Faulkner, *Competitive and Corporate Strategy* (London: Irwin, 1997).
19. S.G. Amin, A.F. Hagen and C.R. Sterrett, 'Co-operating to Achieve Competitive Advantage in a Global Economy: Review and Trends', *SAM Advanced Management Journal*, 60, Issue 4 (1995), pp. 37–41.
20. Ibid., pp. 37–41.
21. B. Piachaud and F. Moustakis, 'Is there a Valid Case for Mergers within the Defence and Pharmaceutical Industries? A Qualitative Analysis', *Journal of World Affairs and New Technology*, 3, Issue 4 (2000), pp. 1–7.
22. P.S. Briggs, *Major Mergers in the Pharmaceutical Industry*, Scrip Reports (London: PJB Publications Limited, 1993), pp. 19–43.

23. PriceWaterhouse Coopers Report, *Pharmaceutical Sector Global Market and Deal Survey* (London: PriceWaterhouse Coopers, 1997), pp. 1–20.
24. Ibid., pp. 1–20.
25. Ibid., pp. 1–20.
26. W. Bogner and H. Thomas, *Drugs to Market: Creating Value and Advantage in the Pharmaceutical Industry* (Oxford: Pergamon, 1996).
27. S. Barley, J. Freeman and R. Hybels, R. 'Strategic Alliances in Commercial Biotechnology', in N. Nohria and E. Eccles (eds), *Networks and Organisations* (Cambridge: Harvard University Press, 1992), pp. 314–47.
28. M. Sharp, 'The New Biotechnology: European Governments in Search of a Strategy', *Working Paper No: 15*, Science Policy Research Unit, University of Sussex, Sussex (1985).
29. M. Sharp, 'Technological Trajectories and Corporate Strategies in the Diffusion of Biotechnology', in E. Hornell and G. Vickery (eds), *Technology and Investment: Crucial Issues for the 1990s* (London: Pinter Publications, 1990), pp. 93–114.
30. E. Whittaker and J.D. Bower, 'A Shift to External Alliances for Product Development in the Pharmaceutical Industry', *R&D Management*, 24, Issue 3 (1994), pp. 249–61.
31. H. William, 'Strategic Choices in Technology Management: Lessons from Biotechnology', *Review of Business*, 14, Issue 3 (1993), pp. 14–19.
32. M. Sharp, 'Collaboration and the Pharmaceutical Industry: Is it the Way Forward?', *Unpublished Papers*, Science Policy Research Unit, University of Sussex, Sussex (1989), pp. 1–33.
33. M. Sharp, 'Pharmaceuticals and Biotechnology: Perspectives from the European Industry', in C. Freeman, M. Sharp and W. Walker (eds), *Technology and the Future of Europe: Global Competition and the Environment in the 1990s* (London: Pinter Publications, 1991), pp. 213–30.
34. Ibid., Sharp *et al.* (1991).
35. B. Piachaud and M. Lynas, 'The Biotechnology Revolution: Implications for the Pharmaceutical Industry', *The International Journal of Biotechnology*, 2, Issue 3/4 (2001), pp. 350–61.
36. W.W. Powell, 'Learning from Collaboration: Knowledge and Networks in the Biotechnology and Pharmaceutical Industries', *California Management Review*, 40, Issue 3 (1998), pp. 228–40.
37. J. Child and D. Faulkner, *Strategies of Co-operation: Managing Alliances, Networks and Joint Ventures* (Oxford: Oxford University Press, 1998).
38. D. Collis, 'Organisational Capability as a Source of Profit', in B. Moingeon and A. Edmondson (eds), *Organisational Learning and Competitive Advantage* (London: Sage Publications, 1996), pp. 139–63.
39. J. Child and D. Faulkner, *Strategies of Co-operation: Managing Alliances, Networks and Joint Ventures* (Oxford: Oxford University Press, 1998).
40. M.E. Gordon, 'Strategic Alliances in the Pharmaceutical Industry: A Qualitative Examination', in *American Marketing Association (AMA) Educators Conference*, Enhancing Knowledge Development in Marketing, Conference Proceedings, Illinois (1995), pp. 553–8.
41. G. Devlin and M. Bleackly, 'Strategic Alliances: Guidelines for Success', *International Journal of Strategic Management: Long Range Planning*, 21, Issue 5 (1988), pp. 18–23.

42. A. Parkhe, 'Inter-Firm Diversity, Organisational Learning and Longevity in Global Strategic Alliances', *Journal of International Business Studies*, 22, Issue 4, pp. 579–601.
43. L. Segil, *Intelligent Business Alliances: How to Profit Using Today's Most Important Strategic Tool* (London: Century Business, 1996).
44. Ibid., Segil (1996).
45. L.G. Herbiniak, 'Implementing Global Strategies', *European Management Journal*, 10, Issue 4 (1994), pp. 392–403.
46. J. Howells and M. Wood, *The Globalisation of Production and Technology* (London: Belhaven Publishers, 1992).
47. F. Todtling, 'Firm Strategies and Restructuring in a Globalising Economy', *IIR Discussion Paper No: 53* (1995), pp. 1–15.
48. R. Nelson, 'Recent Evolutionary Theorising about Economic Change', *Journal of Economic Literature*, 33, Issue 1 (1995), pp. 48–90.
49. J.H. Dunning, *Economic Analysis and the Multinational Enterprise* (London: Allen and Unwin, 1974).
50. J. Child and D. Faulkner, *Strategies of Co-operation: Managing Alliances, Networks and Joint Ventures* (Oxford: Oxford University Press, 1998).
51. F.J. Contractor and Lorange P. 'Why should Firms Co-operate? The Strategy and Economic Basis for Co-operative Ventures', in F.J. Contractor and P. Lorange (eds), *Co-operative Strategies in International Business* (New York: Lexington Books, 1988), pp. 3–27.
52. B. Kogut, 'Joint Ventures: Theoretical and Empirical Perspectives', *Strategic Management Journal*, 9, Issue 4 (1988), pp. 319–32.
53. M.E. Porter and M.B. Fuller, 'Coalitions and Global Strategy', in M.E. Porter (ed.), *Competition in Global Industries* (Cambridge: Harvard University Press, 1985).
54. W.W. Powell K. Koput and L. Smith-Doerr, 'Inter-organisational Collaboration and the Locus of Innovation: Networks of Learning in Biotechnology', *Administrative Science Quarterly*, 41, Issue 1 (1996), pp. 116–45.
55. Ibid., pp. 116–145.
56. O. Williamson, *Markets and Hierarchies: Analysis and Antitrust Implications* (New York: Freepress, 1975), pp. 116–45.
57. M. Sharp, 'Collaboration and the Pharmaceutical Industry: Is it the Way Forward?', *Unpublished Papers*, Science Policy Research Unit, University of Sussex, Sussex (1989), pp. 1–33.
58. V. Chiesa and R. Manzini, 'Organising for Technological Collaborations: A Managerial Perspective', *R&D Management*, 28, Issue 3 (1998), pp. 199–212.
59. Ibid., pp. 199–212.
60. K. Arrow, 'Innovation in Large and Small Firms', in J. Ronen (ed.), *Entrepreneurship* (London: Lexington Books, 1983).
61. F. Della Valle and A. Gambardella, 'Biological Revolution and Strategies for Innovation in Pharmaceutical Companies', *R&D Management*, 23, Issue 4 (1993), pp. 287–302.
62. Ibid., pp. 287–302.
63. A. Arora and A. Gambardella, 'New Trends in Technological Change: Towards an Innovative Division of Labour', *Working Paper No: 92–37*, John Heinz III, School of Public Policy and Management, Carnegie Mellon University, Pittsburgh (1992), pp. 259–77.

64. F. Della Valle and A. Gambardella, 'Biological Revolution and Strategies for Innovation in Pharmaceutical Companies', *R&D Management*, 23, Issue 4 (1993), pp. 287–302.
65. A. Arora and A. Gambardella, 'New Trends in Technological Change: Towards an Innovative Division of Labour', *Working Paper No: 92–37*, John Heinz III, School of Public Policy and Management, Carnegie Mellon University, Pittsburgh (1992), pp. 259–77.
66. F. Della Valle and A. Gambardella, 'Biological Revolution and Strategies for Innovation in Pharmaceutical Companies', *R&D Management*, 23, Issue 4 (1993), pp. 287–302.
67. A. Gambardella, 'Competitive Advantages from In-house Scientific Research: The US Pharmaceutical Industry in the 1980s', *Research Policy*, 21, Issue 5 (1992), pp. 391–407.
68. B. Piachaud and M. Lynas, 'The Biotechnology Revolution: Implications for the Pharmaceutical Industry', *The International Journal of Biotechnology*, 2, Issue 3/4 (2001), pp. 350–61.
69. K. Arrow, 'Innovation in Large and Small Firms', in J. Ronen (ed.), *Entrepreneurship* (London: Lexington Books, 1983).
70. S. Barabaschi, 'From In-house R&D to a Multi Channel Knowledge Acquisition System', in *European Industrial Research Management Association (EIRMA) Annual Conference*, Mastering the Growth of Scientific and Technological Information, Conference Proceedings, Berlin (1990), pp. 80–8.
71. S. Barley, J. Freeman and R. Hybels, R. 'Strategic Alliances in Commercial Biotechnology', in N. Nohria and E. Eccles (eds), *Networks and Organisations* (Cambridge: Harvard University Press, 1992), pp. 314–47.
72. M. Sharp, 'Technological Trajectories and Corporate Strategies in the Diffusion of Biotechnology', in E. Hornell and G. Vickery (eds), *Technology and Investment: Crucial Issues for the 1990s* (London: Pinter Publications, 1990), pp. 93–114.
73. J. Hagedoorn, 'Inter-Firm Partnerships and Co-operative Strategies in Core Technologies', in C. Freeman and L. Soete (eds), *New Explorations in the Economics of Technological Change* (London: Pinter Publications, 1990), pp. 3–37.
74. B. Piachaud and M. Lynas, 'The Biotechnology Revolution: Implications for the Pharmaceutical Industry', *The International Journal of Biotechnology*, 2, Issue 3/4 (2001), pp. 350–61.
75. E. Whittaker and J.D. Bower, 'A Shift to External Alliances for Product Development in the Pharmaceutical Industry', *R&D Management*, 24, Issue 3 (1994), pp. 249–61.
76. J. Drews, 'Pharmaceutical Industry in Transition', *Drug News and Perspectives*, 5, Issue 3 (1992), pp. 133–8.

4
The Core Competency Framework and Approaches to R&D

The decision to outsource has traditionally been made on the basis of comparative cost. However it has been recognised that if properly implemented, outsourcing can provide a number of strategic benefits which include improved quality, focus, flexibility and leverage. If companies are to reap these benefits, it is essential that strategic sourcing decisions are based on sound strategic principles. It is important that managers consider the protection, development and exploitation of core activities, as well as the need to relate such sourcing decisions to the competitive advantage of the firm. Arguably then, the decision to 'make or buy' can be regarded as one of the most fundamental components of manufacturing strategy, as well as the most complex.

4.1 Pharmaceutical research: a definition

The role of research in the pharmaceutical industry takes its orientation from two opposing viewpoints that, for the sake of brevity could be described as 'originality' and 'independence' on the one hand, and 'emulation' and 'dependence' on the other.[1] A dynamic research idea that creates products can lead to the foundation of a company, allow diversification and open up new fields of activity. It could be said that research plays a central role in companies formed to realise specific scientific or technical projects, and it is both the powerhouse and the heart of the company, as well as the mainspring of strategy.[2] Such companies have existed through the ages and they are very much a part of the present day economy. The pharmaceutical industry provides an excellent case in point as it is a science-based sector whose pivotal function is R&D.

According to Drews (1989), research in the industrial context can be driven either by forces that are inherent in science and technology or by customer needs. In the first instance, research will generate a culture of the 'technically feasible'; while in the second, a 'demand culture' will emerge.[3] The emergence of biotechnology and genetic engineering has given rise to the biotechnology industry, which one could argue, symbolises the expression of original, scientific and realisable product ideas. Here, scientists and technologists play a dominant role; there is a mood of 'get up and go' and informality, while the organisation itself embodies a culture of the 'technically possible' – all of which are typical of young companies with a scientific and technological orientation.[4]

However as success increases, such companies begin to acquire a market orientation with the intention of securing continuity and long-term viability. Having achieved success in certain markets, as well as having established good relationships with particular customer groups, companies respond to demand by improving and upgrading the product range. Research in this instance has to attune itself to the market and to customer needs, as well as to the conditions it has itself created. Consequently, a 'demand culture', or a culture of need is established. Taken within this context, research is simply:

> A means to an end whose activities are dictated by market considerations. When applied to the pharmaceutical industry, most pharmaceutical companies contain mixtures of these two prototypes and house both types of research. However, it is the second type of research activity, characterised by emulation and entrepreneurial dependence which is dominant in most cases.[5] (Drews 1989)

In attempting to define what constitutes 'research', Harden *et al.* (1990) categorise research into three groups. These include: (1) Basic, pure or fundamental research which is done primarily to acquire new knowledge with no specific application in mind; (2) Strategic research which is conducted with eventual practical applications in mind although this cannot be clearly defined at the outset; and (3) Applied research which is directed towards specific practical aims and objectives.[6]

When taken in the context of the pharmaceutical industry, 'Research and Development' activities refer to the entire process whereby a drug is brought to market. Although R&D has traditionally been treated as one function in which are concentrated the firm's activities devoted to the development of new products and technologies, over time this R&D function has played different roles within the firm and has accordingly been managed in different ways. Roussel *et al.* (1991) have identified three approaches to R&D management which reflect three different points of view: (1) R&D as the ivory tower, where new product ideas are produced and developed, isolated from the rest of the company; (2) R&D as a function that is integrated with business management and is therefore strongly market orientated; and (3) R&D as a function which balances market-driven exploitation of technological opportunities and the exploration of new findings, and is thus linked in an operational and strategic partnership with business management.[7]

Although approaches to managing R&D have changed over time, it has always been viewed as one function from an organisational point of view. The taxonomy of R&D organisations is usually input-orientated (that is by scientific discipline), and output-orientated (that is by product line) and matrix organisations.[8] Yet in the past few years, other approaches have emerged. Firms have either changed the ways in which R&D is organised or have re-thought the overall structure of R&D on the basis of technological competence. This indicates that within R&D, there are activities that are very different in nature and would thus require different organisation and managerial approaches.

4.2 The research and development process

The R&D process as pertinent to the pharmaceutical industry is briefly outlined in Figure 4.1. It is composed of two distinct phases: drug discovery which aims at *discovering* a new compound and the development phase which aims at *evaluating* the effectiveness of the new compound.[9]

Phase 1: drug discovery

The process of developing a new drug can only begin once a compound containing potentially valuable medicinal properties has been discovered. Before this stage is reached, many years would have been spent investing in research in order to learn more about the aetiology and pathogenesis of the particular disease for which the drug is suited. Over the course of the past few decades, advances in molecular and cellular biology have contributed to a far better understanding of many diseases. In the past, the main sources of new drugs were often serendipity, folk medicine or trial and error, whereas today, drug design is much more directed.[10]

The pre-clinical phase The aim of the pre-clinical development phase for a potential new medicine is to explore the drug's efficacy and safety before it is administered to patients. In this phase, varying drug doses are tested on animals and/or in vitro systems such as yeast or bacteria. Here, various types of safety studies are required, which relate to acute,

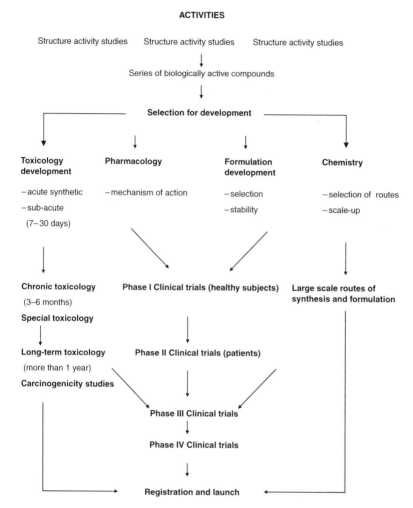

Figure 4.1   The pharmaceutical research and development process

sub-acute and chronic toxicity tests to detect unwanted general and organ-specific effects; reproductive toxicity tests to reveal the effects on fertilisation, the developing embryo, the foetus, and the new born offspring; mutagenicity tests to identify any damaging effects on DNA, genes and chromosomes; and prolonged carcinogenicity tests to discover whether the drug has the potential to cause any tumours.[11]

In addition, biological studies are carried out on animals to investigate absorption from the site of administration into the bloodstream, subsequent distribution to other parts of the body, drug metabolism, and finally, the excretion of the compound and its metabolic products. These studies which investigate how the drug and its metabolites behave in the body are referred to as pharmacokinetic (PK) studies, while those that investigate the therapeutically intended effects on the targeted organs or systems are referred to as pharmacodynamic (PD) studies.[12]

The technical development of a new medicine also begins in the pre-clinical phase, and continues during subsequent clinical phases. It includes (1) chemical development (which involves the determination of new manufacturing processes so that production can be increased in scale, while at the same time limiting impurities and degradation products); (2) analytical development (quality assurance of the compounds and the form of delivery, including stability under various conditions and over time); (3) pharmaceutical development, also known as the drug formulation process, which includes making choices about the route of administration and the dosage form (tablets, soluble tablets, capsules, suspension forms); (4) the use of excipients, which are other substances mixed with the drug as well as coatings); and (5) packaging.[13]

Phase 2: drug development

Compounds that survive the high attrition rate in the pre-clinical phase then undergo clinical investigations involving human subjects. The clinical development period is usually divided into a number of phases, with each phase progressively testing the safety and efficacy of the compound.

Phase I: clinical pharmacology & toxicity   During Phase I, which lasts an average of one year; the drug is tested on a small number of healthy (non-patient) volunteers. Participants are usually male, because at this stage it is unlikely that all reproductive toxicity tests would have been completed. These participants are also young, since the likelihood of ill-health increases with age. The main aim of these trials is to obtain data on the compound's safety, appropriate dosage range and pharmacokinetic properties. However it must be noted that in this phase, not all types of drugs are tested on non-patient volunteers. In the case of anti-cancer drugs for example, medicines are only tested on patients.

Phase II: initial clinical investigation for treatment effect   In Phase II which usually lasts approximately two years, the drug is tested in controlled studies involving 100 to 300 patient volunteers. These controlled studies have a strict inclusion and exclusion criteria, as well as treatment protocols. The principal aims in Phase II are to assess the drug's effectiveness on patients; to collect dose-response information in order to establish the dose that produces the desired effect; and to collect additional information on safety.

Phase III: full scale evaluation of treatment   Phase III studies typically last approximately three years, and involve large scale trials on a more heterogeneous patient population that better reflects the actual population. Thus, it is normal that 1000 to 3000 patients are involved in these multi-centre trials. In Phase III, the drug's effectiveness is defined more precisely, which means that information about optimum dosage and indications for use is refined. During this stage, the drug is also compared with a placebo or an available alternative drug. This process is carried out using a Randomised Clinical Trial (RCT), which is the corner stone of the clinical development phase and is accepted as the method of choice for the evaluation of new therapeutic remedies.

Collecting further information on drug safety is another function of Phase III studies. Due to the large numbers of patients involved, it is expected that the more common adverse side effects will be detected at this stage. However, the monitoring for rarer side effects that are unpredictable from the pharmacology continues in subsequent phases of development and even after the medicine has been launched. As a general rule, clinical trials continue until enough evidence has been obtained to file a New Drug Application (NDA) with the appropriate regulatory authorities. An NDA is used for applications made within the United States, while in the United Kingdom a Product Licence Application or (PLA) is required. These applications contain all the scientific data for both pre-clinical and clinical phases, as collected by the sponsor.

Phase IV: post marketing surveillance   After an NDA has been filed, the purpose of Phase IV studies is to provide data on the long-term safety and efficacy of a drug. This phase is also designed to collect new types of information, such as data on the impact of the drug on quality of life parameters (both functioning and well-being), or pharmaco-economic statistics (to assess if the drug provides value for money compared with other available therapies). Once a new drug has been approved, new clinical Phase II and III studies are initiated to develop new indications or formulations. The manufacturing company and the healthcare authorities will monitor the drug after it has been approved and marketed in order to discover whether its use may lead to any adverse reactions. Consequently, new drug development is a lengthy process.

According to the Tufts Centre for the Study of Drug Development, new drugs approved by the FDA between 1990 and 1994 took an average of twelve years from the pre-clinical development stage of a new compound to the date on which the drug received marketing approval. Since pharmaceutical innovation is associated with a high risk of failure, on average only 1 out of every 1000 compounds that enter pre-clinical testing survive to the clinical phase. Of this, just 1 out of every 5 will eventually receive regulatory approval.[14]

Such failure can be due to overly negative side effects (such as unacceptable toxicity or unwanted side effects) or because of insufficient therapeutic effects. Even for those drugs that do reach the clinical testing phase, obtaining market approval remains uncertain. It is common that, for every one hundred drugs that enter clinical studies, an average of 30 per cent will be rejected during Phase I, a further 37 per cent during the course of Phase II, 6 per cent in Phase III, and an additional 7 per cent during the regulatory review period.[15] In total, only 20 per cent of drugs that reach the stage of being tested on humans are approved for marketing.[16]

4.2.1   Differentiating between research and development

Although R&D is concerned with the discovery and exploitation of promising new candidates, the objectives and characteristics of discovery are significantly different to those of development.[17] The critical mass *per se* comprises a different meaning for 'research' and 'development'. While the critical mass of drug discovery can be measured as the 'weight of the average human brain' involved with the research process; development is strongly dependent on the number of people comprising the development team and the extent to which the project team is focussed and structured.[18] In the case of development, a large increase in personnel and funds would have a significant impact on the speed at which the project would proceed; whereas with research, a similar investment would not raise the percentage of new ideas produced. In addition, the average pharmaceutical company spends a greater proportion of its R&D budget on development; with estimates varying from 60 to 90 per cent of the total investment made.[19] Accordingly, research takes by far the smaller portion of the total R&D budget. In the case of development, the completion time of an activity can be predicted with reasonable accuracy, whereas it is totally arbitrary in research. The degree to which an activity can be formalised in development is also very high, as opposed to research where it is very low. These differences are summarised in Table 4.1.

Traditionally, research in the pharmaceutical industry consisted of the random screening of thousands of compounds, aimed at finding the one compound with specific therapeutic and biological properties. The

Table 4.1 Main differences between research and development activities

Characteristics	Research	Development
Objectives	Drug discovery	Drug development
Timing	Unpredictable	Predictable
Formalisation	Low	High
Expenditure	Modest	Substantial
End results	Unpredictable	Planned

discovery of a certain therapeutic compound was a 'casual' event which resulted from a trial-and-error approach. The research effort therefore required large laboratories and significant human, financial and technological resources. In order to protect the intellectual property rights of innovations, research was carried out in 'secret' within the firm's own laboratories, and contact with external sources was greatly limited.

Over time however, the nature of pharmaceutical research has changed through the application of two novel approaches. First, research has shifted from a trial-and-error approach to becoming a scientific, deductive process. 'Discovery by Design', where the causes of a particular pathology are examined and an 'ideal' compound is virtually created through electronic design is one such approach. Second, the adoption of 'High Throughput Screening' has radically altered the face of research. Once the medical target has been defined, automated systems systematically screen a number of molecules to check whether they meet the required criteria. Such techniques have dramatically reduced the time needed to search for potential new drugs (from years to months), as well as the total number of scientific researches needed. The production of different applications of the same compound has therefore been made much easier. This is because a compound can now be rationally modified to select different actions of the molecule so that the drug may be adapted in such a way as to obtain different therapeutic effects.[20]

As for the development process, emphasis is placed on the clinical testing of new compounds. This involves highly standardised large-scale operations which require a significant amount of resources in terms of people, technologies and finance. It is also a process that generates highly codified knowledge.

The efficiency of development activities strongly depends on the achievement of critical mass and the 'size' factor. Consequently, the greater the amount of resources, the faster the process (reducing time-to-market); and the more rational use of resources (fully exploiting the capacity of specialised assets).[21] (Chiesa *et al.* 1997)

The combination of falling drug prices together with the rise of restrictive legislation that governs the approval process, has exerted pressure for spanning the window of commercial exploitation of a new drug, and has therefore reduced the time-to-market. As a result, pharmaceutical firms have been required to enter into collaborative agreements in order to achieve the required critical mass; to access complementary resources (such as the capacity to conduct certain clinical tests); to outsource well defined stages of the development process, as well as to speed up the development process itself.[22]

4.2.2   Forms of collaborative agreements in R&D

In the research phase, there are three principle methods for accessing external resources: (1) *Fund novel research* which involves the financing of research activities within the laboratory of another company. This approach generally implies that the company financing the research project will hold the intellectual property rights to any discovery arising from the research; (2) *Monitor and license-in* which involves the monitoring of research activities carried out in external organisations and the subsequent licensing-in of any research that appears promising; and (3) *Joint research* which refers to the conducting of research in collaboration with another organisation, through the establishment of joint research teams in a given area.

Similarly in the development phase, other methods are used for accessing external resources. Although the development phase is composed of a number of different stages, the form of collaboration and the methods used to access external resources is common throughout the developmental process: (1) *Outsourcing* is a method of accessing external resources where pre-clinical and clinical activities are provided by an external organisation on a contract basis. Rather than conducting highly codified activities internally, companies can assign a Clinical Research Organisation (CRO) the task of conducting a particular activity within the development process; (2) *License-in* which involves licensing-in a drug at a particular stage of the development process. Here, the risks and costs involved vary dramatically according to the particular stage of the development process. For example, if a drug is licensed-in at an early stage of its development, the associated risk is very high, while the cost involved is comparatively low. Conversely, if the development process is at Phases III or IV, then the degree of risk is much lower, while the associated costs significantly high; and (3) *Joint ventures* which refer to agreements between companies to jointly develop or commercialise a new compound.

4.3   The core competency framework

The basic ideas behind core competencies and strategic outsourcing have been well supported by research extending over a twenty-year period.[23] In 1974, Rumelt noted that neither strategies of unrelated diversification or vertical integration, which were both favoured at the time, yielded consistently high returns.[24] Having observed the failure of many conglomerates in the 1960s and 1970s, both financial theorists and investors turned their attention to more focussed company concepts.[25] This approach simply meant a move towards 'doing what one does best' by retreating to fewer product lines. Nevertheless it was observed that, although many of the highly successful Japanese and American companies did have wide ranging product lines, these firms were not highly vertically integrated. Although the Japanese automobile industry was considered vertically integrated, it was in fact, structured around a 'mother company' which primarily performed design and assembly functions with a number of independent suppliers and alliance partners, all of which did not have ownership bonds with the 'mother company'.[26] Many other high-technology Japanese firms, particularly the more innovative ones such as Sony and Honda, also used comparable strategies to leverage a few core skills against multiple markets through the use of extensive outsourcing. Thus, the term 'core competency strategies' was later used to describe these and other less diversified strategies developed around a central set of corporate skills.[27]

Two new strategic approaches have thus emerged. When properly combined, these new options give managers the freedom to leverage their organisation's skills and resources well beyond levels obtainable through other strategic directions. The first approach refers to the identification of a company's *core competencies*. Here, the firm's own resources are concentrated on a set of core skills so that it may achieve definable pre-eminence and thereby provide unique value for customers.[28] The second refers to the *strategic outsourcing* of other non-core activities. This includes those activities traditionally considered integral to any company for which the firm has neither a critical strategic need, nor unique capabilities.[29]

In trying to assess how managers can successfully combine core competency concepts and strategic outsourcing for maximum effectiveness,

Quinn *et al.* (1994),[30] suggest that careful attention must be paid to assessing the (1) nature of the core competency framework; (2) means through which managers could analytically select and develop the core competencies that would provide the firm with uniqueness, competitive edge and the basis of value creation in the future; (3) types of non-core activities that could be outsourced; and (4) means by which managers could determine strategically (rather than in a short-term or ad-hoc fashion), the activities to be maintained internally, and those to be outsourced.[31]

Companies must therefore follow a two-pronged strategy before arriving at the decision to outsource. It is essential that management *define*, and *identify* core competencies prior to *determining* which activities it wishes to maintain in-house, and which activities it wishes to outsource.

4.3.1 Identifying core competencies

The analysis of firm strategies in terms of core competencies is invaluable in that a core competence provides a firm with a competitive distinction and thereby a gateway to new opportunities.[32] The core competence approach therefore allows for a framework that addresses key dimensions of strategic management and competition since it requires that managers and researchers think of competition not primarily as a battle for market share but as a contest for opportunity share in future markets.[33]

In order to understand and implement strategies based upon a core competence framework, the roots of core competence must be examined. Since a study of core competence is much more than merely asking the question 'what do we do well?' managers must therefore go well beyond looking at traditional product or functional strategies to the fundamentals of what the company can do better than anyone else.[34]

When reviewing the literature on what constitutes a core competence, a number of view points emerge. For example, if taken from an economic perspective, Teece *et al.* (1997) suggest that a competence is created when firm specific assets are assembled into integrated clusters spanning individuals and groups, thereby allowing distinctive activities to be performed.[35] Core competencies are those activities that are critical to a firm's survival, and should therefore be derived with reference to opportunities and threats facing the firm. If taken from the technology management approach, Leonard-Barton (1995) defines core capabilities as the knowledge set that distinguishes and provides competitive advantage.[36] However when taken from the perspective of corporate strategic management, Prahalad and Hamel (1990) define competencies as the collective learning in the organisation, especially in relation to co-ordinating diverse production skills and integrating multiple streams of technology.[37] However regardless of the specific approach adopted, core competencies must be viewed as sources of competitive advantage which when identified, should pass three qualifying tests: (1) provide access to a wide variety of markets (2) contribute towards perceived customer benefits, and (3) be difficult for competitors to imitate.[38] However Quinn *et al.* (1994), who through a study of both successful and unsuccessful corporate examples provide a comprehensive analysis of what constitutes core competencies in a firm. Accordingly, core competencies may comprise some or all of the following:

1. Skills or knowledge Competencies are sets of skills that transcend traditional business functions, which enable an organisation to consistently perform an activity better than competitors and to continually improve on the activity as markets, technology and competition evolve. Competencies could involve activities such as product or service design, technology creation, customer service or logistics that are based on knowledge, rather than on the ownership of assets or intellectual property *per se.*

2. Limited in number It is important that companies target two or three activities in the value chain that are considered most critical to future success. If this specialisation is spread to beyond three to five activities, the companies will eventually be unable to match the performance of its more focussed competitors or suppliers, since each set of skills requires total management dedication.

3. Unique sources of leverage For a strategy to be effective, management must seek out instances where there are imperfections in the market, or gaps in the knowledge base, which the company is uniquely qualified to fill and where investments in intellectual resources can be successfully leveraged.

4. Effective domination Essentially, each company is in competition with all potential suppliers of each activity in its value chain. Management must therefore benchmark its selected core competencies against all other potential suppliers of a particular activity and continue to build on those core competencies until it is demonstrably the best. Due to this, the basic nature of strategic analysis changes from the perspective of industry analysis to that of horizontal analysis, which encompasses capabilities across all potential providers of an activity regardless of which industry the supplier is located. True strategic focus therefore means the capacity to bring more power to bear on a selected sector than any competitor can.

5. *Customer focus* At least one of the firm's core competencies should directly relate to understanding and serving the needs of its customers. By aggressively examining its customers' value chains, a company can identify areas in which it can specialise and thereby provide an activity at a lower cost more effectively to them.

6. *Embedded in the organisation* When a strategy is greatly dependent on creativity, personal dedication and initiative, or on the attraction of high calibre professionals; core competencies must be captured within a company's systems. Broadly defined, this should include its values, organisational structures and management systems. With regard to actual competencies, these may include the recruiting and training of personnel, marketing, innovation and the control of remote and diverse operating sites within a common framework and philosophy.

What is clear is that competencies and capabilities are not given to a firm, but must instead be built from within. The critical task for management therefore is to create an organisation capable of infusing products with irresistible functionality or to create products that customers need but have not yet imagined.[39] Once a set of core competencies has been selected, the firm must ensure that it preserves its absolute pre-eminence in those chosen areas. Management may even need to surround those competencies with defensive positions both upstream and downstream in the value chain. It is consequently vital that managers consciously develop their core competencies so as to strategically block competitors and avoid outsourcing these functions or give suppliers access to the knowledge bases or skills that comprise these core competencies.[40]

4.3.2 Identifying Core Competencies in Relation to Pharmaceuticals

Traditionally, core competencies in pharmaceuticals have rested on the skills involved in R&D, marketing and promotion. However studies conducted by Bognor *et al.* (1994) suggest that these broad descriptions are much too general.[41] A more focussed assessment of core competency concepts in relation to the pharmaceutical industry suggests that:

1. Core R&D skills must be interpreted in relation to the various therapeutic classes of drugs that exist. It is true that differing therapeutic classes not only recognise the different pockets of demand that exists for drugs, but also the different R&D skills required to manufacture such therapies. For example, the skills required to develop antibiotic drugs are significantly different from those used to produce psychotropic drugs.

Furthermore, these therapeutic classes have also changed in their relative importance within the overall pharmaceuticals market over the years. In the 1940s and 1950s antibiotics were regarded as the primary new drug; while in the 1960s a wave of psychotropic drugs provided significant advances in dealing with mental and emotional problems. Subsequently in the 1980s, a new generation of cardiovascular drugs replaced older therapies; while in the 1990s a revolution in the biosciences led to an explosion in drug design.[42]

2. Such skills must also be interpreted in relation to the changing character of the research methodologies required to identify new drug compounds. Prior to the Second World War, skills in molecular manipulation and mass-assay testing which were originally derived from organic chemistry dominated pharmaceutical R&D. Later in the 1950s, the soil screening and fermentation techniques utilised by antibiotic manufacturers provided an alternative research base for some firms, especially those in the USA. Subsequent to this, a major shift occurred from large-scale 'trial-and-error' techniques as a result of developments in the life sciences of biology and chemistry, which by then had advanced very rapidly. These advances allowed researchers to develop drugs based on the knowledge of how the body's systems functioned, thus allowing for more concentrated research. Eventually this increased knowledge of biology led to a more radical change during the 1980s with the emergence of biotechnology as an alternative to organic chemistry, which formed the general basis for pharmaceutical research as depicted in Table 4.2.

As with changes in research methodology, a similar pattern of competence changes also occurred over time within the area of sales and promotion. Prior to the 1950s, direct selling to the physician did not exist. However the creation of 'prescription only' medicines in the USA prior to the Second World War, together with an increased flow of new synthetic antibiotics, brought about the need to develop skills for influencing the physician.[43] Since this time, pharmaceutical firms have assembled an increasing sales force with the aim of selling directly to physicians. Thus over the past fifteen years, at least two major shifts have occurred in relation to the selling pattern of pharmaceuticals. This has helped to create new platforms in the development of selling competencies, while at the same time making older methods of selling redundant.

3. There is a new and growing source of competence, which is the ability to cope effectively with external collaboration and strategic sourcing partnerships. One of the most important outcomes of the 'biological revolution' for the pharmaceutical industry has been the need to enter

Table 4.2 Core competency changes in research and development

Technology	Time scale	Effect	Function
Organic chemistry	1870–present	Established firms in Central Europe skilled in molecular manipulation and trial-and-error techniques	Hoechst & Ciba-Geigy: Sustained competencies in product development for over a century
Fermentation and soil screening techniques	1940s–present	Established firms in the USA skilled in antibiotics which is a narrow competence not widely transferable to other drug groups	Lilly & Squibb: Their leading products brought both companies industry leadership for 20 years which later began to lag
Rational drug design	1970s–present	High cost of product development was driven by advances in biochemistry	SmithKline & Merck: Able to develop drugs which required cutting-edge research across therapeutic classes
Biotechnology	1980s–present	Non-organic approaches to drug therapy meant that focus moved from protein manipulation to receptor antagonists	Genetech & Amgen: Both had specialised cutting-edge research as well as knowledge and insight

Source: Bogner, W.C. and Thomas, H. 'Core Competence and Competitive Advantage: A Model and Illustrative Evidence from the Pharmaceutical Industry' in G. Hamel and A. Heene (eds), *Competence Based Competition: Towards the Roots of Sustainable Competitive Advantage* (1994). Copyright John Wiley & Sons Limited. Reproduced with permission.

into external partnerships for product development. This move away from the traditional practice of internally conducted R&D has required that managers examine matters relating to outsourcing, partner selection and partnership management. The shift towards external collaborative ventures is irreversible owing to the dynamics of the modern pharmaceutical environment. In an industry that is as technologically diverse, and technologically reliant as pharmaceuticals, the ability to effectively manage complex corporate networks is essential and therefore a key ingredient of success for managers operating in 'virtual' organisational settings of a globalised market.

Competitive advantage must therefore be based on distinctive set of core competencies if it is to be sustained over time. However since such relationships are neither stable over time nor uniform at any given point in time, the skills which underpin the core products and services of the firm must constantly change and improve over time via learning. The implications of this are that competencies should always be viewed in dynamic terms rather than the static.

> In the short-run, a company's competitiveness derives from the price / performance attributes of current products. However in the long-run, competitiveness derives from an ability to build, at lower cost and more speedily than competitors, the core competencies that spawn unanticipated products. The real sources of advantage are to be found in management's ability to consolidate corporate-wide technologies and production skills into competencies that empower individual businesses to adapt quickly to changing opportunities.[44]
> (Prahalad and Hamel 1990)

From the perspective of strategic outsourcing, core competencies should be viewed as those activities that offer long-term competitive advantage and which therefore, *must* be rigidly controlled and protected.[45]

4.4   Appraising the sourcing decision

The practice of outsourcing select applications to external suppliers while retaining other applications in-house disregards the 'all-or-nothing' approach in favour of a more flexible and modular method of outsourcing. Although selective outsourcing can provide managers with a greater array of options, it is inevitably more confusing. This may lead to wrong decisions being made about which services should be outsourced and which should be retained in-house; to neglect the technical issues involved with outsourcing; and to miscalculate the long-term economic consequences.[46] Thus it is important to consider the wider implications of the move towards outsourcing, with regard to factors such as design, R&D, engineering, manufacturing and assembly, as well as the technology positions of competitors and potential competitors.[47] It is imperative that managers draw up an effective framework that will examine the complex issues and assumptions associated with all sourcing decisions since an analysis based exclusively on relative costs will only help provide one dimension of the answer. To this end, managers must assess the following criteria in terms of the wider implications to both the strategy and structure of the organisation.

1. Will the company achieve a competitive edge?   One of the most important factors that must be considered in relation to the question of insourcing versus outsourcing, is whether the company can achieve a sustainable competitive edge by performing an activity internally – either cheaper, better, faster or with some unique capability – on a systematic basis.[48] If one or more of these dimensions is critical to the customer, and if the company can perform a particular function uniquely well, then the activity should be retained within. Nevertheless, through careful investigation and rigorous benchmarking, it is important to ascertain if internal capabilities are indeed on a par with the best quality suppliers since it is often assumed that because a company has performed an activity internally, or if it is considered vital to the business, that activity should be kept within the domain of the firm.

2. How vulnerable will the firm be?   Quinn *et al.* (1994) identify two causes of vulnerability. The first occurs when there are *many suppliers* in the marketplace. In this case, it is unlikely that the company will be more efficient than the best available supplier. However if there is insufficient depth in the market, overly powerful suppliers could hold the company to ransom. The second cause of vulnerability derives from *a lack of information* in the marketplace. Here, problems could arise if a supplier has unique information that the purchasing company does not hold. Suppliers may then be able to charge what are essentially considered monopoly prices, which could nevertheless be less costly than reproducing the service internally. Stuckey *et al.* (1993) identify three forms of 'asset specificity' that commonly create market imperfections: (1) *Site specificity* where a group of suppliers locate costly fixed assets in close proximity to the buyer, thus helping to minimise both transport and inventory costs for the supplier; (2) *Technical specificity* where one or both parties are required to invest in equipment that can only be used by the two parties concerned. In most instances, such technology has a low alternate use; and (3) *Human capital specificity* where employees are required to develop in-depth skills that are specific to a particular buyer or customer relationship.[49]

3. *How much control will the company want to maintain?* When deciding on a sourcing strategy for a particular segment of the business, managers have a number of control options to choose from. Where there is a high potential for vulnerability, combined with a high potential for achieving a competitive edge, stringent control measures are required. The opposite is true for more basic tasks. Between these two extremes however are opportunities for developing special incentives or more complex contracts to balance intermediate levels of vulnerability against more moderate prospects for competitive edge.[50] In working through the available options, Quinn *et al.* (1994) suggest that managers should ask themselves the following questions:

a. Does the company truly want to produce the product or service internally in the long term? If so, can the company provide the supporting investments necessary to sustain a position of pre-eminence? Is this critical to defending core competencies? *Or,*

b. Can the company license-in technology or purchase knowledge that would enable it to be the best over the long term? *Or,*

c. Can the company buy the item as a complete product or service from the best supplier? Would this be a viable long term option as volume and complexity levels grow? *Or,*

d. Can the company establish a joint development project with a knowledgeable supplier that would eventually provide it with the capability to be best in the particular activity? *Or,*

e Can the company enter into a long-term development or purchase agreement that would provide it with a secure source of supply and a proprietary interest in knowledge, or other property of vital interest to both the supplier and the firm? *Or,*

f. Can the company acquire and manage a best-in-class supplier to its advantage? If not, can the company establish a joint venture or partnership that avoids the possible limitations of each of the above? *If so,*

g. Can the company establish controls and incentives that would reduce total transaction costs below the level of producing the same goods or services internally?[51]

4. *Could an internal department provide the service more efficiently than an outside supplier?* The common assumption is that economies of scale, highly skilled personnel, and superior practices allow external suppliers

to provide a service more efficiently than an internal department possibly could. However evidence from a survey conducted by Lacity *et al.* (1995) suggests that many departments do in fact have equally successful technologies and adequate economies of scale, but are not allowed to adopt the best practices that would help them match or defeat a supplier's tender. In other words, internal departments were not allowed to compete. However if a company should choose to invite internal departments to bid for specific contracts, managers should accomplish two things. First, employees should be motivated to find novel ways of providing the same service at lower cost; and second, management should gain a much deeper understanding of the costs of a given service and the best ways in which it should be provided, thereby placing themselves in a stronger position to evaluate future bids more effectively and to write contracts that would better serve the interests of the firm should management decide to outsource in the future.[52]

5. How will changes in the business environment affect overall strategy? The decision to outsource must be assessed in relation to its effect on competitive advantage and to possible changes in the organisation's business environment.[53] All sourcing decisions must support business strategy, and should be revised as competitive conditions change. Since strategy is a way of responding to changes in the business environment, Jennings (1997) suggests that management must (1) develop a clear understanding of the unit's business strategy; (2) consider all potential environmental changes that may alter the competitive forces in the industry, which will require a subsequent change to the business strategy of the firm; (3) consider the implications of the sourcing strategy in relation to achieving the business strategy, including the effect upon cost, quality and flexibility; and (4) question the merits of investing in in-house facilities when fluctuations in demand make the economies of their utilisation uncertain.[54]

6. Is there an economic rationale?   All businesses, including those that compete through differentiation, need to achieve the lowest level of cost consistent with the business strategy. Outsourcing allows the company to benefit from a superior set of cost drivers, which include factors such as scale, learning and location, all of which are available to the supplier.[55] Because of this, outsourcing can make a significant contribution towards reducing cost. However cost considerations require a careful evaluation of service levels and the various components that make up that cost. This is because the costs of delivering a defined level of service are far ranging and include both explicit and implicit costs.[56] The company must therefore (1) recognise the importance of cost, and the potential cost savings that could be made in terms of the organisation's competitive strategy and profitability; (2) fully define the service provided, including aspects such as 'free' advice and flexibility; (3) include all costs in the costing exercise, including the alternative net revenue available through the releasing of staff and facilities; and (4) avoid developing cost penalties for those activities that are retained in-house that could arise through increasing cost allocations or loss of economies of scale.[57]

It is therefore important that the sourcing decision makes economic, if not economical sense. Before an activity is outsourced it is essential that the implications of proposed actions and any proposals by potential suppliers are thoroughly examined. Willcocks *et al.* (1995) suggest that four key issues must be explored. (1) Are projected in-house costs static, or can action be taken to reduce them? (2) Will supplier motivation to increase profit through the reduction of cost affect the quality of the service provided? (3) How 'fixed' is the price? (4) Will there be expensive add-ons and how does the price compare to what else is available on the market?[58]

7. How will outsourcing affect organisational capabilities? Although reducing cost is an important consideration, comparative cost is not a sufficient justification for outsourcing. Evaluating all activities purely on the basis of cost fails to recognise the strategic significance of some activities and may lead to the loss of strategically important capabilities.[59] Firms must instead distinguish between core and peripheral activities so as to avoid losing their distinctive capabilities through misguided outsourcing. Quinn *et al.* (1990) suggest that if utilised correctly, outsourcing should reduce the scope of an organisation's activities, thereby allowing management to achieve increased focus upon the development and exploitation of core capabilities and increased leverage.[60] Therefore when considering the outsourcing of near to core activities, Jennings (1997) recommends that (1) great care must be taken to protect and develop core capabilities and the integration of the activities that provide capability; (2) outsourcing decisions must be viewed as opportunities to improve the organisation's focus upon its distinctive capabilities and to further the leverage of those capabilities; and (3) the creation of a competitor through the leakage of knowledge concerning essential technologies or customer information must be avoided.[61]

8. How will the company manage supplier relationships? The relationships that develop between an organisation and its suppliers can provide the opportunity for improving performance and competitive advantage, and may also lead to far reaching change. However supplier relationships could also expose the organisation to new dangers, especially in relation to the potential power of suppliers. Should an outside supplier prove disappointing, or attempt to impose price increases, the contracting firm may face considerable switching costs, which include the cost of negotiation with new suppliers.[62] In the event that a suitable replacement cannot be found, the company will have to consider returning to in-house supply. However, the need to re-develop the required expertise can prove both difficult, as well as an unattractive use of scarce resources. In order to avoid potential future difficulties, both parties to a supply agreement must establish clear and shared expectations concerning the levels of service. The contracting company must also give consideration to the strategic intent of potential suppliers, including the possibility of the outsourcing arrangement creating a competitor in the future.[63]

The long-term aspirations of the organisation to reduce cost, improve quality, make technical progress, as well as to develop products and services all contribute to shaping supply arrangements. Since such relationships are designed to be long term, it leads to advantages that arise from the adaptation between supplier and customer, whereby each organisation in the supply network is able to develop its own expertise while adapting to the requirements of other members.[64] Through improved flexibility and learning, these networks improve the organisation's ability for self-renewal and adaptation without the loss of effectiveness.[65]

Because such close working relationships create significant levels of dependence and vulnerability for both parties, while increasing the opportunity and incentive for opportunistic behaviour, Jennings (1997) recommends that management should (1) identify a number of viable suppliers; (2) ensure that there is effective future competition in the supply market, or that the power of suppliers can be counteracted; (3) evaluate the cost of having to switch suppliers; (4) avoid creating a monopoly in supply; (5) carefully select the supplier, evaluate the supplier's capability and culture as well as its compatibility with the contracting organisation; and (6) explicitly state and agree expectations concerning levels of service and their development.[66]

9. How will the company successfully exploit technology sourcing? For a business to develop and sustain a competitive advantage, it needs to have access to one or more technologies, and be able to benefit from, or even lead in technology creation. Therefore the decision of which technologies should be developed in-house, and which must be outsourced, must be made selectively so as to ensure support for sustaining the competitive advantage of the firm. In light of this, Welch *et al.*

(1992)[67] suggest that for each technology, attention must be given to:

a. The importance of the technology for competitive advantage: The organisation must focus investment and management attention on those technologies that provide distinctive product and service characteristics, since changes in the competitive environment can dramatically alter, and even reduce, the importance of a particular technology for competitive advantage.

b. The maturity of the process technology: This could be determined by scanning other industries, as well as the industry in which the company operates. It is important to carry out this assessment process in order to avoid recreating developments that have been achieved elsewhere, and to discover technologies that might be available through purchasing, licensing or other supply agreements.

c. The company's relative technological performance versus that of competitors: If the company's technological performance lags in relation to its competitors, it may be impossible to bridge this gap through internal development alone. As a result, the technology may have to be accessed through an outside supply arrangement.

10. What are the issues concerning the transferring of people and assets? A key concern of any company should be the risk of being bound to an irreversible contract, which questions the astuteness of transferring the ownership of assets, along with personnel to the supplier. To reduce the probability of unforeseen obstacles, Willcocks *et al.* (1995) recommend that management consider the (1) the advantages to be gained from transferring all or some personnel, and assets to the vendor; (2) what critical skills and assets should not be transferred; and (3) the identifiable risks of making the specific transfers planned.[68]

Quinn *et al.* (1994) therefore suggest that the main concern should not be whether a company should make or buy an activity *per se*, but rather how it would be able to structure internal versus external sourcing arrangements on an optimal basis. Due to increasing complexity, greater specialisation, and the proliferation of new technical capabilities, outside suppliers are able to perform many such activities at lower cost and with a higher added value than most fully integrated companies can. In some cases, new production technologies have moved manufacturing economies of scale towards the supplier.

In certain specialised niches, outside companies have grown to such size and sophistication that they have developed economies of scale, scope and knowledge intensity so formidable that neither smaller nor more integrated producers can effectively compete with them. Therefore, to the extent that knowledge about a specific activity is more important than knowledge about the end product itself, specialised suppliers can often produce higher value added at a lower cost for that activity than almost any integrated company.[69] (Quinn and Hilmer 1994)

Ranganath Nayak (1993) therefore suggests that the 'make or buy' decision should be viewed as a process of continual strategic analysis. For what may seem a sensible course of action at a given point in time, may not be so in the future due to changes in technology, markets, suppliers and (or) competitors. Due to the inherent difficulties involved with the decision making process, it is considered prudent to buy from external sources when the (1) technology is of low significance to competitive advantage; (2) supplier has proprietary technology that is needed; (3) supplier's technology is better and (or) cheaper than that of the purchasing company, and is relatively easy to integrate; (4) core of the strategy is based on system design, marketing, distribution and service, rather than on development and manufacturing; (5) technology development process requires special expertise; and (6) technology development process requires external accountability.[70]

It is clear that over the past few decades, advances in technology have enabled managers to effectively segment their value chains, which has presented companies with a number of flexible options. This has enabled management to maintain key strategic elements internally, while at the same time outsourcing some, or all, remaining components to suppliers anywhere in the world with the minimum of transaction costs. It is therefore not unusual that many companies have reduced their functions to those deemed essential for providing customers with the greatest possible value from its core skills. To achieve this however, companies must follow a two-step strategy. First, the management must concentrate on identifying those few core service activities, in which it has, or can at least develop unique capabilities. Second, management must aggressively seek ways to eliminate, limit, or outsource those remaining functions in which the company cannot attain superiority. This helps management to focus on what it does best, as well as to leverage its organisational and financial resources far beyond what traditional strategies allow.

Thus, the benefits of successfully combining the two approaches are considerable since it allows managers to leverage company resources in four key ways. First, to maximise returns on internal resources by concentrating investments and energies on what the organisation does best. Second, such well-developed core competencies provide formidable barriers against present and future competitors that seek to expand into the company's area of interest. This helps to facilitate and protect the strategic advantages of the market share. Third, the company is able to fully utilise a supplier's investments, innovations and specialised professional capabilities which would otherwise be prohibitively expensive, or even impossible to duplicate internally. Fourth, in rapidly changing markets and technological situations, this joint strategy decreases risks, shortens product cycle times, lowers investments and creates better responsiveness to customer needs.[71]

In answering the question 'is the company truly competitive and how can intelligent outsourcing improve productivity and the company's competitive position over the long-term?' Quinn *et al.* (1990) suggest that competitive analyses should not only consider competitors within the company's own industry or the exclusive providers of a service, but all potential providers and industries that might cross-compete in the activity, using relevant benchmarks. The rational for this is multifaceted. On the one hand, this approach broadens the analytical process and gives it a much more external, market-driven orientation, while on the other, it also introduces new objectivity into the evaluation process, and at a minimum, generates strong pressures for productivity gains if management decides to continue sourcing internally. In the end, the central issue should not be whether or not to outsource a particular function. Rather emphasis must be placed on *how* a company will be able to use the market and associated services for organisational advantage, if it chooses to follow an outsourcing strategy. To determine this will therefore require careful thought and consideration about the costs and benefits associated with the strategic sourcing process.

Notes

1. J. Drews, 'Research in the Pharmaceutical Industry', *European Management Journal*, 7, Issue 1 (1989), pp. 23–30.
2. Ibid., pp. 23–30.
3. Ibid., pp. 23–30.
4. Ibid., pp. 23–30.
5. Ibid., pp. 23–30.
6. D. Harnden and D. MacArthur, *The Management of Pharmaceutical R&D: The Keys to Success*, Scrip Reports (London: PJB Publications Limited, 1990), pp. 14–31.
7. P.A. Roussel, K.N. Saad and T.J. Erickson, *Third Generation R&D* (Cambridge: Harvard University Press, 1991).

8. B. Twiss, *Managing Technological Innovation*, Fourth Edition (London: Pitman Publishers, 1992).
9. J. Drews, 'Research in the Pharmaceutical Industry', *European Management Journal*, 17, Issue 1 (1989), pp. 23–30.
10. K.I. Kaitin and H. Houben, 'Worthwhile Persistence: The Process of Developing New Drugs', *Odyssey: The GlaxoWellcome Journal of Innovation in Healthcare*, 1, Issue 3 (1995), pp. 54–9.
11. Ibid., pp. 54–9.
12. Ibid., pp. 54–9.
13. Ibid., pp. 54–9.
14. D.E. Wierenga and C.E. Eaton, 'The Drug Development and Approval Process', Office of Research and Development, Pharmaceutical Research Association (1999), http:www.allp.com
15. K.I. Kaitin and H. Houben, 'Worthwhile Persistence: The Process of Developing New Drugs', Odyssey: The *GlaxoWellcome Journal of Innovation in Healthcare*, 1, Issue 3 (1995), pp. 54–9.
16. Ibid., pp. 54–9.
17. V. Chiesa, 'Separating Research from Development: Evidence from the Pharmaceutical Industry', *European Management Journal*, 14, Issue 6 (1996), pp. 638–47.
18. Ibid., pp. 638–47.
19. 'Pharmaceutical Companies Confront High Costs of Drug Development', *R&D*, 38, Issue 11 (1996), pp. 17.
20. V. Chiesa and R. Manzini, 'Managing Virtual R&D Organisations: Lessons from the Pharmaceutical Industry', *International Journal of Technology Management*, 13, Issue 5/6 (1997), pp. 471–85.
21. Ibid., pp. 471–85.
22. Ibid., pp. 471–85.
23. O. Williamson, *Markets and Hierarchies: Analysis and Antitrust Implications* (New York: Free Press, 1975).
24. R. Rumelt, Strategy, *Structure and Economic Performance* (Cambridge: Harvard University Press, 1974).
25. P.Y. Barreyre, 'The Concept of Impartation Policies: A Different Approach to Vertical Integration Strategies', *Strategic Management Journal*, 9, Issue 5 (1998), pp. 507–20.
26. J.B. Quinn, and F.G. Hilmer, 'Strategic Outsourcing', *Sloan Management Review*, 35, Issue 4 (1994), pp. 43–55.
27. C.K. Prahalad, and G. Hamel, 'The Core Competence of the Corporation', *Harvard Business Review*, 68, Issue 3 (1990), pp. 79–91.
28. J.B. Quinn, T.L. Doorley and P.C. Paquette, 'Technology in Services: Rethinking Strategic Focus', *Sloan Management Review*, 31, Issue 2 (1990), pp. 79–88.
29. J.B. Quinn, 'Leveraging Knowledge and Service Based Strategies Through Outsourcing', in J.B. Quinn (ed.), *Intelligent Enterprise: A Knowledge and Service Based Paradigm for Industry* (New York: Free Press, 1992).
30. J.B. Quinn and F.G. Hilmer, 'Strategic Outsourcing', *Sloan Management Review*, 35, Issue 4 (1994), pp. 43–55.
31. Ibid., pp. 43–55.

32. P. Stonham, 'The Future of Strategy: An Interview with Gary Hamel', *European Management Journal*, 11, Issue 2 (1993), pp. 150–57.
33. H.E. Post, 'Building a Strategy on Competencies', *The International Journal of Strategic Management: Long Range Planning*, 30, Issue 5 (1997), pp. 733–40.
34. J.B. Quinn, T.L. Doorley and P.C. Paquette, 'Beyond Products: Service Based Strategies', *Harvard Business Review*, 68, Issue 2 (1990), pp. 58–67.
35. D.J. Teece, G. Pisano and A. Shuen, 'Dynamic Capabilities and Strategic Management', *Strategic Management Journal*, 18, Issue 7 (1997), pp. 509–34.
36. D. Leonard-Barton, *Wellsprings of Knowledge: Building and Sustaining the Sources of Innovation* (Cambridge: Harvard University Press, 1995).
37. C.K. Prahalad and G. Hamel, 'The Core Competence of the Corporation', *Harvard Business Review*, 68, Issue 3 (1990), pp. 79–91.
38. Ibid., pp. 79–91.
39. Ibid., pp. 79–91.
40. J.B. Quinn and F.G. Hilmer, 'Strategic Outsourcing', *Sloan Management Review*, 35, Issue 4 (1994), pp. 43–55.
41. Bogner, W.C. and Thomas, H. 'Core Competence and Competitive Advantage: A Model and Illustrative Evidence from the Pharmaceutical Industry' in G. Hamel and A. Heene (eds), *Competence Based Competition: Towards the Roots of Sustainable Competitive Advantage* (Chichester: John Wiley and Sons, 1994).
42. Ibid., Bognar *et al.* (1994).
43. P. Temin, *Taking your Medicine: Drug Regulation in the United States* (Cambridge: Harvard University Press, 1980).
44. C.K. Prahalad and G. Hamel, 'The Core Competence of the Corporation', *Harvard Business Review*, 68, Issue 3 (1990), pp. 79–91.
45. J.B. Quinn and F.G. Hilmer, 'Strategic Outsourcing', *Sloan Management Review*, 35, Issue 4 (1994), pp. 43–55.
46. M.C. Lacity, L.P. Willcocks and D.F. Feeny, 'The Value of Selective IT Sourcing', *Sloan Management Review*, 37, Issue 3 (1996), pp. 13–25.
47. P. Ranganath Nayak, 'Should you Outsource Product Development?' *Journal of Business Strategy*, 14, Issue 3 (1993), pp. 44–5.
48. J.B. Quinn and F.G. Hilmer, 'Strategic Outsourcing', *Sloan Management Review*, 35, Issue 4 (1994), pp. 43–55.
49. J. Stuckey and D. White, 'When and When not to Vertically Integrate', *Sloan Management Review*, 34, Issue 3 (1993), pp. 71–84.
50. J.B. Quinn and F.G. Hilmer, 'Strategic Outsourcing', *Sloan Management Review*, 35, Issue 4 (1994), pp. 43–55.
51. Ibid., pp. 43–55.
52. M.C. Lacity, L.P. Willcocks and D.F. Feeny, 'IT Outsourcing: Maximise Flexibility and Control', *Harvard Business Review*, 73, Issue 3 (1995), pp. 84–93.
53. R. Rumelt, *Strategy, Structure and Economic Performance* (Cambridge: Harvard University Press, 1974).
54. D. Jennings, 'Strategic Guidelines for Outsourcing Decisions', *Strategic Change*, 6, Issue 2 (1997), pp. 85–95.
55. M.E. Porter, *Competitive Advantage*: *Creating and Sustaining Superior Performance* (New York: Free Press, 1985).
56. D. Jennings, 'Strategic Guidelines for Outsourcing Decisions', *Strategic Change*, 6, Issue 2 (1997), pp. 85–95.

57. Ibid., pp. 85–95.
58. L.P. Willcocks, G. Fitzgerald and D.F. Feeny, 'Outsourcing IT: The Strategic Implications', *International Journal of Strategic Management, Long Range Planning*, 28, Issue 5 (1995), pp. 59–69.
59. D. Jennings, 'Strategic Guidelines for Outsourcing Decisions', *Strategic Change*, 6, Issue 2 (1997), pp. 85–95.
60. J.B. Quinn, T.L. Doorley and P.C. Paquette, 'Technology in Services: Rethinking Strategic Focus', *Sloan Management Review*, 31, Issue 2 (1990), pp. 79–88.
61. D. Jennings, 'Strategic Guidelines for Outsourcing Decisions', *Strategic Change*, 6, Issue 2 (1997), pp. 85–95.
62. J. Stuckey and D. White, 'When and When not to Vertically Integrate', *Sloan Management Review*, 34, Issue 3 (1993), pp. 71–83.
63. R.A. Bettis, P. Bradley and G. Hamel, 'Outsourcing and Industrial Decline', *Academy of Management Executive*, 6, Issue 1 (1992), pp. 7–23.
64. D. Jennings, 'Strategic Guidelines for Outsourcing Decisions', *Strategic Change*, 6, Issue 2 (1997), pp. 85–95.
65. R.R. Miles and C.C. Snow, 'Causes of Failure in Network Organisations', *California Management Review*, 34, Issue 4 (1992), pp. 53–72.
66. D. Jennings, 'Strategic Guidelines for Outsourcing Decisions', *Strategic Change*, 6, Issue 2 (1997), pp. 85–95.
67. J.A. Welch and P. Ranganath Nayak, 'Strategic Sourcing: A Progressive Approach to the Make-or-Buy Decision', *The Academy of Management Executive*, 6, Issue 1 (1992), pp. 23–32.
68. L.P. Willcocks, G. Fitzgerald and D.F. Feeny, 'Outsourcing IT: The Strategic Implications', *International Journal of Strategic Management: Long Range Planning*, 28, Issue 5 (1995), pp. 59–69.
69. J.B. Quinn and F.G. Hilmer, 'Strategic Outsourcing', *Sloan Management Review*, 35, Issue 4 (1994), pp. 43–55.
70. P. Ranganath Nayak, 'Should you Outsource Product Development?' *Journal of Business Strategy*, 14, Issue 3 (1993), pp. 44–5.
71. J.B. Quinn and F.G. Hilmer, 'Strategic Outsourcing', *Sloan Management Review*, 35, Issue 4 (1994), pp. 43–55.

5
Outsourcing Pharmaceutical Product Development

Outsourcing has become an essential business tool for the biotechnology, pharmaceutical and medical devices industries. The traditional vertically integrated, self-sufficient organisational model is all but obsolete. Today, companies experiment with strategic alliances, networks and other forms of commercial relationships to discover more efficient ways of managing the organisation. The era of virtual integration and that of the 'virtual organisation' has dawned, and has rapidly gained momentum. In this modern epoch, a new philosophy has emerged which defines the ingredients for management success: speed, expertise, flexibility and innovation.

5.1   An introduction to strategic outsourcing

Historically, large manufacturing companies conducted almost all of their production in-house, thereby enabling management to exert control over all phases of the production process. The rationale for this lay in the expectation that the manufacturer would be able to reap the benefits of economies of scale, and secure a greater degree of consistency over supply. At a time when most firms enjoyed limited competition and a relatively stable demand for products, outsourcing was not considered a desirable nor profitable business choice.[1] Instead, the focus of production lay on control.

The advent of global competition and its subsequent growth in the 1990s provided the impetus for firms to streamline their internal operations and to concentrate more closely on those activities deemed 'core'. Those that were not, were essentially suited for outside supply. The formation of strategic supplier partnerships has therefore become an integral component of business strategy for most firms.[2] For if implemented correctly, such partnerships had the potential to offer those companies a tremendous competitive advantage.[3]

Although the growth of outsourcing has significantly increased in both absolute and relative terms over the past decade, the concept of 'outsourcing' itself is in fact not a new phenomenon. According to Howell (1999), industry today has witnessed a return towards the 'norm' for industrial R&D that existed at the turn of the twentieth century. Since in-house R&D laboratories were considered novel during this period, it was common for most firms to conduct research by contracting out such undertakings to universities or independent research scientists when necessary.[4] Even in the pharmaceutical industry, which is a sector with a long scientific tradition, this was considered the most appropriate method for conducting research up until the First World War.[5] With regard to the United Kingdom, the problem was more acute as the emergence and development of in-house R&D departments occurred at a much later date. These laboratories were less adequate in nature when compared to those that had emerged in the United States and especially Germany.[6] It was during the interwar years however, that the USA, and the UK, established a tradition of large, centralised R&D laboratories.[7]

Although there is ample evidence that companies today experiment with various forms of external collaborations in order to access innovative technology and expertise; it appears that a re-learning process of the collaborative practices used in the late nineteenth and early twentieth centuries is taking place. As companies seek a more balanced and mature approach to their research and technological requirements, a new era relating to the acquisition of such competencies, and patterns of collaboration have emerged.[8] Firms have come to realise that it is not only necessary to have the internal capacity to adequately appraise, select and then utilise 'imported' research, but the knowledge to retain selected core technological competencies within the firm so that research can be undertaken more effectively on a hierarchical, non-contractual basis.

This appreciation of the importance of innovation and new product development as a means to creating effective competitive advantage has resulted in a significant repositioning of the ways in which some companies actually organise for R&D. With the efficiency of the R&D pipeline under increasing scrutiny, a trend towards the 'virtual R&D' organisation has occurred. According to Bone (1996), the virtual R&D organisation, therefore, behaves quite differently from the traditional firm since it generates maximum business advantage from the application of technology by (1) accessing the most relevant technology from the most competent sources; (2) developing and using a formal technology management process; (3) installing formal processes for finding and integrating external technologies; (4) replacing fixed costs of capital, internal R&D and equipment with variable costs; (5) managing virtual teams across commercial and national boundaries; and (6) creating a culture focussed on speed, excellence and networks.[9]

The reasoning behind the move towards 'virtual R&D' is clear. Creativity, combined with technology, is undoubtedly an important determinant of competitiveness, since all companies seek more effective ways of responding to changing market situations.[10] Furthermore, the results of past rationalisation of R&D groups have left some companies struggling to maintain a position of strength in important areas of development. This is especially true in the case of pharmaceuticals. Managed outsourcing is therefore a means to preserving the necessary critical mass.

5.1.1 Towards a definition of outsourcing

Outsourcing has often been referred to as everything that an organisation purchases from outside suppliers (see Figure 5.1) and is viewed as a function that encapsulates the many forms of organising work, which include the production of goods and services. For the purpose of this book however, it is appropriate that the term 'outsourcing' be properly defined and understood. In view of this, outsourcing essentially involves:

> Turning over a part of, or all of those functions that fall outside the organisation's chosen core competencies to an external supplier whose core competencies are the functions being outsourced[11] (Sharpe 1997)

Similarly, Brancaccio (1998) also offers an insightful definition of what constitutes the outsourcing process. To this end, strategic outsourcing may be viewed as the desire to make, implement and review informed sourcing decisions based on an (1) agreed and communicated current set of core competencies; (2) understanding of short, medium and long-term resource demands; (3) understanding of the quality, quantity and cost of the available internal resource and the external supply base; (4) current knowledge of best sourcing strategy, practice and behaviours gleaned from inside and outside the organisation.[12] However, this does not imply that all outsourcing decisions must or will be 'strategic'.

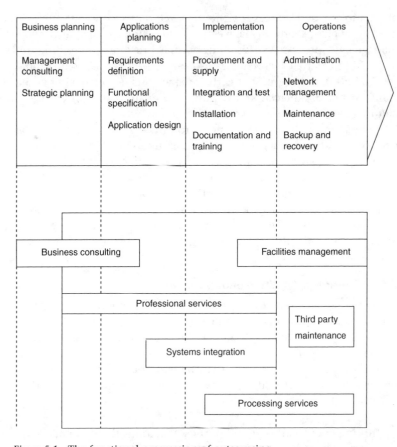

Figure 5.1   The functional progression of outsourcing

Source: J. Gantz, 'Outsourcing: Threat or Salvation?' *Networking Management* (1990). Copyright John Gantz. Reproduced with permission.

Tactical relationships are equally important and must also be managed professionally. Therefore, the ultimate aim of strategic sourcing must be to:

> Successfully leverage internal and external skills, knowledge and technology; to enhance the effectiveness of development thereby helping the company to realise and sustain a competitive advantage[13] (Brancaccio 1998)

Although the pharmaceutical industry is one of the world's most profitable sectors, it is also one of the most isolated. Historically, the brains in research, development, sales and marketing have been developed in-house. The pride taken in home-grown skills has to a great extent acted as a deterrent for pharmaceutical firms to outsource any of these components.[14] Since today the technologies required for discovering new drugs have rapidly proliferated, it has made it impossible for pharmaceutical firms to conduct all R&D activities alone. Through outsourcing, firms have therefore been able to access a variety of techniques and methodologies which it could otherwise not hope to achieve on its own.

5.1.2 Rational for outsourcing

Studies relating to the motives for outsourcing have sought to emphasise 'push' and 'pull' factors as possible causes for externalising a part of the R&D portfolio. With regard to 'push' factors, the most frequently cited causes are the increasingly complex and fast changing nature of research, together with the high costs and risk associated with the R&D process.[15] For many companies, this is an intractable problem since novel technical discoveries demand that firms cope with difficult and complex scientific problems. At the same time, the product offerings of firms have also become more sophisticated as companies strive to cater to changes in production techniques, and to consumer demand.[16] As for 'pull' factors, these refer to the relative attractiveness of external sources of expertise as opposed to the internal resources of the firm. Howell (1999) suggests that outsourcing provides the firm with the opportunity to network with other agents, which would permit in-house staff to become part of a wider 'invisible college' within a specific research community.[17]

Thus it may be argued that the rise of outsourcing is not the consequence of a sudden technical breakthrough but rather the result of market forces creating a new and specific type of demand.[18] The convergence of these 'push' and 'pull' factors have made companies realise that they simply do not have all the necessary resources within the firm to effectively cover all aspects of the R&D process, which encompass a range of scientific and technological disciplines. The desire to satisfy this need has therefore provided the impetus for further collaboration.

When taken within the context of the pharmaceutical industry, traditional wisdom dictates that (1) with high fixed costs and a correspondingly high level of government intervention, it would be difficult to realise manufacturing economies without jeopardising standards of quality or future capacity; (2) for companies committed to innovation as a source of growth, it would be irrational to restrict investment in R&D; and (3) with intense competition and longer development times, a high promotional spend is the only means of achieving a reasonable return in the time allowed.[19] Therefore rather than store resources with a view to meeting all possible demands, it would be optimal to retain sufficient resources in-house while contracting out supplementary requirements. With this in mind, Griggs (1993)[20] and Taaf (1996)[21] suggest that the use of external resources by pharmaceutical companies is driven by the desire to acquire:

1. Extra capacity   Outsourcing is primarily driven by a need to overcome a lack of capacity within the pharmaceutical firm. In times of peak activity, outsourcing enables a rapid response to a surge in demand for a given product or service since the excess work can be turned over to an external contractor.

2. Backup capacity   Although a company can invest in its own support facility for use in the event that a primary site or supplier fails, this service can be provided much more economically by contractors.

3. Multi-sourcing capability   Under this arrangement, products or services can be drawn from several sites in line with commercial and strategic requirements.

4. Access technologies and skills   The decision to use an outside supplier must take into account a number of variables which include, the entry cost for that technology; the availability of facilities for installation; the lead time for acquiring, installing and commissioning the equipment; the availability of suitable staff to manage the technology; and anticipated capacity utilisation. If a company lacks a competence or presence, it can be filled through outsourcing, especially in areas of innovation or specialist expertise provided that the framework for its effective utilisation is present.

5. Cost control   The outsourcing of many activities within pharmaceutical organisations enables firms to ensure that their departments and associated functions experience as little 'downtime' as possible. This is possible due to the fact that outsourcing converts the fixed costs of maintaining a department with a particular competence into variable costs that are incurred only when that particular skill or service is required.

Studies conducted by Tapon *et al.* (1997) also highlight two important motives for the outsourcing of R&D within the pharmaceutical industry. The first is that leading edge research has for the most part been carried out within universities and other specialist research laboratories; while the second arises from an unusual feature inherent in biotechnology itself – that of the blurring border between basic and applied research.[22]

According to Pisano *et al.* (1988), this implies that since advances in basic research often lead directly to the synthesis of a new compound with commercial potential, this provides the stimulus for external collaboration with academic and (or) external research laboratories for the purpose of keeping abreast with the latest theoretical developments.[23]

5.2 Outsourcing research and development activities

There are many different sources of external R&D available to the firm. These range from universities and other higher educational research institutes, to government and private research laboratories, and other industrial organisations that may be suppliers, customers or competitors.[24] Each of these providers is individual in nature and so it is important to be aware of the different characteristics and capabilities of each. Table 5.1 therefore highlights the relative capabilities of each of these different sources as viewed from the perspective of the outsourcing organisation.

Table 5.1 The relative capabilities of various sources of external R&D

Sources of R&D	Quality of science	Innovation	Delivery	Privacy	Knowledge	Cost
Universities	H	H	L	L	H	H
Government laboratories	M	M	M	M	H	L
Independent research organisations	M	M	H	H	M	M
Industrial organisations (non competitor)	M	M	H	H	M	M
Industrial organisation (competitor)	M	M	M	L	M	L
Independent contract researchers	L	L	M	M	L	H

Key: H = High, M = Medium, L = Low.

Source: M. Pilbeam, 'Outsourcing R&D' in *European Industrial Research Management Association (EIRMA) Annual Conference*, The Evolution of Industrial R&D, Conference Proceedings, Venice, (1997). Copyright European Industrial Research Management Association (EIRMA). Reproduced with permission.

5.2.1 Outsourcing research activities

Although the motives for outsourcing elements of research vary from one company to another, the general areas in which research can be outsourced include biotechnology, new discovery techniques and pre-clinical investigations such as animal testing and formulation. Of these, the principle areas of interest for pharmaceutical firms are twofold. The first is gene technology, which includes gene sequencing, genomics and antisense technology; while the second is that of enabling technologies such as combinatorial chemistry and computer aided drug design. Enabling technologies are those that 'enable' or facilitate more efficient drug development, the most noteworthy of which is combinatorial chemistry.

1. Outsourcing to biotechnology firms Since the 1970s, the growth of the biotechnology sector has transformed the opportunities of the pharmaceutical industry in terms of the potential to discover new products and techniques, which occurred at a time when many of the large, pharmaceutical manufacturers found themselves falling behind in a number of areas that had previously yielded promising new products and the development of NCEs (see Table 5.2).

In stark contrast to the pharmaceutical sector, these smaller biotechnology firms focussed on a small number of selective skills in specialist technologies, which provided them with a significant competitive edge over their much larger rivals. Although rich in talent, many of the new biotechnology start-ups lacked the capital required to bring their pioneering products to fruition. Conversely, the wealthy pharmaceutical firms lacked some of the innovative flair embodied within these smaller firms. As a result, a symbiotic relationship developed between the two sectors, which stimulated the formation of alliances and outsourcing agreements.

Table 5.2 Top 10 global biotechnology firms

Rank	Company	Country
1	Amgen	USA
2	Genetech	USA
3	Chiron	USA
4	British Biotech	UK
5	Biogen	USA
6	Genzyme	USA
7	Biocompatibles International	UK
8	Scotia Holdings	UK
9	Celtech Group	UK
10	Qiagen	Germany

Pharmaceutical companies therefore benefited from an enriched research programme, while the biotechnology firms now had the opportunity to further the development of its products. As a result, the 1990s witnessed an increase in partnership activity between these two sectors as the large pharmaceutical firms sought to strengthen their R&D base.

Taafe (1996) suggests that the outsourcing of research to biotechnology companies has a number of advantages as opposed to a strategy of acquisition. (1) The capital expenditure required to form a partnership is far lower than that of acquiring a firm. This saving in revenue thereby enables the pharmaceutical firm to construct a larger portfolio of projects drawn from a number of sources, in contrast to having a smaller number of projects derived from a single firm. This then allows for greater diversity and choice. (2) By partnering with biotechnology firms, pharmaceutical companies can assemble a product portfolio of choice, thereby avoiding the burden of having unpromising candidates within their own R&D portfolios. (3) In the event that a product or technology should fail, it is less costly for a pharmaceutical firm to disengage itself from the partnership than if it had the failing technologies or products in-house. (4) The benefit of remaining independent inspires the spirit of innovation within biotechnology firms, and through this, its entrepreneurial flair. Evidence suggests that the entrepreneurial spirit contained in these firms does not survive the more formal culture of the pharmaceutical organisation.[25]

2. Outsourcing research into genomics The roots of genomics are to be found in the Human Genome Project (HGP) which is an international effort to sequence the three billion nucleotides that comprise the human genome.[26] The aim of the HGP is to produce a complete map of the human genome, which comprise over one hundred thousand genes. The term genomics refers to the large-scale sequencing of disease causing genes, as well as to the discovery of the cellular function of these genes.[27] In the field of genetic science, genomics and the sequencing of the human genome have therefore emerged as the most important areas of genetic research.

Taking the field of genetics as a whole, interest in the science has risen sharply since the 1990s due to the increasing numbers of new drugs designed to match the active sites of enzymes or receptors. Therefore, what companies hope to achieve from this research is twofold. The first is to identify a gene for a particular protein or enzyme that would enable the clarification of the structure of the protein. The second is the ability to produce in vitro, and then test candidate compounds for specific pharmacological activity. Recent estimates place the number of genes whose structure has been partly explained at 65 000.[28] Although the actual function of many of these genes is still unknown, this expansion of the knowledge base nevertheless represents significant progression in pharmaceutical research.

The potential to form partnerships with firms, whose expertise is primarily in genomics, represents a considerable advantage to pharmaceutical firms since they do not have to invest extensively in developing or acquiring genomics capability in-house. For the pharmaceutical industry, the ability to tap into genomics research is significant in that genomics can provide better validated targets against which pharmaceutical companies can screen their chemical libraries. If companies can identify very specific targets that interfere exclusively in processes that contribute to diseases, such firms have the potential to discover more important drugs than market competitors. Alliances in genomics should therefore be designed to not only bring genomic technologies in-house so as to enable scientists to discover proprietary new drugs, but to also bring proprietary new targets that external partners have developed into internal drug screening operations. Effective outsourcing, coupled with the recruitment of new staff expert in genomic technologies, therefore have the potential to make pharmaceutical firms very strong in this area of scientific research.

By the end of the 1990s, ten major pharmaceutical companies were involved in various collaborative agreements with Incyte Pharmaceuticals with the aim of having access to the company's genomic databases. These companies included Abbot Laboratories, Hoechst, Johnson & Johnson, NovoNordisk, Pfizer, Pharmacia and Upjohn, BASF AG, Hoffman La Roche, Shering AG, and AstraZeneca.[29] Further examples of companies with specialised genomic capabilities are contained in Table 5.3.

3. Outsourcing enabling technologies such as combinatorial chemistry   All major pharmaceutical firms have actively searched for ways to gain access to, and control of the rapidly expanding technology of combinatorial chemistry. This technology, which involves the application of genetic engineering, has the potential to dramatically increase the number and type of molecules available for research. Combinatorial chemistry is essentially the process of synthesising, screening and optimising large numbers of chemical compounds aimed at drug discovery. As such, this technology directly addresses some of the inefficiencies present in traditional drug discovery techniques, which is both a costly and time-consuming process. By using combinatorial techniques, a single chemist therefore has the potential to synthesise a greater number of

Table 5.3   Specialist providers of genomic research

Company	Location	Country
Acadia Pharmaceuticals	San Diego	USA
Affymax Research Institute	Palo Alto	USA
Affymetrix Inc.	Santa Clara	USA
Ariad Pharmaceuticals	Cambridge	USA
Axys Pharmaceuticals	San Francisco	USA
Aurora Biosciences	San Diego	USA
Cubist Pharmaceuticals	Cambridge	USA
Exelexis	San Francisco	USA
Gene Trace Systems	Alameda	USA
Genetech Inc.	San Francisco	USA
Genetics Institute Inc.	Cambridge	USA
Genome Systems Inc.	St. Louis	USA
Genome Therapeutics Corporation	Waltham	USA
Human Genome Sciences	Rockville	USA
Lawrence Berkeley Laboratory	Berkeley	USA
MetaXen	San Francisco	USA
Millennium Pharmaceuticals Inc.	Cambridge	USA
National Centre for Genome Research	Santa Fe	USA
Pangaea Pharmaceuticals	Cambridge	USA
R.W. Johnson Pharmaceutical Research	San Diego	USA
Institute	Palo Alto	USA
Stanford Human Genome Centre		
Synthetic Genetics Molecular Biology	San Diego	USA
Resources Inc.		
Washington University Genome	St. Louis	USA
Sequencing Centre		
Zeneca	Washington	USA
3D Pharmaceuticals	Exton	USA

distinct compounds than the entire compound collection assembled by large pharmaceutical companies over decades of research.[30]

Using traditional methods, pharmaceutical firms could take between three to five years to identify a lead compound, at a cost of approximately $2000 per compound. However through the use of combinatorial techniques, a chemist is able to simultaneously synthesise thousands of related molecules at a cost of less than $1 per compound.[31] This methodology can thereby shorten the drug discovery process by one to two years, thus lowering overall development costs while expediting the introduction of a new drug on the market.

Due to the difficulties associated with developing combinatorial capability in-house, many pharmaceutical companies chose to either acquire the capability, or to outsource their requirements in this area. One such example was GlaxoWellcome's acquisition of Affymax in 1995, a California based biotechnology company that was specialised in the field. Although GlaxoWellcome had been developing its own combinatorial technology prior to the acquisition of Affymax, it did in fact trail about three years behind Affymax in terms of its own capability. As with all pharmaceutical firms who ventured into such agreements, it was the desire to close the technology gap which acted as the principle motive for collaboration. With the passing of time, the outsourcing of combinatorial capabilities has gained further momentum and a greater number of outsourcing agreements formed between pharmaceutical firms and specialist providers. Examples of such arrangements are contained in Table 5.4.

It is estimated that the rate of growth of four of the most important drug discovery markets – bioinformatics, combinatorial chemistry, genomics and high through-put screening – will more than double by 2005. At the same time, it is also expected that the market for combinatorial chemistry will increase to $2.5 billion by 2005, while the market for high through-put screening will rise to $1 billion worldwide. As for genomics-based technologies, it is expected that the market for this resource will dramatically increase as well. Since genomics based

Table 5.4   Providers of combinatorial chemistry expertise

Company	Major partners
Affymax	GlaxoWellcome
Alanex	Astra – NorvoNordisk – Hoffman La Roche
ArQule	Pharmacia & Upjohn – Abbot Laboratories – Hoffman La Roche
Arris Pharmaceuticals	Bayer – Pharmacia & Upjohn
Chiron	Ciba Geigy – Organon
CombiChem	Hoffman La Roche
Houghten Pharmaceuticals	Osiris Therapeutics – NovoNordisk – Proctor & Gamble
Isis Pharmaceuticals	Boehringer Ingelheim
Oncogene	BioChem Pharmaceuticals
Oxford Diversity	Pfizer
Peptide Therapeutics	Alizyme
Pharmacopoeia	Schering Plough – Sandoz – Organon
Pharma Genics	Boehringer Mannheim
David Sanoff Research Centre	SmithKline Beecham
Selectide	Hoechst Marion Roussel
Signal Pharmaceuticals	Tanabe Pharmaceuticals
Sphinx	Eli Lilly

research is one of the major causes for the exponential growth of drug targets, it is expected that the market for bioinformatics will also increase to $4 billion by 2005.[32] Thus, it appears that the revolution in genomics and associated technologies has had a profound effect on the pharmaceutical industry, with alliances and outsourcing agreements viewed as standard vehicles for accessing these technologies across several platforms.

4. Outsourcing to academia   Over the past few decades, intense competition in both industry and academia has radically changed the way in which industrialists and academics interact.[33] This strategic re-focusing has affected academic–industry research arrangements in that academic researchers have re-aligned much of their research to coincide with the needs of industry.[34] The move towards rationalising internal resources and the wide dispersion of knowledge has inevitably led research-based companies to commission more of their work from universities and other academic institutions (see Table 5.5).

Although the principle motives for outsourcing research to academic institutions are similar to those that have spawned collaborative agreements between biotechnology firms and the pharmaceutical sector, when taken from an organisational point of view, the reasons for engaging in outsourcing agreements arise from the need to (1) enhance research capacity in areas of interest to the company; (2) expand existing research programmes more rapidly than could otherwise be

Table 5.5   Research collaborations between industry and academia

Interaction	Agreement type
Exchange information and ideas without financial commitment	Confidential disclosure agreement
Sponsor post-graduate award	Award a PhD studentship
Research collaboration with one or more academic researchers over a two-year period	Award a project grant
Research collaboration with a number of academic researchers and technicians over a three-year period	Award a research programme grant
Draw on academic advice in a particular area of expertise	Consultancy agreement
Provide biological or chemical agents for use in research	Material transfer agreement
Support a university lectureship	Create a lectureship position
Bestow a university professorship	Charitable donation

accomplished through internal means; (3) add to an existing research programme a new dimension that is more readily available from academia; and (4) serve identifiable science objectives that complement the major scientific thrusts of a company, as well as existing scientific arrangements.[35]

If properly implemented, the benefits to be gained from this form of partnership are wide ranging. From an industry perspective, research conducted within universities helps strengthen the firm through the provision of trained researchers, new ideas and a medium for the development of emerging technologies.[36] Conversely, industrial associations with academia often help to shape, and provide direction to the research being undertaken within those institutions. This meeting of minds between academics and industrialists therefore has a synergistic effect. Bodnar (1990) suggests that one of the benefits of having a strategic alliance with an academic institution is that it provides one of the most effective means to maintaining contact with, and to eventually having a claim to other areas of research, which would develop to a point that would justify bringing it in-house.[37] The enhanced prospect for recruitment, the creation of a willing community of researchers, and the broadening of potential points for interaction with academia in the future are all additional benefits that could be gained.

It is therefore not surprising that over the years, universities and the pharmaceutical industry have developed a wide variety of research connections as illustrated in Table 5.6. The most frequently used methods of interaction are the establishment of industrial research parks near university campuses and the development of technology transfer units by universities. It is also common for companies to negotiate exclusive licenses on patents, or to set up agreements for the purchase of marketable results in exchange for academic research funding.

Although the procurement of funding for research represents a major objective for most academic institutions, many research departments also seek to locate companies that are willing to commercialise their research. To this end, agreements with pharmaceutical firms can help satisfy both needs. Today, collaborations with leading academic departments are seen as much more important to a company's R&D programme than were previously considered, and have as a result increased in number.[38] One such example is GlaxoWellcome, which in 1996 spent more than £10 million on research project grants and studentships within UK institutions. Further examples are contained in Table 5.6.

Table 5.6   Examples of academic research partnerships funded by GlaxoWellcome

Institute	Location	Therapeutic area
Duke University	USA	Alzheimer's disease
Harvard University	USA	Cardiovascular disease
Institute for Cancer Research	UK	Cancer
Jackson Institute	USA	Genetics and Genomics
Melbourne University	Australia	HIV infection
Oxford University	UK	HIV infection
Scripps Institute	USA	Cancer
University College London	UK	Cardiovascular disease
University of California	USA	Cancer
University of Gothenburg	Sweden	Genetics and Genomics
University of Wales, Cardiff	UK	Genetics and Genomics
University of Wisconsin	USA	Diabetes

5.2.2   Outsourcing development activities

Of the two production phases, 'development' comprises the more expensive element of the R&D process. It is estimated that of a given R&D budget, approximately 70 per cent of the total is spent on development while the remaining 30 per cent is spent on research.[39] Since the production of pharmaceuticals is strictly defined and governed by the American FDA and other regulatory bodies, much of the development process is generic in nature. This has aided the establishment of an entire industry whose specialisation rests on clinical trial testing, and whose function is to perform contract services for companies that do not choose, or do not have the necessary resources to conduct such trials internally.

Outsourcing to clinical research organisations

The term Clinical Research Organisation or CRO is applied to any organisation that performs R&D work for a sponsor company. However when used within the context of the pharmaceutical industry, the term strictly refers to development projects only, since most of the R&D projects undertaken by CROs involve Phase III clinical trials. The clinical trial process, and in particular Phase III of these trials, comprise an important element of the total R&D budget of the pharmaceutical firm. Because of this, careful consideration is given to contracting out this aspect of the drug development process. Clinical R&D accounts for 30 per cent of all R&D spending with 23 per cent spent all scientific and professional R&D personnel.[40]

Due to variations in the number of development projects undertaken at any given time, the work carried out within these departments is not always maintained at a consistent level. In the case of a company that does not always operate its development facilities at optimum capacity the contracting out of clinical research provides an opportunity of converting fixed costs into variable costs. Furthermore, significant time can also be saved by having clinical trials conducted by CROs rather than by in-house departments, since the pharmaceutical company will not require additional time to recruit the necessary medical staff to manage the trial.

The services provided by CROs essentially involve managing the administration of the clinical research conducted by independent doctors in hospitals, as well as those in general practice. In essence CROs perform the task of data processors, whereby the clinical data supplied by the research network is collected, collated and analysed. According to Colburn *et al.* (1997) the basic services offered by the CRO industry are: (1) quality assurance and control; (2) pre-clinical pharmaco-kinetic, pharmacology and toxicology studies; (3) to design, conduct and analyse sophisticated Phase I and Phase II pharmacokinetic and pharmacodynamic decision making studies; (4) management of multi-centre studies; (5) manufacture and data base management; and (6) statistical analysis and reporting.[41]

With the growth of the CRO industry, many of these organisations have attempted to create market differentiation by providing additional services that could be supplied more cost-effectively to the larger pharmaceutical firms. The services most frequently contracted out to CROs include laboratory tests, toxicology, clinical pharmacology and pharmacokinetics. More recently however, CROs have also assumed responsibility for a growing number of studies designed to support new drug and product licence applications, as well as the design and implementation of entire development programmes with the assistance of the corporate sponsor.[42] Some examples of this are contained in Table 5.7.

Services currently available through outsourcing cover almost the entire spectrum of activities conducted within the pharmaceutical industry. Due to the growth of the contract service market, it is now possible to outsource almost every functional activity traditionally the domain of the pharmaceutical firm. It is therefore not inconceivable for a major pharmaceutical company to take on the role of co-ordinator whose function is to direct outsourcing activities from discovery through to post marketing surveillance.

Table 5.7   Areas of clinical development expertise

Clinical stage	Specialised CROs
Pre-clinical and toxicology	Pharmacopoeia, Huntington International Holdings, International Research and Development Corporation, Phoenix International, Quintiles International
Phase I	Pharmacopoeia, Corning Pharmaceutical Services, Parexel International, Phoenix International, Quintiles International
Phase II to Phase IV	Pharmacopoeia, Corning Pharmaceutical Services, Parexel International, Pharmaceutical Product Development, Phoenix International, Quintiles International
Clinical site operators	Clinical Studies Limited

When determining the degree to which outsourcing is required, it is important that the firm focuses on the needs of its core competencies rather than on all of the services that the contract services industry has to offer. This strategy of 'selective' outsourcing thereby facilitates the outsourcing of non-core activities to specialist providers whose core competencies are the servicing of those outsourced activities.

5.3   The advantages and disadvantages of an outsourcing strategy

For the most part, many of the problems associated with outsourcing are due to the nature of the process itself; it is time consuming and requires dedicated expertise to achieve desired outcomes. Failure to clearly define performance expectations and measurement criteria contained in the outsourcing contract has led many companies to lose sight of the most basic purchasing and partnership principles involved: the tendency to virtually abdicate the management function, thereby creating an environment in which the supplier manages the outsourcing agreement.[43]

Although many companies have in truth pursued outsourcing as a means of disengaging from essential processes that are not deemed critical to the core business, the eventual success of an outsourcing agreement depends on how well the partnership is managed. To this end, supplier performance must be continually assessed, while specifications defining the level of service to be provided must be periodically revised. Inevitably, such requirements hold important ramifications for the outsourcing company. While a new set of skills will be required to manage outsourcing agreements, a new kind of manager will also be required to oversee the partnership.[44] This implies that effective in-house management must continue to remain an important element of the outsourcing process.

A crucial factor often overlooked by management when assessing the potential benefits of an outsourcing strategy is that by nature, outsourcing trades the problems associated with managing a specific function for those of managing a specific type of partnership. Although a company may delegate the responsibility of managing a number of infrastructure services to an outside supplier, it nevertheless remains accountable for (1) establishing the procedures and mechanics for working with strategic partners; (2) managing the individual agreements; (3) streamlining the overall number of alliances, given that outsourcing suppliers may also be competitors; (4) recognising potential changes that may be required in a partner's organisation; and (5) redefining supplier relationships.[45] Given the complexity of managing the outsourcing process, a number of critical success factors must therefore be considered if a successful outcome is to be ensured.

5.3.1   The advantages of an outsourcing strategy

The outsourcing of research and development activities to an external agent can provide the outsourcing company with a number of tangible benefits. Taken within the context of the pharmaceutical industry, Tapon *et al.* (1999) suggest that an effective outsourcing strategy can enable the company to:

1. *Keep abreast of novel research*   Rapid advances in the field of science and technology has made it practically impossible for firms to keep abreast of such changes in isolation. By outsourcing research at the early and risky stages of drug design, a company can enjoy a more cost-effective way of exploring new technologies without having to commit resources and hire new researchers, as well as experiment on a small scale with major changes in research directions and processes prior to being implemented within the internal laboratories of the firm.[46]

2. *Develop new capabilities*   By developing new capabilities, the company will be able to reposition its research efforts in line with competitive expectations, as well as have a wider range of research approaches. Through outsourcing, a company can therefore learn new types of research from its outsourcing partner with a view to bringing in-house the most promising research programmes.[47]

3. Re-invent core capabilities Collis (1994) suggests that over time, all resources tend to acquire a negative value, either because they erode or become less effective, or because they are replaced by a different and better set of capabilities.[48] As such, very few firms are able to sustain a competitive edge over a long period of time. Through outsourcing, a firm can continuously improve its core competencies by encouraging in-house research departments to remain as, or become more competitive, than external research laboratories.

4. Benchmark with external laboratories Competition with external research laboratories encourages internal departments to consistently meet the standards of world class research. It also creates awareness of novel research techniques that may surpass current thinking and practice. Outsourcing therefore creates an atmosphere where success is never taken for granted and acquired positions are never kept for long.[49]

5. Understand the relative costs of research By outsourcing various components of an R&D programme, the relative costs of different types of research are made apparent. This provides the firm with a better understanding of the expenses that would be incurred if a new research methodology was pursued, without actually having to commit to the research programme itself. If the new approach requires more resources than the firm has, or necessitates those that it could not acquire or manage, the outsourcing relationship can be terminated without cost to other components of the business.[50]

6. Improved efficiency and flexibility As advances in science have facilitated a broadening of the knowledge base and the introduction of novel research techniques, pharmaceutical firms have become obliged to look for personnel specialised in cutting-edge research techniques. In areas of monoclonal antibodies, tissue targeted pro-drugs, gene therapy and drug delivery systems, services are often better provided by individual specialists who are expert in the field and its application, rather than by one company alone.[51] By providing a 'window on science', outsourcing therefore enables the firm to exploit faster, and more effectively, the results of basic research conducted in universities and external laboratories.[52] Such efficiency gains invariably lead to lower costs as resources are better utilised within the firm. Outsourcing also allows the sponsor to invest in a number of smaller projects with different research centres, rather than make a single investment with a single company. This strategy allows for flexibility, and also provides an alternative to acquisition. For an industry such as pharmaceuticals, flexibility is especially important since new avenues for research are discovered almost daily, and companies must therefore be free to pursue them.[53] This offers pharmaceutical companies a route into new areas of research with minimum outlays and with maximum return.

7. Flexible resource allocation   The budgetary resources made available to project managers for the administering of R&D projects is often determined by senior management. Of the total budget allocation, up to 90 per cent can comprise fixed costs, while the portion owed to coping with bottlenecks in R&D projects, comprises the remainder of the total spend. This of course, has two significant drawbacks. First, the capacity to allocate resources to more important projects is restricted. Second, a percentage of resources may in fact be allocated to projects with a lower priority. This could result in the company having to bear the cost of mediocre projects that do not offer the best chance of success, while impeding the diversion of additional resources to those that do. The need to temporarily allocate substantial research staff from one project to another in order to ease such bottlenecks is a common problem with pharmaceutical R&D. For this reason, a 'lack of capacity' is often cited as the single most important reason for outsourcing a particular area of research. It is therefore advisable, that internal resources be used for coping with the 'troughs' of a project, while the 'peaks' are catered for externally. This holds well as an argument for outsourcing parts of clinical development, as well as particular stages of pre-clinical work.

8. Access to facilities   Constraints on conducting particular phases of R&D is often caused by physical limitations such as inadequate space and (or) equipment, rather than by a lack of appropriate personnel. In the case of pharmaceutical research, problems arise when existing facilities become overloaded. Outsourcing during periods of over capacity helps alleviate this problem since it can be implemented on an 'as-required' basis without large financial outlays.

9. Greater speed   Speed is a crucial element in drug development. Through outsourcing much more could be achieved in parallel than what could possibly be accomplished within the individual firm. Problems of recruiting high calibre research staff, particularly at short notice are also averted.

10. Minimise risk   For the pharmaceutical manufacturer, risk is an inherent feature of the drug development process. When taken from the standpoint of the industry, risk can be divided into two elements. The first is the probability of clinical success at each stage of the development process, and the second is the probability of success in a commercial context.

a. Risk associated with clinical failure   Risk in this case derives from two aspects that are crucial to clinical success. In the first instance, the company needs to choose the right project, while in the second it also needs to choose the right drug candidate for development. Since recent estimates suggests that small specialist companies will supply at least half the expertise for the discovery and development of the next generation of new medicines, outsourcing provides pharmaceutical manufacturers with the opportunity to broaden their research potential without having to establish any long-term commitments that may be discontinued in the future.[54] These companies will also be free to retain in-house a greater interest in more fundamental research than could otherwise be justified.

b. Risk associated with commercial success If taken from a purely financial perspective, pharmaceutical companies can gain access to high quality research for a smaller sum and at a risk premium than could otherwise be obtained from within. In other words, a company that is in the process of finding a research partner can have the freedom to carefully select the project which promises maximum probable return, while at the same time absolving itself of the need to decide how and when internal assignments should be terminated.[55] Although a pharmaceutical firm cannot entirely eliminate risk from the R&D process, by exporting risk to smaller companies and to academic institutions, it is able to reduce it by a certain degree.

5.3.2   The disadvantages of an outsourcing strategy

Working in collaboration with external agents is both challenging and risky since the opening up of channels of co-operation brings with it a new dimension to the overall business. Research conducted by Cavalla (1997) highlights a number of disadvantages associated with outsourcing, most of which are essentially related to effective partnership management.

1. Suitable partner The cost of an unsuccessful partnership is more than just the financial, since the company would also lose crucial time and opportunities that it could have fruitfully been engaged in elsewhere.[56] Although, the ambitions and goals of each party are to a greater extent guided by financial considerations, it is natural that both parties should view the factors that determine the commercial merit of the collaboration from fundamentally different perspectives. Therefore it is important to have an acute awareness of the probable partners available, as well as an understanding of the rationale for the work itself. To successfully accomplish this requires extensive knowledge, which needs to be complemented by an effective system of information gathering.

2. Cost   Outsourcing research entails both direct and indirect costs. However, it is the indirect costs and risks that are by far the most significant since companies tend to underestimate the start-up costs, which include redeployment costs, relocation costs and unanticipated parallel running costs.[57] Companies also tend to underestimate the costs of managing the outsourcing agreement since without effective management and monitoring mechanisms, the company would benefit little from the research conducted outside the firm. As significant financial outlays increasingly become necessary, the average pre-commercial payment extracted from pharmaceutical firms are also increasing due to the increased demand for contractor services which permits such inflation.[58]

3. Loss of control   In outsourcing arrangements, partial control of the project inevitably passes from the client to the provider. As a result, the information available to the project manager would be less complete and detailed than would otherwise be if the project was retained in-house. Furthermore, many of the difficulties encountered by the provider are often not seen or even understood by the contracting firm. This lack of effective communication often leads to problems with quality and to delays, and invariably to suspicion of the provider's true capabilities. Although all collaborative agreements experience a loss of control to a greater or to a lesser extent, the degree to which the contracting firm may effectively control an external project crucially depends on the quality and the quantity of information, and on the advance warning of problems. Although similar rules do apply to internal projects, such problems are exacerbated between partners who do not know each other well, and who have not developed a trusting relationship.[59]

4. Conflicting research culture   Approaches to conducting research work within a university environment is different to that in industry since academics tend to adhere to a much purer research discipline than is required by the commercial partner. This often leads to problems involving an unwillingness to repeat tried and tested techniques in favour of continually pursuing innovative areas of research.[60] Such expectations lead to difficulties in incorporating the principles of screening and the repetitive evaluation of drugs as dictated by the discovery programme, into the traditional academic–industry alliance. Furthermore, the goals of both parties are also fundamentally different. For an academic, one of the principal objectives of conducting research is to publicise the results in peer-reviewed journals and books; while the aim of the industrialist is to obtain patent protection or to submit the findings for regulatory approval. In addition, concerns over confidentiality breaches together with academic bureaucracy, are often cited as major causes of frustration inherent in industry–academic collaborations.[61]

5. *Time* One of the fundamental determinants of success in the pharmaceutical industry is the speed at which a new drug is brought to market since fast and efficient delivery is vital in securing a competitive advantage over rivals. Although various modes of collaborative agreements are used to speed up the drug discovery and deployment process, such arrangements are also the cause of unforeseen delays that result in significant setbacks. In reality, a considerable amount of time is required to establish a contractual arrangement. The complexity of the work involved and the nature of the contract frequently combine to make these arrangements more difficult.

6. *Co-ordination and expertise* When a project is moved to a different location, the geographical separation may lead to an intellectual and technological schism.[62] For one, the gap between the expertise of both the internal and external collaborators may become quite pronounced the further the project strays away from the knowledge base of those within the contracting firm. As increasingly novel methods of pharmaceutical R&D are discovered, it is vital that the knowledge and experience that are to be found in a project are not solely contained within external sources. The increased level of work performed outside the organisation could also make the training of new employees more difficult if particular aspects of drug development are regularly performed by the service provider. As a result, a lack of expertise may develop within the pharmaceutical firm. Since it is difficult to replicate within collaborative work the multidisciplinary nature that is prevalent in large pharmaceutical organisations, it is necessary to maintain a core of qualified personnel and expertise in-house in order to maintain a minimum amount of directionality, interpretative capability and control.[63] To this end, an experienced co-ordinator must be present within the pharmaceutical firm to effectively incorporate the results of the outsourced work with components from in-house research.

7. *Instability* A degree of instability is also inherent in R&D outsourcing partnerships and can pose a significant disadvantage to both large and small firms alike. In the case of the smaller firm, it is often more dependent on employees who are critical to the company's operation. Therefore in the event of their departure, such individuals could take with them project specific expertise that may be difficult to replace. Similarly, when two large companies merge, the fusion of the companies' research strategies inevitably creates a 'knock-on' effect, with the most likely outcome being the termination of some research projects. As

a result, both these factors could be the cause of instability for large and small firms.

8. *Potential competitors*   Through outsourcing, a firm may inadvertently create a competitor. This can occur when the results of a particular research programme are difficult to appropriate, enabling the service provider to gain insights which would allow it to establish itself in an existing or new area of research that the pharmaceutical firm had hoped to preserve or gain a position in.[64]

9. *Monopoly supply*   Contracting out important components of research to the same laboratory over long periods of time may place the purchasing firm in a vulnerable position and thereby under the influence of a monopoly supplier. This over dependency can be caused by the supplier possessing capabilities that are important to the client, but which the client itself lacks.

10. *Lack of organisational learning*   Much of the learning that takes place within an organisation is experimental since management do not fully appreciate the nature of a task until it has been experienced. Therefore what may be classified as tactical, commodity, or of low value today, may in fact become strategic, core, or high value tomorrow.[65] In such an eventuality, there is no reason why a third party could not operate, enhance, or rebuild an application that has been reclassified as strategic. However the contracting firm could thereby run the risk of losing valuable expertise by not retaining the activity in-house.

5.3.3   The effect of outsourcing on organisational behaviour

According to Marcella (1995), the effects of outsourcing on organisational behaviour are both considerable and far reaching given that it can influence a number of factors pertaining to managerial behaviour. For example (1) Organisations often do not communicate the intention to outsource for fear of losing key employees should early negotiations fail. This approach could have serious repercussions once the decision to outsource is made. (2) Outsourcing compels management to closely examine matters concerning staff and other personnel, which can encourage more open communication with employees. (3) Outsourcing can provide the organisation with a period of reorientation, or a chance to view it from a different perspective. The can lead to a re-assessment of customer–supplier relations in the hope that such efforts will be mutually reciprocated by the service provider. (4) At the business level, outsourcing can play an important role in managing acquisitions, decentralisation initiatives, leveraged buyouts, divesting operations and other forms of organisational restructuring. (5) Outsourcing encourages management to carefully examine each and every operation. This directs attention to the core of the business, while providing the impetus to being efficient in those particular competencies. (6) Outsourcing also encourages management to view every action, and every operation, from the perspective of a cost-benefit relationship.[66]

Irrespective of whether innovative ideas for research originate internally or externally, outsourcing is an essential component for keeping abreast with the latest scientific developments, and is a useful tool for challenging the established notions of in-house scientists. Nevertheless, the firm must have in place a few, select core capabilities that must be consistently exploited regardless of the number of outsourcing agreements already formed. It is essential that the firm clearly understands the direction and scope of its R&D programme, for outsourcing should be used as a *complement* to the research effort, rather than as a substitute for it. Therefore it is important that companies realise that:

> Strategic outsourcing is **not** a panacea for whatever ails the company. Rather, it a sophisticated approach to the strategic use of non-core business functions.[67] (Marcella 1995)

5.4 Outsourcing: implications for the pharmaceutical industry

During the past century, the pharmaceutical industry has experienced a series of dramatic changes as a result of developments in science and technology, which have spawned new opportunities for innovation. Traditionally, the R&D activities of large pharmaceutical firms were kept within the boundaries of the organisation, with various forms of collaborative agreements seen only as second best to the option of conducting these activities alone. More recently however, the external contribution from the perspective of the firm to the creation and successful application of technology has significantly increased, and the innovation process has become much more interactive. From the standpoint of the pharmaceutical industry, a number of reasons are responsible for this change in behaviour (see Table 5.8). This impetus for change is the result of a combination of political, economic, technological and social factors; all of which have helped redefine the dynamics of this particular industry.

Over time, the growth of the pharmaceutical industry worldwide has been slower than the increases in R&D costs, and this has led to a cost-earnings differential that cannot be sustained indefinitely. Rapid

Table 5.8 A synopsis of changes affecting the pharmaceutical industry

Political	Economic
Requirements of regulatory bodies	Globalisation of pharmaceutical companies
Harmonisation of regulatory requirements	Rising costs of Research and Development
Price and profit controls	Increasing competition
Decreased effective patent life	Greater generic competition
Technological	**Social**
Emergence of biotechnology	Changing population demography
Growth of information technology	Closer scrutiny of the cost of drugs
Impact of genomics	Emergence of alternatives to traditional therapies

advances in the fields of science and technology, especially within the disciplines of biotechnology and genetics, have made it impossible for even the largest pharmaceutical manufacturers to conduct internally, all activities associated with the R&D process. Pure in-house research is now no longer an option for several reasons. First, it is impossible to assemble under one roof all the skills required along the spectrum of R&D. Second, the total R&D costs for assembling all the necessary skills and resources are unaffordable. Due to these pressures on pharmaceutical earnings, together with rising R&D costs, pharmaceutical firms have found it necessary to adopt a number of cost containment measures, in addition to those pertaining to the safety and efficacy of drugs. The need to demonstrate 'value' to the consumer has now become imperative.

5.4.1 Changing R&D management practices

For the pharmaceutical industry, one of the spill over effects of these heightened pressures has been the need to change the ways in which R&D has been traditionally managed. The demand for innovation in an increasingly complex and global business environment has necessitated new approaches to managing R&D because the requirements for success in the marketplace have changed in a number of profound ways. In addition to demands for efficiency, quality and flexibility; companies are also required to simultaneously cut costs, improve standards of quality, shorten product development times, and introduce innovative products that are valued by the customer.[68] As a result, the environment for product development in technology-based industries is now defined by the following key factors: (1) Increased domestic and global competition; (2) Continuous development of new technologies that make existing products obsolete; (3) Changing customer requirements that truncate product life cycles; (4) Higher product development costs; (5) Increased pressure on R&D to be accountable to the needs of the business; (6) Increased sensitivity to social and environmental concerns; and (7) Increased need for involvement of external organisations in the new product development process.[69]

These changes to the business environment, together with the new criteria for commercial success, have required that companies re-think the ways in which industrial R&D should be managed. Studies conducted by Gupta *et al.* (1996) highlight a number of major changes that have taken place within the R&D environment, all of which have served to alter the R&D management practices of technology-based companies.[70] Such changes have necessitated an increased focus on:

1. Cross-functional teamwork   The research process now involves non-R&D personnel in areas such as new product development, project prioritising and assessment, and in the formation of the company's technology strategy. There is greater emphasis on cross-functionality as opposed to being purely 'technology driven' or 'production driven'.

2. Achieving business results   In both the short and long term, it is important that R&D is held accountable for directly contributing to the overall business. This has led to a greater awareness of the need to streamline efforts on a few high impact, customer directed projects rather than on a number which are unconnected.

3. Development speed   The desire to swiftly bring new products to the market that customers will value is an important consideration for all companies. This emphasis on speed has required that R&D managers learn efficiently, experiment frequently, and quickly incorporate learning into the next generation of products.[71]

4. The constraints on R&D resources   Greater constraints on R&D resources have improved the ways in which R&D is managed. For example, R&D departments have begun to forge closer links with business units and are more open to external sources of technology.

5. R&D alliances   R&D intensive organisations are global in nature. In order to increase speed to these global markets, firms have sought partners who can complement their capabilities and thereby provide significant windows of opportunities for future research.

Since much of current management thinking and practice as well as the operating culture of large industrial research laboratories evolved prior to the 1970s, some of the institutions and instincts developed in this early period are now at odds with current realities (see Table 5.9).

Table 5.9   R&D's emerging scope

	Moving from	Moving towards
Emphasis	Individual researcher	Cross-functional teamwork
Performance measurement	Contribution to science	Contribution to profits
Foremost priority	Improve professional standing	Improve business performance
Driving force	Science and technology	Markets and customers
Innovative focus	Breakthroughs and radical 'R'	Continuous and incremental 'D'
Aspiration	Technological excellence	Customer value
Time horizon	Long-term	Short-term
Sources of ideas	Own efforts internally generated	Alliances from multiple sources
Scope	Local and isolated	Global and integrated
Type of innovation	Product	Product and processes
Resources	Abundant	Scarce

Source: Gupta, A.K. and Wilemon, D. 'Changing Patterns in Industrial R&D Development'. *Journal of Product Innovation Management* (1996). Copyright Blackwell Publishing.* Reproduced with permission.

* Journal Homepage www.blackwell-synergy.com

As a result, a re-examination of the assumptions on which traditional R&D management is based is required. For the pharmaceutical industry, the response to change within both its internal and external operating environments has been the adoption of a number of approaches that have spanned the strategic continuum. These options include the more conventional strategies of mergers and acquisitions, strategic alliances, joint ventures, licensing and consortia. Such considerations have also led to a more progressive method for conducting R&D: that of outsourcing specific functions and processes.

In most pharmaceutical companies, technology and its various processes are being outsourced in two principal ways: (1) *Explicitly* through formal agreements for technology licensing, contract R&D and technology suppliers; as well as through numerous relationships with universities, government laboratories and individual technologists; and (2) *Implicitly* through joint ventures, strategic alliances and globalised networks; as well as through active or passive co-operation with numerous suppliers of different components or systems.[72]

Corresponding to the needs of the pharmaceutical industry, a supplier industry has also emerged, which comprises a number of small, specialist firms chiefly within the biotechnology and clinical development sectors. From their inception, the existence of these specialist firms has come to depend on the custom of the pharmaceutical industry, which in turn has come to view these providers as an extension of the R&D process. Consequently, a symbiotic relationship has evolved between these two sectors: that of mutual dependence between buyer and seller.

For the pharmaceutical industry however, such changes represent a radical departure from the traditional methods of drug discovery whereby the firm controlled all aspects of the pharmaceutical R&D process. The impact of these changes to such long-established business paradigms has therefore been to transform the relative importance of different activities and processes within the firm. By this it is meant that within the pharmaceutical organisation, attention has now had to shift away from the: (a) internal development activities of researchers and engineers *to* the external and collaborative technology activities of both technical and business staff; and (b) internal management decisions of directors of R&D *to* the partnering decisions of chief technology officers and managers of multi-source product teams and supplier relations.

Pharmaceutical innovation is composed of a number of external agents, each responsible for particular aspects of the product development chain. It is important that these external relationships are competently managed if value is to be created in the product development process. For until recently, R&D managers have not been held fully accountable for technology value and performance outside the functional realm of internal R&D.[73] For the most part, managers have tended to focus much of their effort on the effective management of the company's internal R&D competencies and resources since the need to directly manage the new cross-functional and (or) extra-organisational processes necessary for addressing these strategic shifts did not previously exist. Therefore the greatest challenge faced by managers of R&D is to successfully manage this new sourcing environment so that each individual partnership can be utilised in ways that will meet the demands for stronger and more sustainable competitive advantage.

Having established the parameters of the modern pharmaceutical industry, it is apparent that a number of conclusions can be drawn. Advances in the fields of science and technology together with pervasive changes in the industry's operating climate have profoundly and irreversibly altered the composition and the direction of the pharmaceutical sector, with external research organisations taking on the role of suppliers of innovative activity. Since the large pharmaceutical firms can no longer view themselves as the primary innovators in the industry, it appears that a new business strategy towards innovation has evolved.

This then implies that the fundamental challenge for pharmaceutical managers is to effectively *construct*, and *manage*, a portfolio of collaborators with the aim of securing access to the emerging science and technology, as well as the required organisational capabilities.

Outsourcing, by its very definition encompasses these key challenges if it is to be utilised effectively. Therefore it is imperative to understand the nature of the process itself, and what it means to those implementing this strategy, before examining further the ramifications of this novel approach to drug delivery.

Notes

1. R.S.M. Lau and C.N. Hurley, 'Outsourcing Through Strategic Alliances', *Production and Inventory Management Journal*, 38, Issue 2 (1997), pp. 6–10.
2. L.M. Ellram, 'A Managerial Guideline for the Development and Implementation of Purchasing Partnerships', *International Journal of Purchasing and Materials Management*, 27, Issue 2 (1991), pp. 2–8.
3. D.J. Bowersox, 'The Strategic Benefits of Logistics Alliances', *Harvard Business Review*, 68, Issue 4 (1990), pp. 36–43.
4. J. Howells, 'Research and Technology Outsourcing', *Technology Analysis and Strategic Management*, 11, Issue 1 (1999), pp. 17–29.
5. J.M. Liebenau, 'International R&D in Pharmaceutical Firms in the Early Twentieth Century', *Business History*, 26 (1984), pp. 329–46.
6. D.C. Mowery, 'Firm Structure, Government Policy and the Organisation of Industrial Research: Great Britain and the United States: 1900 to 1950', *Business History Review*, 58 (1980), pp. 504–31.
7. J. Howells, 'Research and Technology Outsourcing', *Technology Analysis and Strategic Management*, 11, Issue 1 (1999), pp. 17–29.
8. R. Coombs, 'Core Competencies and the Strategic Management of R&D', *R&D Management*, 26, Issue 4 (1996), pp. 345–55.
9. S. Bone, 'R&D Outsourcing', *International Journal of Physical Distribution & Logistics Management*, 26, Issue 7 (1996), pp. 3–6.
10. Ibid., pp. 3–6.
11. M. Sharpe, 'Outsourcing, Organisational Competitiveness and Work', *Journal of Labour Research*, 18, Issue 4 (1997), pp. 535–50.
12. N. Brancaccio, 'Outsourcing in Drug Development: A Strategic Opportunity', in *Outsource '98*, Conference Proceedings, San Francisco (1998), pp. 1–9.
13. Ibid., pp. 1–9.
14. C. Cookson, 'Research and Development: Industry is Aiming for Harder Target', *Financial Times*, 24 April 1997.
15. F. Sen and A.H. Rubenstein, 'An Exploration of Factors Affecting the Integration of In-house R&D with External Technology Acquisition Strategies of a Firm', *IEEE Transactions on Engineering Management*, 37, Issue 4 (1990), pp. 246–58.
16. J. Howells, 'Research and Technology Outsourcing', *Technology Analysis and Strategic Management*, 11, Issue 1 (1999), pp. 17–29.
17. Ibid., pp. 17–29.

18. M. Sharpe, 'Outsourcing, Organisational Competitiveness and Work', *Journal of Labour Research*, 18, Issue 4 (1997), pp. 535–50.
19. D. MacArthur, *Optimising the Use of Contract Services by the Pharmaceutical Industry*, Scrip Reports (London: PJB Publications Limited, 1994), pp. 1–14.
20. S. Griggs, 'Why Use Contract Services?', in *Interphex '93*, Conference Proceedings, Utrecht (1993).
21. P. Taafe, *Outsourcing in the Pharmaceutical Industry* (London: Financial Times Health and Healthcare Publishing, 1996), pp. 5–44.
22. F. Tapon and M. Thong, 'Outsourcing of Research by Pharmaceutical and Biotechnology Firms: 1988–1996', *Working Paper No: 1997–2*, Department of Economics, University of Guelph, Ontario (1997), pp. 1–52.
23. G.P. Pisano, W. Shan and D.J. Teece, 'Joint Ventures and Collaboration in the Biotechnology Industry', in D.C. Mowery (ed.), *International Collaborative Ventures in US Manufacturing* (New York: Ballinger Publications, 1988), pp. 183–222.
24. M. Pilbeam, 'Outsourcing R&D', in *European Industrial Research Management Association (EIRMA) Annual Conference*, The Evolution of Industrial R&D, Conference Proceedings, Venice (1997), pp. 99–104.
25. P. Taafe, *Outsourcing in the Pharmaceutical Industry* (London: Financial Times Health and Healthcare Publishing, 1996), pp. 5–44.
26. 'The Sequence of the Human Genome', *Science Magazine*, 291, Issue 5507 (2001), pp. 1304–51.
27. Ibid., pp. 1304–51.
28. P. Taafe, *Outsourcing in the Pharmaceutical Industry* (London: Financial Times Health and Healthcare Publishing, 1996), pp. 5–44.
29. R. McNeil, *Pharmaceutical Strategies: Class Acts* (London: Financial Times Health and Healthcare Publishing, 1996), pp. 35–60.
30. 'Reducing Time to Drug Discovery', *Combinatorial Chemistry*, 77, Issue 10 (1999), pp. 33–48.
31. P. Van Arnum, 'The R&D Race is on', *Chemical Market Reporter*, 256, Issue 7 (1999), pp. 1–7.
32. Ibid., pp. 1–7.
33. M. Skingle, 'Developing Effective Partnerships between Industry and Academia', in J. Anderson, R. Fears and B. Taylor (eds), *Managing Technology for Competitive Advantage* (London: Cartermill International & Financial Times Healthcare Publications, 1997), pp. 223–37.
34. Ibid., pp. 223–37.
35. A.G. Bodnar, 'Strategic Alliances for Research', in *Financial Times Annual World Pharmaceuticals Conference*, Conference Proceedings, London (1990), pp. 5.1–5.4.
36. M. Skingle, 'Developing Effective Partnerships between Industry and Academia', in J. Anderson, R. Fears and B. Taylor (eds), *Managing Technology for Competitive Advantage* (London: Cartermill International & Financial Times Healthcare Publications, 1997), pp. 223–37.
37. A.G. Bodnar, 'Strategic Alliances for Research', in *Financial Times Annual World Pharmaceuticals Conference*, Conference Proceedings, London (1990), pp. 5.1–5.4.
38. P. Taafe, *Outsourcing in the Pharmaceutical Industry* (London: Financial Times Health and Healthcare Publishing, 1996), pp. 5–44.

39. G. Haas, 'Increasing Effectiveness in Pharmaceutical R&D', in *European Industrial Research Management Association (EIRMA) Conference*, The Evolution of Industrial R&D, Conference Proceedings, Venice (1997), pp. 85–92.
40. P. Taafe, *Outsourcing in the Pharmaceutical Industry* (London: Financial Times Health and Healthcare Publishing, 1996), pp. 5–44.
41. W.A. Colburn, J.E. McClurg and J.R. Cichoracki, 'The Strategic Role of Outsourcing: CROs and the Outsourcing Phenomenon', *Applied Clinical Trials*, 6, Issue 9 (1997), pp. 68–75.
42. Ibid., pp. 68–75.
43. R. Mullin, 'Managing the Outsourced Enterprise', *Journal of Business Strategy*, 7, Issue 4 (1996), pp. 28–36.
44. The Outsourcing Institute, 'Managing the Outsourcing Relationship: A Shared Vision Producers Greater Rewards', *http://www.outsourcing.com/content.asp?page=01i/articles/process/tarsh_managing_outsourcing.html&nonav = true*
45. J. Gantz, 'Outsourcing: Threat or Salvation?' *Networking Management Journal*, 8, Issue 10 (1990), pp. 25–40.
46. R. Henderson and I. Cockburn, 'Scale, Scope and Spill-Overs: The Determinants of Research Productivity in Drug Discovery', *Rand Journal of Economics*, 27, Issue 1 (1996), pp. 32–59.
47. E. Whittaker and D.J. Bower, 'A Shift to External Alliances for Product Development in the Pharmaceutical Industry', *R&D Management*, 24, Issue 3 (1994), pp. 249–60.
48. D.J. Collis, 'How Valuable are Organisational Capabilities?' *Strategic Management Journal*, 15, Special Issue (1994), pp. 143–52.
49. F. Tapon and M. Thong, 'Research Collaborations by Multi-National Orientated Pharmaceutical Firms: 1988–1997', *R&D Management*, 29, Issue 3 (1999), pp. 219–32.
50. Ibid., pp. 219–32.
51. D. Cavalla, *Modern Strategy for Pre-Clinical Pharmaceutical R&D: Towards the Virtual Research Company* (Chichester: John Wiley and Sons, 1997).
52. F. Tapon and M. Thong, 'Research Collaborations by Multi-National Orientated Pharmaceutical Firms: 1988–1997', *R&D Management*, 29, Issue 3 (1999), pp. 219–32.
53. M.C. Lacity, L.P. Willcocks and D.F. Feeny, 'IT Outsourcing: Maximise Flexibility and Control', *Harvard Business Review*, 73, Issue 3 (1995), pp. 84–93.
54. Lehman Brothers Report, '*Pharma Pipelines*' (London: Lehman Brothers, 1996).
55. D. Cavalla, *Modern Strategy for Pre-Clinical Pharmaceutical R&D: Towards the Virtual Research Company* (Chichester: John Wiley and Sons, 1997).
56. R. Arnold and J. Grindley, 'Matchmaking: Identifying and Evaluating Drug Discovery Partners', *Drug Discovery Today*, 1, Issue 79 (1996).
57. M.J. Earl, 'The Risks of Outsourcing IT', *Sloan Management Review*, 37, Issue 3 (1996), pp. 26–32.
58. D. Cavalla, *Modern Strategy for Pre-Clinical Pharmaceutical R&D: Towards the Virtual Research Company* (Chichester: John Wiley and Sons, 1997).
59. Ibid., Cavalla (1997).
60. D. Blumenthal, N. Causino, E. Campbell and K.S. Louis, 'Relationships between Academic Institutions and Industry in the Life Sciences: An Industry Survey', *New England Journal of Medicine*, 334, Issue 6 (1996), pp. 368–73.

61. Ibid., pp. 368–73.
62. D. Cavalla, *Modern Strategy for Pre-Clinical Pharmaceutical R&D: Towards the Virtual Research Company* (Chichester: John Wiley and Sons, 1997).
63. Ibid., Cavalla (1997).
64. F. Tapon and M. Thong, 'Research Collaborations by Multi-National Orientated Pharmaceutical Firms: 1988–1997', *R&D Management*, 29, Issue 3 (1999), pp. 219–32.
65. M.J. Earl, 'The Risks of Outsourcing IT', *Sloan Management Review*, 37, Issue 3 (1996), pp. 26–32.
66. A.J. Marcella, *Outsourcing, Downsizing and Re-Engineering: Internal Control Implications* (Florida: The Institute of Internal Auditors, 1995).
67. Ibid., Marcella (1995).
68. T. Kumpe and P.T. Bolwijn, 'Toward the Innovative Firm: Challenge for R&D Management', *Research Technology Management*, 37, Issue 1 (1994), pp. 38–44.
69. F.P. Boer, 'R&D Planning Environment for the 90s: America and Japan', *Research Technology Management*, 34, Issue 2 (1991), pp. 12–15.
70. A.K. Gupta and D. Wilemon, 'Changing Patterns in Industrial R&D Development', *Journal of Product Innovation Management*, 13, Issue 6 (1996), pp. 497–511.
71. Ibid., pp. 497–511.
72. R.S. Jonash, 'Strategic Technology Leveraging: Making Outsourcing Work for You', *Research Technology Management*, 39, Issue 2 (1996), pp. 19–25.
73. Ibid., pp. 19–25.

6
Guide to Strategic Outsourcing and Partnership Management

The prevailing economic environment offers more interesting and valuable opportunities for strategic outsourcing than ever before. The increasing popularity of outsourcing strategies reflects the concurrent growth of the partnership approach to managing supplier relations. More importantly, it also reflects the rising influence of strategy concepts like core competencies, which encourage companies to compete for the future by focussing on developing depth of learning in carefully selected core activities, while creating value for customers through a network of supply partnerships with other similar focussed firms.[1]

The strategic logic of this approach is that partners with complementary competencies can create more value for customers than the equivalent resources contained within a vertically integrated company.[2] Although outsourcing provides a powerful means to maintaining an organisation's focus, it is a tool that is most effective when its strengths are exploited and its limits understood. An outsourcing strategy that is based on the premise that the cost of an internal service can be reduced by externalising the function (thereby transferring the financial burden of personnel and technology to the service provider), must be viewed as a simplistic approach.[3] Caution must be applied if long-term competitiveness is not to be sacrificed for short-term advantage.

As with other industries, the pharmaceutical industry has also realised the value of effective outsourcing, and that more importantly, such relationships must be developed and monitored for cost effectiveness and value.[4] To this end, outsourcing management is in search of the best balance of internal resources and external services with which to match corporate culture and goals. In order to meet these objectives, strategic planning is necessary to manage the process – equilibrium between outsourcing and insourcing must be part of the overall project development plan and management strategy if future success is to be ensured.[5]

6.1 Changing competencies in the pharmaceutical industry

Research within the pharmaceutical industry has been transformed into a richly innovative synergy between a very few large companies and a host of smaller firms. Given the level of co-dependency among operators in the industry, the key challenge facing the pharmaceutical sector is how best to manage these collaborations with external agents. An understanding of the dynamics of the buyer-supplier relationship is imperative if firms are to construct a portfolio of collaborators that will provide access to the emerging science and technology, as well as the necessary organisational capabilities.

With this in mind, the adoption of some degree of 'virtual' R&D, even if applied only selectively, must be underpinned by a sound set of management principles that will be pertinent to formulating an effective sourcing strategy. This is especially important when applied to three key areas:

The sourcing strategy

a. A clear set of strategic intents and a realistic set of management expectations must drive all technology sourcing efforts since random or unguided activities will inevitably produce poor results;
b. External sourcing activities must complement the strengths and weaknesses of internal R&D efforts. The organisation must therefore maintain a strong internal R&D function so as to derive maximum benefits from all outsourcing activities;
c. Commitment to the sourcing effort must be sustained over the long term;
d. The search for useful technologies must be both broad and focussed. It must be 'broad' in terms of technologies, geographies and sources; and 'focussed' in terms of the business and technology strategies employed, their priorities and available resources.

The organisation and its people

a. Whatever the organisational model chosen, management strategies and expectations must be made clear to the personnel involved, and the level of resources available appropriate to the scope of the effort;

b. Outsourcing efforts require experienced R&D professionals with good commercial sense and investigative skills;

c. The success of external sourcing activities depends on early procurement from all key individuals from within and outside the R&D function.

Processes and systems

a. Multifunctional co-operation is essential for the speedy and objective evaluation of potential opportunities identified by the search process;

b. Outsourcing agreements often involve prolonged negotiations that require managerial patience, flexibility and creativity.

c. Nurturing an outsourcing arrangement requires careful treatment of any resistance or resentment demonstrated by internal R&D staff;

d. The successful internalisation and commercialisation of acquired technology requires early implementation of cross-functional teamwork, as well as close attention to communication and decision making processes.[6]

What can be assumed with a greater degree of certainty is that the successful innovative pharmaceutical company will be the one that develops capabilities across a wide array of disciplines. These will include networking and partnering, project and knowledge management, the ability to manage across virtual organisations, and most importantly, the capacity to channel these combined resources into delivering value to the production process and to the organisation as a whole.[7] These combined factors will comprise the core competencies of the future – those that will drive the industry forward and be the determinants of business success in the years to come. Inevitably, the adoption of strategic outsourcing tacitly implies capabilities across all these areas of expertise. Like other fundamental shifts in management thinking, effective outsourcing requires the development of new skills, mindsets and corporate architectures – qualities that are not readily present in most organisations.

6.2   The strategic sourcing model

What has emerged from this study of outsourcing practices within the R&D environment of the pharmaceutical industry is that the ability to forge, manage and sustain strategic sourcing relationships is now an important ingredient of commercial success. Therefore the aim is to provide a mechanism by which the pharmaceutical firm can implement and sustain a strategic sourcing partnership. To this end, the *Strategic*

Sourcing Model provides a systematic framework designed at facilitating a coherent and holistic approach to implementing and managing the buyer–supplier relationship (see Figure 6.1). This model is comprised of seven distinct stages:

1. The decision to make internally or buy from external sources
2. Distinguish between core and non-core activities
3. Select a partner
4. Manage the outsourcing arrangement
5. Evaluate performance
6. Work together
7. Organisational learning

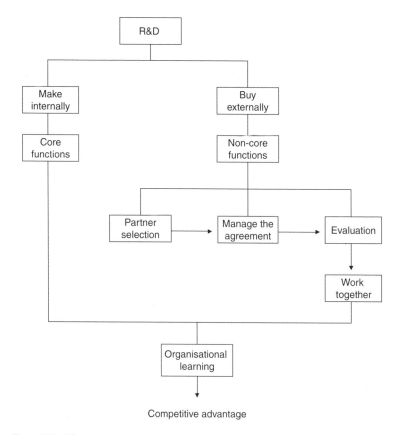

Figure 6.1   The strategic sourcing model

Stage 1: the decision to make internally or buy from external sources

In reaching a decision on whether or not to outsource, management must consider the wider implications of this option, not merely on the R&D activities of the firm, but also on aspects such as design, engineering, manufacturing and assembly, as well as the technology positions of all competitors and potential competitors within the industry. To achieve this, it is important that management formulate an outsourcing *mission statement* which incorporates the organisation's outsourcing intentions as well as the strategic rationale behind the decision to outsource. This is a necessary first step if managers are to understand why a specific function or process is to be supplied by external sources.

When devising an outsourcing mission statement, Blumberg *et al.* (1999) suggest that the document must accurately describe the (1) processes to be outsourced and the broad objectives for outsourcing; (2) relationship of outsourcing to the overall strategy of the firm; (3) links between the outsourced process and the company's core competencies; (4) strategic forces that direct the organisation towards an outsourcing relationship; (5) expected positioning of the relationship along the strategic sourcing spectrum; (6) scope of coverage; (7) critical risks involved; and (8) expected duration of the relationship.[8]

The objective of this mission statement is to define the scope, the approach, the resources and the internal cross-functional and cross-organisational linkages that would be utilised if promising opportunities were identified. It is therefore important that any sourcing strategy is directly aligned with the company's overriding mission, strategies and innovation objectives. Managers who are responsible for constructing this document must have a clear understanding of the principals governing the overall strategy of the firm, and the relevance of outsourcing within it.

Millson *et al.* (1996) point out that a clear definition of the 'need to align' is the single most important activity that management must undertake prior to forming any outsourcing agreement, since this helps to clarify the purpose of the programme.[9] One of the reasons why outsourcing arrangements fail is because of a lack of careful, mindful analysis of the ramifications of the partnering process before an alliance is formed.[10] Thus it is vital to select only those relationships considered sufficiently important so that they will be entered into with full commitment and with a willingness to invest the resources, as well as make the internal changes that successful external partnerships entail – the sharing of information, the linking of systems, and the establishment of agreements for governing the partnership.[11]

Stage 2: distinguish between core and non-core activities

The ability to effectively select and develop core competencies is a fundamental requirement of every firm regardless of the markets or industry served, since it provides the building blocks upon which competitive advantage is built and protected. Nevertheless, the identification of core competencies is often a difficult task given that the principle functions of the organisation are frequently confused with core activities. This is particularly true in an industry such as pharmaceuticals whose functions span a spectrum of capabilities, ranging from the purely scientific, to the marketing and selling of the finished product. In general terms, the particular areas and (or) functions that may be deemed as core capabilities for the *modern* pharmaceutical firm are: (1) knowledge pertaining to distinctive therapeutic classes; (2) project management capabilities; (3) the ability to access external sources of expertise and technology; (4) managing collaborative partnerships; (5) integrating and co-ordinating all activities, both domestic and global; (6) R&D methodologies; (7) knowledge management; and (8) sales and promotion techniques.[12]

When taken specifically within the context of pharmaceutical R&D, a company's core capabilities also include NCE library acquisition and management, high throughput-screening, understanding of disease mechanisms, neurosciences, genomics, and computer-aided molecular design.[13] Other possible core competencies can also include animal toxicology studies, pharmacokinetics design and studies, data entry and the management of laboratory systems.[14] Given the diversity of operational activities and knowledge sets required, an accurate identification of pharmaceutical core capabilities is both a difficult and complex process. However if strategic outsourcing is to be achieved, this is a necessary action that must be fulfilled.

One way of determining the core capabilities of the firm is through a value chain analysis. Put simply, the value-added chain is the process by which technology is combined with material and labour inputs, whereby processed inputs are then assembled, marketed and distributed.[15] By analysing each link and comparing it to prevailing competitors, the firm can determine where its own strengths lie along the value-added chain. These identifiable areas of expertise are the areas in which the firm will wish to concentrate its in-house resources, thereby building a distinctive competitive advantage that will differentiate it from its competitors. As for the other links in the value-added chain, these represent the areas in which the firm is not strong enough relative to its rivals. Therefore rather than attempt to control and perform all functions internally, the new streamlined organisation can focus its resources only on those factors of production in which it has pre-eminence, with the remainder left to specialist experts.[16] This not only adds value to both internal and external processes, but also to strengthening competitive advantage.

Outsourcing must therefore be conducted carefully, systematically and with explicit goals. The primary motives for considering a sourcing option should include strategic and tactical considerations at both the department and organisational level. Accordingly, management should not view outsourcing as an excuse to relinquish control of poorly managed, costly or misunderstood functions. Rather, management should consider (or re-consider) every three to four years, the overall merits of having an outsourcing strategy, especially when there have been changes in the market or when internal, industry or technological changes have taken place.

Stage 3: select a partner

Because partners with different expertise can fulfill particular outsourcing requirements better than others, management must be acutely aware of the prospective partner's resources, motives, competencies and weaknesses. The attributes of all potential partners must therefore be assessed in terms of (1) Physical factors such as capital, employees, geography and physical assets; (2) Technological factors such as product lines, process capabilities, patents and R&D; (3) Marketing factors such as distribution channels, customer knowledge and brand image; (4) Existing alliances with competitors, customers and suppliers; and (5) Similarities and differences in corporate cultures.[17]

A fundamental objective of any alliance is to further the strategic business objectives of the partnering firms. Thus, a prime consideration in partner selection should be to ascertain if prospective partners are a good fit strategically. Such an assessment should be based upon a shared understanding of the business rationale for the alliance, where the partners not only understand each other's reasons for forming the alliance, but also the strategic rationale behind the formation of the alliance itself.[18] Although the individual reasons do not have to be similar in nature, the motives themselves must be clearly understood by all participants. To achieve this, good strategic fit therefore requires as much self-examination as that of prospective partners.

a. Partner capability   During the early stages of the appraisal process, individuals who will take leadership responsibility, perform analysis, and be accountable for decision making must be identified. This decision must be based on the function to be outsourced and the circumstances surrounding the sourcing decision. Although a project leader or champion is desirable, in the case of large outsourcing contracts, senior management must play a pivotal role. In any event however, the team should consist of a mix of managerial and technical talent. In terms of the size of the team, this depends on the scope and the size of the project, although it is generally accepted that smaller teams are more effective than larger groups. Klepper *et al.* (1997) recommend that it is highly beneficial to have persons experienced with outsourcing on the team due to their past experience and insight, and to this end, outside consultants are highly desirable.[19] Those individuals that comprise the team should also include members responsible for initially drafting the contract so as to ensure continuity in the relationship.

According to Gay *et al.* (2000), the formal assessment of partner capability only begins once a specification of service document has been drafted. This is the 'brief' that the service provider will need to subsequently follow, and possibly improve upon according to its own area of expertise and level of experience. The formulation of the service specification document requires knowledge of the full extent of what is to be produced in order to ensure that nothing is excluded. This requires the contribution of a joint team, together with external advisors as well as training programs specialised in the principles of specification production. Therefore in general terms, the contents of this document must be drawn up to include an assessment of: (1) *Introduction* stating the purpose of programme and a structure of the statement of service; (2) *Background and objectives* pertaining to the motives for outsourcing; (3) *Existing circumstances* based upon quantitative and qualitative analyses; (4) *Statement of requirements* which summarises the requirements of the service provider, as well as the services that will be excluded and included; (5) *Service level requirements*, which identify current service levels and forms of measurement, service measurement systems, and the future level of service to be provided; (6) *Phased implementation and transition planning*, which details transition planning, post-contract verification methods, the location of multiple business units on a single site, Human Resource and communication issues; (7) *Communications and Human Resources* to include the transfer of undertakings and the protection of employment; and (8) *Contractual matters* detailing the background to the relationship, general contract objectives, principles governing the relationship, contract monitoring, the supplier's financial well-being, quality, staff training, allocation of the supplier's key employees to the contract, procurement and engagement of subcontractors, invoicing, payment terms, changes in control, problem management and resolution, service continuity, disaster recovery, contingency and transition planning.[20]

b. Partner compatibility   An issue that merits significant consideration at the outset of any collaboration is the compatibility of potential partners and their respective organisational cultures.[21] For organisations to work together it is important that there is a degree of cultural fit and compatibility between firms. The member organisations must be able to communicate with each other having a 'language' that is understood by all participants. The partners must also have a working style that is complementary in the way in which decisions are reached and problems resolved; and above all else, their behavioural styles must also be compatible.[22] Thus the importance of collaborating with an organisation with a compatible culture and mode of operation, as well as complementary areas of strength and expertise that is based on mutual understanding cannot be over stated. However since it is likely that differences in culture and operating styles will only emerge as the collaboration evolves, much depends on the ability to identify such differences speedily and to resolve any potential difficulties that may arise. It is therefore necessary to choose a partner(s) that will present a minimum of inherent conflict, and a maximum of mutual comprehension and respect if day-to-day conflicts are to be resolved expediently.[23]

c. Partner commitment   Dedication to a partnership agreement comprises two principle features. The first relates to the level of resources and effort committed to the partnership on a continuous basis. The second is associated with how readily the partner will leave the alliance once unexpected difficulties arise. It is therefore necessary to examine whether both parties are truly willing and able to commit the necessary resources and time required to make the partnership a success. If the dissolution of the alliance or even its under-performance is likely to create significant difficulties for the partnering firm, it is probable that the collaborating firm will contribute to the partnership on a regular basis, and will also be willing to commit extra effort and resources to the partnership should difficulties arise.[24] This is because in most instances, collaborative relations prosper as long as the supplier and the customer each have significant and roughly the same dependence upon the relationship.[25]

d. Partner control   When considering aspects of control in an alliance, the fundamental question that arises is how the pattern of control that will emerge, will affect the dynamics of the relationship. In the event that one partner may dominate the relationship, it is important to ascertain the implications of this (either positive or negative), on the success of the relationship. Wolff (1994) therefore suggests that in the case of a two-partner alliance, it is preferable that neither partner should dominate. The affairs of the alliance must instead be conducted on an equal partnership basis, for the greater the differences in *de facto* power, the less desirable the alliance will be.[26]

Since a planned pharmacological study cannot proceed until an appropriate CRO has been selected, the evaluation and selection procedures must be efficient and accurate, if the clinical project is to be a success. While the research involved is expensive, the cost in lost sales revenue for the pharmaceutical firm can be much greater if the study is significantly delayed or has to be repeated. Therefore when selecting a contractor for a specific project, a number of criteria must be taken into consideration prior to selecting a suitable CRO candidate.

Research conducted by PJB Publications Limited (1995)[27] and Vogel *et al.* (1993)[28] suggest that the following must comprise the critical success factors of successful partner selection:

1. *Cost* – It is very important that cost comparisons are made using comparable benchmarks so that costs cover similar functions and levels of service. The pharmaceutical firm must also establish a mechanism for measuring all variable costs incurred;
2. *Financial well-being* – If there are concerns about the risks of contracting with a subsidiary supplier, then guarantees must be obtained from the parent company. In the event of the sub-contractor going out of business, the parent company could ensure continuity by taking over responsibility for the initial contract;
3. *Resources* – This relates to the size of the service provider, the company's financial strengths, technical and (or) specialist equipment as well as available data resources;
4. *Human Resources* – In the event that staff will be transferred from the pharmaceutical firm to the supplier, the company must examine what opportunities exist for staff career development, pensions and other transfer benefits. The company must also examine whether the service provider has invested sufficient resources that would support the outsourced function;
5. *Competencies* – This relates to the qualifications and (or) competencies gained by the service provider's management and staff;

6. *Quality* – Management must determine if the function or service to be outsourced requires specific standards of certification, if the contractor is suitably qualified for the specific tasks, and if appropriate systems are in place for the monitoring and setting of such standards of quality;

7. *Company History* – The pharmaceutical company must establish the track record of the service provider, and the number of years experience the firm has within the outsourcing market. It is also important to determine if outsourcing is core to the supplier's business, or is part of a wider array of services;

8. *Methods* – The pharmaceutical firm must select the supplier on the suitability of the proposed R&D methodologies to the specific project;

9. *References* – The pharmaceutical firm must be able to obtain information pertaining to previous services rendered. When the contract is large in scale, it may be beneficial to visit past clients, as well as to ascertain how many other clients the service provider is contracted with in order to determine if these are current competitors. The possible implications of this to the firm must then be considered;

10. *Interviews* – As with all business partnerships, the key to a successful relationship is the degree of personal chemistry and rapport between the partners involved. This can only be truthfully assessed through personal meetings with key individuals;

11. *Compatibility* – The client and the service provider must have shared views in terms of corporate culture, ethos towards employees, codes of practice, management style, compatible technology and congruent goals; and

12. *Flexibility* – The pharmaceutical firm must establish whether the supplier will be able to support future expansion or alterations to the original contract. This will determine if the supplier is capable of true innovation, or is just a supplier of proprietary services.

Stage 4: manage the outsourcing arrangement

Because every aspect of the outsourcing arrangement is governed by the contract, both the pharmaceutical firm and the service provider must agree on all of the features contained in the document. Management must also consider every possible contingency that may arise, including the resolution of disputes once the contract has been executed. It is also advisable that internal as well as external legal experts are utilised at this stage of the outsourcing process.

To this end, Klepper *et al.* (1997) identify a number of essential criteria that must be included in the terms of the contractual agreement:

1. *Terms of the agreement* – Management must ensure that the contract will only be renewed once a renewal clause has been inserted into the contract, and that prior notice is issued;
2. *Performance measurement* – It is essential that the contract specifies as accurately as possible the services that will be provided under the terms of the contract, the volume of work to be undertaken, the frequency with which specific tasks must be carried out, the R&D methodologies to be used, and the time period in which results must be delivered;
3. *Ownership and confidentiality of the data* – The pharmaceutical firm must ensure that it will retain the intellectual property rights of all the data submitted to the service provider, and that the information provided will be kept strictly confidential;
4. *Infrastructure* – This must include issues pertaining to the physical location of the project. For example, the need for the outsourced team to remain on-site or relocated must be ascertained. The need for new facilities to be built, the type of training that is required, and the party that will pay for specialist infrastructure or equipment must be also be determined;
5. *Reporting and communication* – The contract should also specify how the two parties should communicate in order to effectively assess performance and take remedial action. This could include aspects such as the frequency of reporting and timing, what feedback this should contain, as well as the frequency of such meetings;
6. *Monitoring* – The contract must also include the arrangements made by the pharmaceutical firm for monitoring the services provided in order to ensure that appropriate service levels are met, as well as the criteria for measuring success;
7. *Warranty* – Management must have the service provider certify that all services will be provided as defined in the contractual agreement, and that accommodation will be made for any subsequent increases in requirements;
8. *Incentives* – The pharmaceutical firm should offer the service provider with an incentive to perform, which could include guaranteed savings and the sharing of benefits and risks;
9. *Disclaimers* – Although this must be included in the contract, care should be taken that the disclaimer does not void the warranty of the service agreement; and

10. *Anticipated change* – The outsourcing contract should provide for all eventualities and must therefore include a termination agreement if necessary.[29]

In addition to the terms defined in the contractual agreement, both the pharmaceutical firm and the service provider will also have to agree on the standards of quality that are to be met and delivered. Fromson (1995) therefore suggests that the following must comprise the criteria for quality assurance for any R&D project that is to be outsourced:

1. *Qualifications and experience* – The contract should specify to what degree staff must be qualified, and the minimum levels of experience required;
2. *Confidentiality* – Standards of confidentiality must be maintained in terms of business processes and information so as to ensure that the Data Protection and Intellectual Property Right laws are observed;
3. *Codes of practice* – Management must stipulate that the service provider will work in accordance with relevant codes of practice, professional standards of organisations and (or) associations. When applied to CROs, this refers to international regulatory standards as defined in Good Laboratory Practice (GLP), Good Clinical Practice (GCP) and Good Manufacturing Practice (GMP); and
4. *Health and safety issues* – The contract should also stipulate that the service provider will work in compliance with all relevant health and safety regulations and legislation.[30]

Therefore the purpose of the contract is to establish clearly, comprehensively and unambiguously exactly what the service provider is meant to do for the client. Because the Service Level Agreement (SLA) is not a separate contract, but comprises part of the overall contractual agreement, it must reflect and be consistent with it.[31] In general, the SLA is a factual document stipulating what the supplier does, when and where, and to what standards the task must be completed. It should also make clear who is to be responsible for producing the required data for monitoring and compliance, and the measures to be taken if either party does not comply. To this end, there should be an automatic mechanism in place linked to performance relative to the SLA, so that there is no room for deviation or possible legal dispute. However a degree of flexibility must also be drawn into the contract so that it does not become so prescriptive that it ultimately hinders innovative solutions.[32]

When considering the day-to-day administering of the sourcing partnership, Liedtka (1996) proposes a core set of sound management principles that could be applied to improving the outsourcing agreement.[33] The author suggests that for successful alliance management, the following principles must provide the framework for governing the partnership:

1. *Supported by organisational architecture* – If partners are to create the mindsets, goals, processes and outcomes that will determine the success of the partnership agreement, they must be supported by the larger organisational architecture of the collaborating firms. This organisational architecture must include all elements of design relating to both social and work systems, operating styles and processes for selection, socialisation, development and reward, a culture steeped in honesty, committed leadership, congruent processes for measurement, reward and budgeting, and the provision of time and information.[34]

2. *Belief in honest communication* – Concerns about the political costs of honesty often exacerbates the difficulty of collaboration because such concerns deprive the corporate effort of a very crucial ingredient – accurate information. The need for frequent and open communication between partners is therefore essential. Related to this is the need to establish a degree of trust between partners, which is a vital ingredient for the continuation and effectiveness of inter-organisational relationships.[35] Dodgson (1993) emphasises the importance of developing not only a degree of trust between the *individuals* involved in the collaboration, but also a broader sense of *organisational* trust that would survive the departure of key employees.[36] Thus, it is important to create a climate where the ability to raise sensitive issues exists if effective project management is to be achieved.

3. *Committed leadership* – Both the active and visible support of senior management is essential if the strategic purpose of the partnership is to be reiterated clearly and frequently. It is also important that senior management holds the service provider accountable for meeting performance expectations, and in the event of non-compliance, enforcing the necessary penalties as stipulated in the contractual agreement.

4. *Joint planning and budgeting* – Given that most commitments are crystallised during the formal planning and budgeting stages, this provides crucial opportunities to recognise and incorporate inputs from all parties to the outsourcing arrangement.

5. *Congruent measurement and reward systems* – It is important to ensure that there is at least perceived equality of contribution and benefits from all stakeholders since inequalities can often lead to dissatisfaction, resentment and possibly the termination of the outsourcing

agreement. Lynch (1990) sees the creation of a 'win-win' situation whereby all the partners gain as an important pre-requisite for alliance management given that a partner who believes that he is loosing will not perform well and may eventually terminate the alliance.[37] One way of overcoming this is to frequently conduct 'mutual benefit' assessment exercises so as to reduce the risk of a partner unexpectedly withdrawing from the relationship.

6. *Regular progress reviews* – Regular progress reviews are vital for monitoring prospective opportunities and potential pitfalls that may arise during the course of the outsourcing partnership. In this instance, auditing is critical to ensuring that

   a. progress is being made;
   b. the collaboration is still beneficial to all participants,
   c. potentially profitable opportunities are capitalised upon and,
   d. problems are detected early on in the relationship.[38]

A point of further consideration is the human resource element of the partnership since the size and composition of the outsourcing team depends on the nature of the function to be outsourced. Those personnel who can oversee and manage the contract, as well as handle relations with the service provider must be identified, and their roles clearly defined. For example

1. *Senior Management* must make sure that proper objectives are set;
2. *Current line managers* must provide background information and advice on the standards that are to be set;
3. *Future service managers* must ensure that future cost, quality and contractual issues are clearly understood;
4. *Financial staff* must ensure a full costing of the service to be provided, and include all hidden costs;
5. *Procurement managers* are required to provide effective negotiation skills;
6. *End users* are required to ensure that appropriate service level agreements are developed;
7. *Legal advisors* are required to cover contractual and employment law issues;
8. *Human Resource personnel* are necessary to provide employee relations advise and support; and
9. *Public relations* staff are required to deal with external enquiries.[39]

Having these people involved at the initial stages of the negotiation process therefore helps engender relationships between the client and the service provider, and ensures greater continuity over the duration of the relationship.

Although managing the human resource component of the agreement is one of the most important factors in successfully managing the outsourcing process, a number of other factors must also be considered: For example

1. The pharmaceutical firm must understand the service provider's background and track record, the methods it will employ to maximise its profits, achieve economies of scale and other efficiencies;
2. Management must ascertain if the service provider is to make cost savings, and in doing so, if any short-cuts might be taken;
3. Since costs will be incurred in setting up the outsourcing agreement these must be quoted separately from the contract, so as to avoid high prices for commodity services;
4. It is important to plan ahead as much as possible and to discuss the possibility that the requirements of the business may change over time. Solutions to such changes must therefore be identified;
5. The assumptions made by both parties at the start of the outsourcing agreement must be periodically checked and verified;
6. The contract should remain flexible if it is to remain viable over the long term;
7. Both the pharmaceutical company and the service provider must be motivated to improve the level of service provided and to ensure the success of the outsourcing agreement; and
8. Communication channels must be kept open, and all parties must remain honest to each other.[40]

Stage 5: evaluate performance

Although the service provider's current levels of performance must be evaluated and quantified, it is equally important that the long-term performance trends are also monitored since the company will work with the selected service provider on a regular basis. Therefore when both current and long-term performance levels are compared and considered, for internal as well as external sources, it will be clear whether the external provider is indeed the best choice. To this end, Maromonte (1998) identifies four specific criteria that can be applied to evaluating supplier performance:

1. Quality performance   The competitiveness of the company is to a great extent determined by the success of its source for R&D services. This is especially true in the case of pharmaceuticals where if an R&D project is not successfully completed the company's project development objectives will not be supported. If this is to be avoided, the performance of the R&D service provider must be measured, assessed and compared to other lead sources. In the case of suppliers of R&D, quality is defined as the ability to meet the sourcing company's R&D objectives as described by its R&D specifications.[41] The quality performance measures will need to define both the existing levels of quality that are achieved, as well as the supplier's capacity to improve quality over time. In the first instance, the service provider's R&D project yield must be quantified. Of the total number of R&D objectives pursued, the yield is the percentage in full compliance with the company's objectives as defined by its R&D specifications. Therefore the closer the delivered R&D project yield is to 100 per cent, the better the performance of the R&D service provider. Second, it is also necessary to examine the supplier's quality improvement trend, which examines the degree to which the project yield improves or deteriorates over time. This way the pharmaceutical firm will be able to determine whether it wants to continue its contract with the supplier, or to terminate it.

2. *Delivery performance*   The ability to successfully complete an assigned R&D project on time is a crucial element of the new product development programme and to all of the pharmaceutical R&D process. To ensure timely compliance, Maromonte (1998) identifies two delivery performance measurement criteria. The first evaluates the performance of the service provider based on the number of R&D projects successfully completed on time. The second assesses the capacity of the service provider to consistently reduce R&D project cycle times, and is measured as the annual percentage reduction in the life cycle of a project. Such reductions can be achieved only if the service provider is willing to reorganise its manufacturing facilities by adding state-of-the-art equipment, or through the adoption of novel techniques.[42]

3. *Cost performance*   Given that the total expense of an R&D project is predominantly comprised of the cost incurred in developing and producing a product, it is important that the cost competitiveness of the service provider is monitored periodically. In order to determine cost-related performance measurements, it is important to verify the effective cost of the service provider. For external sources of R&D, the 'effective cost' is the price quoted for a given project, minus the amount the contracting company can expect to recover from the service provider to resolve any warranty claims.[43] Accordingly, estimates of this type of cost are based on the service provider's historic warranty expenses. Once adjustments are made to the internal costs and external prices for the completion of an R&D project, it is then possible to draw comparisons between both expenses.

4. *Product advancement performance*   Since the decision to externalise production is based on accruing long-term benefits, it is necessary to assess the capacity of the service provider to advance its product

offerings through improvements in its R&D capabilities and services. In terms of product advancement capabilities, it is important to measure the service provider's financial commitment to advancing those R&D services that would benefit the sourcing company, as well as to quantify its historic progress in actually achieving its commitments.[44] To this end, the capital investment plans of the supplier must be evaluated since it comprises the service provider's entire operations and planned commitments for the next several years. When taken within the context of R&D, the supplier's commitment to product advancement can be measured by the annual budget committed to areas of its operations that would benefit the pharmaceutical firm. Bragg (1998) also suggests that the contracting company should measure all activities in the functional area to be outsourced *prior* to outsourcing the particular function. This provides the company with a wealth of information that could be used to compare the performance of the company with that of the supplier. One way of ensuring the validity of such measurements, is by having the supplier endorse a document containing the agreed baseline measures which would render the supplier incapable of subsequently refuting the information on the grounds of incorrect data collection or calculation methods.[45] Therefore once a function has been outsourced, measurements should be made at least once a month, or more frequently as desired. This would enable measures to be stored in trend lines, where sudden spikes in the measurements could be investigated to reveal if any problems are occurring.[46] It is therefore important that the company have its own staff collect the measurements and perform the calculations if the results are not to be distorted by the suppliers.

Stage 6: work together

Even in the most meticulously planned partnerships, problems will, and do occur. Some of the most common problems that arise between pharmaceutical companies and their clinical research suppliers occur when:

1. The two parties are unable to agree to the terms of the contract, resulting in a delayed start;
2. The service provider subcontracts part of the operation to another supplier;
3. Misunderstandings arise through both written and oral communication;
4. Established processes require modification prior to work commencing on the contractor's equipment;

5. Careless time-keeping means that the target completion date cannot be met;
6. The pharmaceutical company fails to keep the contractor informed of changes in timing or processes;
7. The service provider fails to keep the client informed of changes in key staff, or of recurrent problems within manufacturing; and
8. Personalities clash between the supplier's staff and the pharmaceutical representative.[47]

It is generally agreed that many outsourcing arrangements fail at this stage of the partnership, partly because both the technical and (or) commercial results fall short of expectations, or simply because the two partners do not work well together. Although many of these commonly occurring problems can be overcome through effective planning especially with regard to technical and commercial evaluations, Chatterji (1996) identifies a number of sound practices that can help improve the probability of success:

1. An effective manager must be appointed to lead the sourcing effort. The role of this key individual must be to ensure the timely recognition and resolution of technical, commercial and organisational issues that arise during the course of the partnership. The decision of whether the candidate should be recruited from the client or the service provider will therefore depend on the nature of the relationship established with the supplier;
2. Informal and formal exchanges of personnel between the two partners are beneficial when transferring technology since it helps to promote mutual trust and respect;
3. The recognition of progress must be shared between all parties involved. Conversely, this also corresponds to the sharing of blame, which should not be placed upon any single party. The partnership must instead look at all problems jointly and work together to resolve them;
4. It is important to maintain close interactions with other key departments in order to ensure cross-functional ownership of the alliance and the smooth assimilation of the technology into the mainstream of the company.[48]

Similarly, a study conducted by Forrest *et al.* (1992) also identifies a number of critical success factors deemed essential to partnership success. These include:

1. Open communication between the two parties;
2. Mutual agreement on strategic objectives;
3. Good interpersonal relations between partners;
4. Sustained mutual commitment to finance, technology, human resources and facilities;
5. Good leadership skills and motivation demonstrated by those conducting the alliance;
6. Sound understanding by both parties on matters relating to technologies;
7. Willingness to change strategic objectives when needed;
8. Compatible decision making processes;
9. Compatible organisational cultures; and
10. Consistent direction and involvement by senior management.[49]

These features are fundamental to the well-being of the partnership if both sides are to work collectively to ensure long-term success.

Stage 7: organisational learning

Thompson *et al.* (1996) suggest that the creation of competitive advantage requires two vital elements. First, the organisation must behave in a co-ordinated, synergy creating manner, thereby integrating functions and businesses; and second, the value adding network (the links between manufacturers, retailers, suppliers and intermediate distributors) must be managed as an effective, integrated system.[50] In the supporting literature, Kay (1993) refers to the realisation of these ideals as 'strategic architecture' given that the means to build and control such 'architecture' is only made possible through the development of strong technological competencies as well as effective functional process competencies, both of which combine to produce superior value for the company. Accordingly, the two most important components of this 'architecture' is systematic thinking, which leads to synergy from the fostering of interdependence between people, functions and divisions in organisations; and the establishment of linkages or even alliances between organisations at different stages of the value-added chain.[51]

The degree of organisational success achieved is to a great extent dependent on management's ability to be proactive as well as reactive to the environment in which the firm operates. If the organisation is to achieve growth and prosperity, management must be able to identify and to create competitive opportunities ahead of its rivals and to then capitalise on them. This in turn requires that managers work in harmony with each other, that information and capabilities are shared across departments, and that the practice is extended to outside the organisation so as to encapsulate the whole of the value chain.[52] Therefore if synergy is to be obtained, it is essential that businesses support each other through the transferring of skills, competencies and capabilities, and in some instances, the sharing of common resources. This implies that organisations must be able to learn from these linkages and to share learning with their partners if competitive advantage is to be secured. Powell *et al.* (1996) therefore suggest that organisational learning is both a function of access to knowledge as well as the capabilities for utilising and building on such knowledge. Accordingly, those organisational arrangements that provide access to knowledge quickly and reliably have the greatest capacity to confer competitive advantage.[53] This implies that if competitive advantage is to be secured through strategic outsourcing, then organisational learning must form a fundamental component of the strategic sourcing process.

When knowledge is broadly distributed, as is the case in the pharmaceutical industry, the locus of innovation is found to exist in a network of inter-organisational relationships.[54] If an organisation is to keep abreast of rapid new developments within the fields of science and technology, it is essential that it be involved in the research and development process. In industries such as pharmaceuticals, where knowledge is a crucial component of competitive success, companies must therefore be expert at both in-house research as well as collaborative research with clinical research organisations, biotechnology firms and other specialist external agents. According to Cohen *et al.* (1989), a firm with a greater capacity to learn is adept at both internal and external R&D, thus enabling it to contribute more to a collaboration, as well as to learn more extensively from such participation.[55] Internal capability and external collaboration are therefore not substitutes for one another, but are in fact complementary, and thus form a crucial part of the strategic process.[56] Arora *et al.* (1990) suggest that this is due to a number of reasons. First, internal capability is indispensable in evaluating research conducted outside of the firm, while external collaboration provides access to knowledge and resources that cannot be generated internally. Second, a network serves as a locus of innovation because it provides timely access to knowledge and resources that are otherwise unavailable, while at the same time, testing internal expertise and learning capabilities.[57]

Similarly, Powell *et al.* (1996) also highlight two key observations: inter-organisational collaborations are not simply a means to compensate for the lack of internal skills, and nor should they be viewed as a series of discrete transactions.[58] Although a firm's skill and value as a collaborator is related to its internal assets, collaboration at the same time enhances and strengthens those internal competencies. Consequently, the development of collaborative relationships is much more than simply learning how to manage a number of collaborations. Management must learn how to transfer knowledge across alliances and locate themselves in those network positions that enable them to keep pace with the most promising scientific and technological developments.[59] Conversely, those R&D alliances that are explicitly explorative also play an important part in enabling a firm to keep abreast of rapidly changing developments. Since knowledge facilitates the use of other knowledge, what can be learned is crucially affected by what is already known:

> In order for industrial research organisations to be in close contact with new advances in basic science, it is important to be an active participant at the leading edge of world science. This is because effective technical interchange requires that the industrial organisation have its own basic research results ... to use as a currency of exchange.[60] (Pake 1986).

What emerges is that continuous learning and improvement is the key to long-term partnership success, and therefore forms an integral part of the strategic sourcing process. Organisational learning should be deeply embedded within all business processes, thereby embracing internal R&D facilities and external outsourcing efforts. Such 'learning' is an important feature of the strategic sourcing process since it has the capacity to ensure reciprocal learning between internal and external agents, thus leading to knowledge creation and accumulation within the firm, as well as for those involved in the outsourcing relationship. It also enables those involved in internal R&D to remain at the forefront of rapid new developments, while at the same time allowing for effective comparison and assessment between internal and outsourced services. Organisational learning also facilitates the absorption of knowledge by the outsourced team from their partners, once again reinforcing the knowledge cycle. These mutual benefits, acquired by both internal and external agents, combine to provide a formidable force in the drive to attain competitive advantage for the organisation as a whole.

6.3   Summary of critical success factors

1. It is possible to derive competitive and strategic value from outsourcing provided that the motives for entering into such an agreement

are in harmony with the overall objectives of the organisation. The sourcing effort must have the support of senior management and be guided by clear and precise goals, *vis-à-vis* the department initiating the proposal and the organisation as a whole.

2. Firms exploring outsourcing as a means to enhancing business performance must complete a strategic analysis of all aspects of the business in order to determine the benefits that could be achieved from the outsourcing of selected non-core functions. The decision to 'make or buy' must be implemented through a systematic analysis of what the firm's core competencies are relative to its competition. Pharmaceutical companies must decide what their core competencies are so that they may be superior in what they do, while selectively outsourcing remaining functions so that expert suppliers can contribute to the company's R&D process.

3. Management must understand that outsourcing does not absolve the organisation from its project management duties. Many of the problems frequently associated with the outsourcing process derive from management's tendency to hand over the project management function to the service provider.[61] Although the responsibility of managing a specific function transfers from within the organisation to an external service provider, the contracting firm must still remain accountable for ensuring the successful operation of the outsourcing arrangement. One of the consequences of outsourcing is that it changes the profile and the content of the business to be managed in that the external sources also require management.

4. To successfully manage the outsourcing arrangement, the pharmaceutical firm must have the necessary skills, knowledge and resources to effectively monitor, manage and assess the services provided. It is essential that the firm enters into an outsourcing arrangement with a comprehensive proposal outlining detailed expectations, requirements and expected benefits. The administering of the outsourced project must be consistent to ensure that requirements are met and that potential problems are identified early in the relationship.[62] As with any new management technique, outsourcing also entails a learning curve for the firm adopting it.

5. Outsourcing should not be viewed as an instrument for alleviating problems experienced within the organisation given that internal problems will not be resolved through outsourcing. If the organisation were experiencing problems of managing or understanding an internal operation, such difficulties would be exacerbated if the function were to be externalised.

6. Outsourcing is not a singular effort to improving a particular function or process, but rather a partnership between both buyer and supplier. Outsourcing should allow the company to return to what it does best, while at the same time, reaping the benefits of permitting its outsourcing partners to do the same.

7. In order to achieve the expected outcomes, the outsourcing effort must be strategic in nature. It must be clearly defined, logically implemented and carefully supervised.

Given the fundamentals upon which the principles of outsourcing are based, the adoption of this strategy requires a transformation to the way in which R&D is managed. For the pharmaceutical industry, achieving the critical success factors necessary for successful outsourcing presents a formidable challenge to both firms and managers alike. These difficulties are compounded due to the historic nature of the industry and its inexperience with dealing with this novel approach to drug delivery. What has emerged is that the traditional skills and competencies upon which the industry was built are changing rapidly, with an array of new expertise being required for future commercial success.

Therefore, it is essential to understand that this particular type of partnering cannot be implanted on to traditional ways of thinking and behaving, nor can it be achieved through structure alone. An aptitude for collaboration can only be achieved through new ways of managing and designing organisations, and facilitated through organisational learning and innovation. If the firm is to acquire the strategic benefits of partnering, it must undergo a transformation at both the corporate and departmental level, and should incorporate such elements as managerial control, the structure of the organisation and even the very sources of competitive advantage. Effective outsourcing therefore requires a new management mindset that embraces opportunity, a set of skills that can foster dialogue amongst participants, as well as organisational change. Those companies that fail to develop a competence for this form of collaboration may ultimately be disadvantaged in a competitive marketplace in the same way as those burdened by obsolete management methodologies and technologies:

> In a world of change, the learners shall inherit the Earth, while the learned shall find themselves perfectly suited for a world that no longer exists.[63] (Hoffer 1963)

Notes

1. B. Leavy, 'Outsourcing Strategy and a Learning Dilemma', *Production and Inventory Management Journal*, 37, Issue 4 (1996), pp. 50–2.
2. Ibid., pp. 50–2.
3. J. Smith, 'Outsourcing as a Strategic Tool', *Competitive Intelligence Review*, 7, Issue 3 (1996), pp. 70–4.
4. M.E. Watanabe, 'Research-for-Hire Companies Proliferate', *The Scientist*, 9, Issue 24 (1995), pp. 4–5.
5. D.A. Daniel, N. Nanjo-Jones, J. Kirwin and S.A. Stempien, 'Outsourcing Management in the Pharmaceutical Industry: The Early Stages at Four United States Companies', *Drug Information Journal*, 31, Issue 1 (1997), pp. 111–18.
6. D. Chatterji and T.A. Manuel, 'Benefiting from External Sources of Technology', *Research Technology Management*, 36, Issue 6 (1993), pp. 21–6.
7. G. Fairlough, 'A Marriage of Large and Small: R&D for Healthcare Products', *Business Strategy Review*, 7, Issue 2 (1996), pp. 14–23.
8. L. Blumberg, 'How to Engage in a Strategic Sourcing Relationship', The Warren Company (1999), *http://www.outsourcing.com/articles/strategicoutsourcing/main.html*
9. M.R. Millson, S.P. Raj and D. Wilemon, 'Strategic Partnering for Developing New Products', *Research Technology Management*, 39, Issue 3 (1996), pp. 41–9.
10. C.E. Schillaci, 'Designing Successful Joint Ventures', *The Journal of Business Strategy*, 8, Issue 2 (1987), pp. 59–63.
11. R.M. Kanter, *When Giants Learn to Dance* (New York: Simon and Schuster, 1989).
12. PriceWaterhouse Coopers Healthcare Report, *Pharma 2005: An Industrial Revolution in R&D* (London: PriceWaterhouse Coopers Healthcare Publishing, 1998).
13. D. Boath, P. Hess and C. Munch, 'Virtual R&D: A Core Competency Approach to Outsourcing', *Pharmaceutical Executive*, 16, Issue 6 (1996), pp. 72–8.
14. Ibid., pp. 72–8.
15. B. Kogut, 'Designing Global Strategies: Comparative and Competitive Value-added Chains', *Sloan Management Review*, 26, Issue 4 (1995), pp. 15–27.
16. PriceWaterhouse Coopers Healthcare Report, *Pharma 2005: An Industrial Revolution in R&D* (London: PriceWaterhouse Coopers Healthcare Publishing, 1998).
17. M.R. Millson, S.P. Raj and D. Wilemon, 'Strategic Partnering for Developing New Products', *Research Technology Management*, 39, Issue 3 (1996), pp. 41–9.
18. J.W. Medcof, 'Why Too Many Alliances End in Divorce', *International Journal of Strategic Management: Long Range Planning*, 30, Issue 5 (1997), pp. 718–32.
19. R. Klepper and W. Jones, *Outsourcing Information Technology, Systems and Services* (New York: Prentice Hall, 1997).
20. C.L. Gay and J. Essinger, *Inside Outsourcing: The Insider's Guide to Managing Strategic Outsourcing* (London: Nicholas Brealey Publishing, 2000).
21. J.C. Mason, 'Strategic Alliances: Partnering for Success', *Management Review*, 82, Issue 5 (1993), pp. 10–15.
22. P. Lorange, 'Co-operative Strategies: Planning and Control Considerations', in N. Hood and J.E. Vahlne (eds), *Strategies in Global Competition* (London: Routledge, 1988), pp. 370–89.

23. F. Leverick and D.A. Littler, *The Risks and Rewards of Collaboration: A Survey of Collaborative Product Development in UK Companies'*, Manchester School of Management, Manchester University, Manchester (1993).

24. J.W. Medcof, 'Why Too Many Alliances End in Divorce', *International Journal of Strategic Management: Long Range Planning*, 30, Issue 5 (1997), pp. 718–32.

25. J.C. Anderson and J.A. Narus, 'Partnering as a Focused Market Strategy', *California Management Review*, 33, Issue 3 (1991), pp. 95–113.

26. M.F. Wolff, 'Building Trust in Alliances', *Research Technology Management*, 37, Issue 3 (1994), pp. 12–15.

27. Scrip Report, *Strategic Management of R&D in the Pharmaceutical Industry* (London: PJB Publications Limited, 1995), pp. 167–82.

28. J.R. Vogel and M.I. Linzmayer, 'Achieving Results with Contract Research Organisations: Evaluating and Selecting CROs', *Applied Clinical Trials*, 2, Issue 8 (1993), pp. 36–41.

29. R. Klepper and W. Jones, *Outsourcing Information Technology, Systems and Services* (New York: Prentice Hall, 1997).

29. Ibid., Klepper *et al.* (1997).

30. J. Fromson, 'What is Needed from a CRO: Compare and Contrast the Requirements of a Large Multinational with Venture Capitalist Type Companies' in the *6th International Conference on Contract Research Organisations*, Conference Proceedings, Amsterdam (1995), pp. 57–64.

31. H. Graham and G. Hunter, 'Its All in the Contract', *Human Resources Magazine*, 33 (1997), pp. 73–6.

32. Ibid., pp. 73–6.

33. J.M. Liedtka, Collaborating Across Lines of Business for Competitive Advantage', *The Academy of Management Executive*, 10, Issue 2 (1996), pp. 20–35.

34. Ibid., pp. 20–35.

35. D. Littler and F. Leverick, 'Joint Ventures for Product Development: Learning from Experience', *International Journal of Strategic Management: Long Range Planning*, 28, Issue 3 (1995), pp. 58–67.

36. M. Dodgson, 'Learning, Trust and Technological Collaboration', *Human Relations*, 46, Issue 1 (1993), pp. 77–95.

37. R.P. Lynch, 'Building Alliances to Penetrate European Markets', *The Journal of Business Strategy*, 11, Issue 2 (1990), pp. 4–8.

38. M.P. Lyons, 'Joint Ventures as Strategic Choice: A Literature Review', *International Journal of Strategic Management: Long Range Planning*, 24, Issue 4 (1991), pp. 130–44.

39. Management Today Report, *Outsourcing Strategies: The UK Outsourcing Report* (London: Management Today, 2000), pp. 107–28.

40. Ibid., pp. 107–28.

41. K.R. Maromonte, *Corporate Strategic Business Sourcing* (Connecticut: Quorum Books, 1998).

42. Ibid., Maromonte (1998).

43. Ibid., Maromonte (1998).

44. Ibid., Maromonte (1998).

45. S.M. Bragg, *Outsourcing: A Guide to Selecting the Correct Business Unit, Negotiating the Contract and Maintaining Control of the Process* (New York: John Wiley and Sons Inc., 1998).

46. Ibid., Bragg (1998).

47. D. MacArthur, *Optimising the Use of Contract Services by the Pharmaceutical Industry*, Scrip Reports (London: PJB Publications Limited, 1994), pp. 71–84.
48. D. Chatterji, 'Accessing External Sources of Technology', *Research Technology Management*, 39, Issue 2 (1996), pp. 48–56.
49. J.E. Forrest and M.J. Martin, 'Strategic Alliances between Large and Small Research Intensive Organisations: Experiences in the Biotechnology Industry', *R&D Management*, 22, Issue 1 (1992), pp. 41–54.
50. J. Thompson and B. Richardson, 'Strategic and Competitive Success: Towards a Model of the Comprehensively Competent Organisation', *Management Decision*, 34, Issue 2 (1996), pp. 5–19.
51. J.L. Kay, *Foundations of Corporate Success* (Oxford: Oxford University Press, 1993).
52. J. Thompson and B. Richardson, 'Strategic and Competitive Success: Towards a Model of the Comprehensively Competent Organisation', *Management Decision*, 34, Issue 2 (1996), pp. 5–19.
53. W.W. Powell, K.W. Koput and L. Smith-Doerr, 'Inter-Organisational Collaboration and the Locus of Innovation: Networks of Learning in Biotechnology', *Administrative Science Quarterly*, 41, Issue 1, pp. 116–37.
54. W.W. Powell and P. Brantley, 'Competitive Co-operation in Biotechnology: Learning Through Networks', in N. Nohria and R. Eccles (eds), *Networks and Organisations* (Cambridge: Harvard Business School Press, 1992), pp. 366–94.
55. W. Cohen and D. Levinthal, 'Innovation and Learning: The Two Faces of R&D', *Economic Journal*, 99 (1989), pp. 569–96.
56. A. Arora and A. Gambardella, 'Complementarity and External Linkages: The Strategies of Large Firms in Biotechnology', *Journal of Industrial Economics*, 38, Issue 4 (1990), pp. 361–79.
57. Ibid., pp. 361–79.
58. W.W. Powell, K.W. Koput and L. Smith-Doerr, 'Inter-organisational Collaboration and the Locus of Innovation: Networks of Learning in Biotechnology', *Administrative Science Quarterly*, 41, Issue 1, pp. 116–37.
59. Ibid., pp. 116–37.
60. G.E. Pake, 'Business Payoff from Basic Science at Xerox', *Research Technology Management*, 29, Issue 6 (1986), pp. 35–40.
61. R. Mullin, 'Managing the Outsourced Enterprise', *Journal of Business Strategy*, 17, Issue 4 (1996), pp. 28–36.
62. D. Elmuti, Y. Kathawala and M. Monippallil, 'Outsourcing to Gain a Competitive Advantage', *Industrial Management*, 40, Issue 3 (1998), pp. 20–4.
63. E. Hoffer, *The Ordeal of Change* (New York: Harper and Row, 1963).

Conclusions

Developments in the evolution of the pharmaceutical industry over the past twenty-five years have ushered in a new age of drug development and design, and with it, novel ways of conducting pharmaceutical research. Outsourcing therefore represents an extension of research and development capabilities, and now forms an integral part of the modern pharmaceutical manufacturing process.

While this strategy provides pharmaceutical companies with the opportunity to overcome some of the commercial pressures prevalent within the industry, it does at the same time, necessitate a fresh perspective on how R&D must be organised and managed. This is because fundamentally, outsourcing effectively implies a departure from many of the conventional R&D practices of the firm. Therefore having examined the dynamics of the pharmaceutical industry, the nature and role of outsourcing, and the strategic imperatives it raises for the firm, the most salient findings and conclusions of this book can be summarised as follows:

- *Change in R&D methodologies*

A shift towards biology as the primary science as opposed to the more traditional discipline of organic chemistry has taken place. Consequently, the methodologies employed in pharmaceutical research and development has also changed. This implies that the key competencies required for discovering and developing new products are now fundamentally different. Today, the technology and skills required to produce new innovations are no longer to be found within the exclusive domain of the pharmaceutical firm given that resources are widely dispersed amongst external agents such as the biotechnology sector. This advancement in the scientific base has therefore given rise to a new model for researching and developing compounds.

- *The industry cannot sustain historic levels of growth*

On account of increasing pressure on pharmaceutical earnings caused by pricing constraints due to government policies and generic competition, and the rising cost of R&D brought about by growing legislative requirements and technological sophistication; rapid advances in the field of science and technology have made it impossible for even the largest pharmaceutical firm to conduct internally, all activities linked to the R&D process. The ability to conduct pure in-house research is no longer an option. First, it is now impossible to assemble under one roof all the skills required along the R&D spectrum, and second, the total R&D cost of assembling all the necessary skills and resources is unaffordable. Furthermore, the rise of the cost-conscious consumer has required the industry to demonstrate 'value' to its customers. These combined factors, have therefore compelled pharmaceutical firms to adopt a number of cost-containment measures in the light of growing difficulty of sustaining historic levels of growth.

- *The formation of networks and collaborative agreements*

Traditionally, the R&D activities of the pharmaceutical firm were kept within the boundaries of the organisation, with various forms of collaborative agreements seen as second best to conducting these activities alone. Because of the increasing speed and mounting cost of innovation, the shortening of product life cycles, and the simultaneous and systematic rise in the cost of launching a new product, complete independence is no longer possible. Today, the innovator is no longer the individual firm but rather a group of networked agents with both complementary as well as heterogeneous skills and assets. External organisations have taken on the role of suppliers of innovative activity, and as a result, pharmaceutical innovation is no longer exclusively contained within the domain of in-house research. Pharmaceutical organisations are therefore engaging in an ever-increasing number of partnership and sourcing arrangements.

- *A division of labour*

Such changes have also led to a division of labour within the pharmaceutical industry given that knowledge and capability are no longer exclusively contained within a single firm. The evolution in pharmaceutical R&D has meant that different firms now possess different comparative advantages, resulting in a stronger focus on specific competencies. Accordingly, the industry has witnessed a move towards specialisation amongst firms.

- *Emergence of a new R&D management ethos*

Corresponding to the needs of the pharmaceutical industry, a supplier industry has emerged and this has led to the emergence of a symbiotic relationship between the two sectors. The impact of these changes to long established business practices has been to transform the relative importance of different activities and processes within the pharmaceutical firm. For the most part, managers of R&D were predisposed to focussing much of their effort on the effective management of the internal R&D competencies and resources of the firm. The adoption of outsourcing as an extension to the R&D process has therefore served to re-organise the parameters within which conventional R&D management was set. Through outsourcing, the fundamental challenge that arises is the ability to successfully construct and manage a portfolio of collaborators that would enable access to the emerging science and technology, as well as the required organisational capabilities. This challenge is fundamental given that managers of pharmaceutical R&D did not previously have to manage extra-organisational processes brought about through collaboration.

- *Tactical outsourcing: the raison d'être*

Outsourcing essentially represents a departure from the traditional business practices of the firm. Given the historic nature of the pharmaceutical industry and the novelty of this approach to drug delivery, it is natural that a number of misapprehensions exist about the outsourcing process, particularly in terms of effective project management and evaluation, and dependency upon the supplier given that the pharmaceutical industry has traditionally prided itself on being at the cutting-edge of scientific development through the efforts of its own in-house research. If outsourcing is to take on a more pivotal role within pharmaceutical R&D, then a fundamental change to the prevailing mind-set of R&D managers must take place.

- *Re-inventing the outsourcing process: key challenges*

A key challenge for managers of pharmaceutical R&D is to discover how best to manage these sourcing agreements with external agents. What has emerged for the pharmaceutical industry is that the traditional skills and competencies upon which the industry was built is shifting rapidly, with an array of new expertise required for commercial success. These competencies include networking and partnering skills, project and knowledge management, and the ability to manage across 'virtual' organisations. Most importantly, pharmaceutical managers must also have the capacity to channel these combined resources into delivering value to the production process and to the organisation as a whole. Inevitably, strategic outsourcing tacitly implies capabilities across all these areas of expertise.

- *Important considerations*

The successful execution of an outsourcing project requires detailed planning and dedicated expertise especially since the contracting of external sources necessitates the re-organisation of conventional business practices, and an awareness and willingness to supporting change. For management, this makes the understanding of a number of critical success factors pertinent to sound project management essential:

1. Management must understand that outsourcing does not absolve the organisation from its project management duties. Although responsibility for the specific function moves from within the organisation to an external service provider, the contracting firm still remains accountable for ensuring the effective management of the outsourced project;
2. Outsourcing should not be viewed as an instrument for alleviating problems experienced within the organisation given that problems experienced internally will not be resolved simply because a function is outsourced;
3. The outsourcing effort must be strategic in nature and be in line with the overall strategic objectives of the firm;
4. The decision to outsource must be initiated by a systematic analysis of what the firm's core competencies are, so that existing strengths can be nurtured while selectively outsourcing remaining functions to specialist suppliers;
5. If the sourcing arrangement is to be effectively managed, the pharmaceutical firm must possess the necessary skills, knowledge and resources to successfully monitor, manage and assess the service(s) provided. The pharmaceutical firm must therefore implement the outsourcing agreement with a comprehensive plan outlining detailed expectations, requirements and potential outcomes;
6. The firm must create a management structure that will work with the new organisational arrangement, as well as achieve a new mind set that will encourage innovation, communication, co-operation, learning and trust amongst partners. This is particularly important given that this particular type of partnering cannot be implanted onto traditional ways of thinking and behaving, nor can it be achieved through changes in structure alone.
7. Since outsourcing entails a significant learning curve, organisational learning and a willingness to learn must be actively encouraged between all parties involved;

8. Outsourcing must not be viewed as a singular effort to improving a particular business function or process but as a partnership between buyer and supplier;
9. The outsourcing of pharmaceutical R&D is not a temporary phenomenon. Due to advances in science, and the wider proliferation of knowledge, it will become an even more integral part of the modern pharmaceutical research and development process. Therefore a thorough understanding of the nature of the process and its implications are required if synergy is to be achieved.

This book has attempted to:

- *Examine* the operating environment of the pharmaceutical industry,
- *Assess* the role of outsourcing within the pharmaceutical product development process,
- *Identify* the critical success factors required for effective partnership management,
- *Determine* the impact that outsourcing has had on conventional R&D organisation,
- *Propose* solutions in the form of the Strategic Sourcing Model.

It is clear that a profound technological shift has taken place in the evolution of the pharmaceutical industry, which has fundamentally and irreversibly altered its composition and direction. The industry has witnessed the birth of a new type of supplier relationship, in which large organisations whose core competencies lie in marketing and the co-ordination of development activities, now contract the services of small, innovative suppliers. The emergence of outsourcing has provided a mechanism through which pharmaceutical organisations are better able to cope with the pressures of modern drug development, and it has come to act as an extension of the pharmaceutical research and development process. Most importantly, the adoption of outsourcing has tacitly implied a fundamental change to the ways in which pharmaceutical R&D has traditionally been organised and managed.

While progress has been made towards reaching a better understanding of the competencies required for this form of collaborative R&D, continuous learning of the necessary partnership principles is essential. This book has served to highlight the critical success factors required, from the perspective of the pharmaceutical firm, for effectively managing the outsourcing relationship. However if there is to be a comprehensive understanding of the dynamics of the buyer–supplier relationship, it is imperative that similar research be carried out into the outsourcing practices of the pharmaceutical industry's smaller suppliers – that of biotechnology and clinical research organisations. Only once a greater understanding of the needs of these firms *vis-à-vis* their larger pharmaceutical partners has been ascertained can there be an optimal coming together of both buyer and supplier in the research and development environment of the pharmaceutical industry.

Bibliography

Academic papers

D.L. Alexander, J.E. Flynn and L.A. Linkins, 'Innovation, R&D Productivity and Global Market Share in the Pharmaceutical Industry', *Review of Industrial Organisation*, 10 (1995), pp. 197–207.

S.G. Amin, A.F. Hagen and C.R. Sterrett, 'Co-operating to Achieve Competitive Advantage in a Global Economy: Review and Trends', *SAM Advanced Management Journal*, 60, Issue 4 (1995), pp. 37–41.

J.C. Anderson and J.A. Narus, 'Partnering as a Focused Market Strategy', *California Management Review*, 33, Issue 3 (1991), pp. 95–113.

A. Arora and A. Gambardella, 'Complementarity and External Linkages: The Strategies of Large Firms in Biotechnology', *Journal of Industrial Economics*, 38, Issue 4 (1990), pp. 361–79.

P.Y. Barreyre, 'The Concept of Impartation Policies: A Different Approach to Vertical Integration Strategies', *Strategic Management Journal*, 9, Issue 5 (1998), pp. 507–20.

R.A. Bettis, P. Bradley and G. Hamel, 'Outsourcing and Industrial Decline', *Academy of Management Executive*, 6, Issue 1 (1992), pp. 7–23.

D. Blumenthal, N. Causino, E. Campbell and K.S. Louis, 'Relationships between Academic Institutions and Industry in the Life Sciences: An Industry Survey', *New England Journal of Medicine*, 334, Issue 6 (1996), pp. 368–73.

F.P. Boer, 'R&D Planning Environment for the 90s: America and Japan', *Research Technology Management*, 34, Issue 2 (1991), pp. 12–15.

S. Bone, 'R&D Outsourcing', *International Journal of Physical Distribution & Logistics Management*, 26, Issue 7 (1996), pp. 3–6.

N. Bosanquet, 'From Prairie to Garden: Where Next for Pharmaceuticals in Europe?' *European Business Journal*, 6, Issue 4 (1994), pp. 39–49.

R. Boscheck, 'Healthcare Reform and the Restructuring of the Pharmaceutical Industry', *International Journal of Strategic Management: Long Range Planning*, 29, Issue 5 (1996), pp. 629–42.

D.J. Bowersox, 'The Strategic Benefits of Logistics Alliances', *Harvard Business Review*, 68, Issue 4 (1990), pp. 36–43.

D. Chatterji and T.A. Manuel, 'Benefiting from External Sources of Technology', *Research Technology Management*, 36, Issue 6 (1993), pp. 21–6.

D. Chatterji, 'Accessing External Sources of Technology', *Research Technology Management*, 39, Issue 2 (1996), pp. 48–56.

P. Chaudhry, P. Dacin and J.P. Peter, 'The Pharmaceutical Industry and European Community Integration', *European Management Journal*, 12, Issue 4 (1994), pp. 442–53.

V. Chiesa, 'Separating Research from Development: Evidence from the Pharmaceutical Industry', *European Management Journal*, 14, Issue 6 (1996), pp. 638–47.

V. Chiesa and R. Manzini, 'Managing Virtual R&D Organisations: Lessons from the Pharmaceutical Industry', *International Journal of Technology Management*, 13, Issue 5/6 (1997), pp. 471–85.

V. Chiesa and R. Manzini, 'Organising for Technological Collaborations: A Managerial Perspective', *R&D Management*, 28, Issue 3 (1998), pp. 199–212.

W. Cohen and D. Levinthal, 'Innovation and Learning: The Two Faces of R&D', *Economic Journal*, 99 (1989), pp. 569–96.

W.A. Colburn, J.E. McClurg and J.R. Cichoracki, 'The Strategic Role of Outsourcing: CROs and the Outsourcing Phenomenon', *Applied Clinical Trials*, 6, Issue 9 (1997), pp. 68–75.

D.J. Collis, 'How Valuable are Organisational Capabilities?', *Strategic Management Journal*, 15, Special Issue (1994), pp. 143–52.

R. Coombs, 'Core Competencies and the Strategic Management of R&D', *R&D Management*, 26, Issue 4 (1996), pp. 345–55.

D.A. Daniel, N. Nanjo-Jones, J. Kirwin and S.A. Stempien, 'Outsourcing Management in the Pharmaceutical Industry: The Early Stages at Four United States Companies', *Drug Information Journal*, 31, Issue 1 (1997), pp. 111–18.

F. Della Valle, and A. Gambardella, 'Biological Revolution and Strategies for Innovation in Pharmaceutical Companies', *R&D Management*, 23, Issue 4 (1993), pp. 287–302.

G. Devlin and M. Bleackly, 'Strategic Alliances: Guidelines for Success', *International Journal of Strategic Management: Long Range Planning*, 21, Issue 5 (1988), pp. 18–23.

J. Drews, 'Research in the Pharmaceutical Industry', *European Management Journal*, 7, Issue 1 (1989), pp. 23–30.

J. Drews and S. Ryser, 'Innovation Deficit in the Pharmaceutical Industry', *Drug Information Journal*, 30, Issue 1 (1996), pp. 97–108.

M.J. Earl, 'The Risks of Outsourcing IT', *Sloan Management Review*, 37, Issue 3 (1996), pp. 26–32.

D.M. Eisenberg, R.B. Davis and S.L. Ettner, 'Trends in Alternative Medicine Use in the United States 1990–1997: Results of a Follow-up National Survey', *Journal of the American Medical Association*, 280, Issue 19 (1998), pp. 1569–75.

K.M. Eisenhardt, 'Agency Theory: An Assessment and Review', *Academy of Management Review*, 14, Issue 1 (1989), pp. 57–74.

L.M. Ellram, 'A Managerial Guideline for the Development and Implementation of Purchasing Partnerships', *International Journal of Purchasing and Materials Management*, 27, Issue 2 (1991), pp. 2–8.

D. Elmuti, Y. Kathawala and M. Monippallil, 'Outsourcing to Gain a Competitive Advantage', *Industrial Management*, 40, Issue 3 (1998), pp. 20–4.

G. Fairlough, 'A Marriage of Large and Small: R&D for Healthcare Products', *Business Strategy Review*, 7, Issue 2 (1996), pp. 14–23.

J.E. Forrest and M.J. Martin, 'Strategic Alliances between Large and Small Research Intensive Organisations: Experiences in the Biotechnology Industry', *R&D Management*, 22, Issue 1 (1992), pp. 41–54.

L. Galambos and J.L. Sturchio, 'Pharmaceutical Firms and the Transition to Biotechnology: A Study in Strategic Innovation', *Business History Review*, 72, Issue 2 (1998), pp. 250–78.

A. Gambardella, 'Competitive Advantages from In-house Scientific Research: The US Pharmaceutical Industry in the 1980s', *Research Policy*, 21, Issue 5 (1992), pp. 391–407.

J. Gantz, 'Outsourcing: Threat or Salvation?' *Networking Management*, 8, Issue 10 (1990), pp. 25–40.

A.K. Gupta and D. Wilemon, 'Changing Patterns in Industrial R&D Development', *Journal of Product Innovation Management*, 13, Issue 6 (1996), pp. 497–511.

R. Henderson, and I. Cockburn, 'Scale, Scope and Spill-Overs: The Determinants of Research Productivity in Drug Discovery', *Rand Journal of Economics*, 27, Issue 1 (1996), pp. 32–59.

L.G. Herbiniak, 'Implementing Global Strategies', *European Management Journal*, 10, Issue 4 (1994), pp. 392–403.

J. Howells, 'Research and Technology Outsourcing', *Technology Analysis and Strategic Management*, 11, Issue 1 (1999), pp. 17–29.

M.C. Jensen, 'Eclipse of the Public Corporation', *Harvard Business Review*, 67, Issue 5 (1989), pp. 61–74.

D. Jennings, 'Strategic Guidelines for Outsourcing Decisions', *Strategic Change*, 6, Issue 2 (1997), pp. 85–95.

R.S. Jonash, 'Strategic Technology Leveraging: Making Outsourcing Work for You', *Research Technology Management*, 39, Issue 2 (1996), pp. 19–25.

K.I. Kaitin and H. Houben, 'Worthwhile Persistence: The Process of Developing New Drugs', *Odyssey: The GlaxoWellcome Journal of Innovation in Healthcare*, 1, Issue 3 (1995), pp. 54–59.

B. Kogut, 'Joint Ventures: Theoretical and Empirical Perspectives', *Strategic Management Journal*, 9, Issue 4 (1988), pp. 319–32.

B. Kogut, 'Designing Global Strategies: Comparative and Competitive Value-added Chains', *Sloan Management Review*, 26, Issue 4 (1995), pp. 15–27.

T. Kumpe and P.T. Bolwijn, 'Toward the Innovative Firm: Challenge for R&D Management', *Research Technology Management*, 37, Issue 1 (1994), pp. 38–44.

M.C. Lacity, L.P. Willcocks and D.F. Feeny, 'IT Outsourcing: Maximise Flexibility and Control', *Harvard Business Review*, 73, Issue 3 (1995), pp. 84–93.

M.C. Lacity, L.P. Willcocks and D.F. Feeny, 'The Value of Selective IT Sourcing', *Sloan Management Review*, 37, Issue 3 (1996), pp. 13–25.

R.S.M. Lau and C.N. Hurley, 'Outsourcing Through Strategic Alliances', *Production and Inventory Management Journal*, 38, Issue 2 (1997), pp. 6–10.

B. Leavy, 'Outsourcing Strategy and a Learning Dilemma', *Production and Inventory Management Journal*, 37, Issue 4 (1996), pp. 50–2.

J.M. Liebenau, 'International R&D in Pharmaceutical Firms in the Early Twentieth Century', *Business History*, 26 (1984), pp. 329–46.

J.M. Liedtka, Collaborating across Lines of Business for Competitive Advantage', *The Academy of Management Executive*, 10, Issue 2 (1996), pp. 20–35.

D. Littler and F. Leverick, 'Joint Ventures for Product Development: Learning from Experience', *International Journal of Strategic Management: Long Range Planning*, 28, Issue 3 (1995), pp. 58–67.

R.P. Lynch, 'Building Alliances to Penetrate European Markets', *The Journal of Business Strategy*, 11, Issue 2 (1990), pp. 4–8.

M.P. Lyons, 'Joint Ventures as Strategic Choice: A Literature Review', *International Journal of Strategic Management: Long Range Planning*, 24, Issue 4 (1991), pp. 130–44.

T.W. Malone, M.S. Scot-Morton and R.R. Halperin, 'Organising for the Twenty-First Century', *Strategy & Leadership*, 24, Issue 4 (1996), pp. 6–11.

J.C. Mason, 'Strategic Alliances: Partnering for Success', *Management Review*, 82, Issue 5 (1993), pp. 10–15.

A. McGahan, 'Industry Structure and Competitive Advantage', *Harvard Business Review*, 72, Issue 6 (1994), pp. 115–24.

J.W. Medcof, 'Why Too Many Alliances End in Divorce', *International Journal of Strategic Management: Long Range Planning*, 30, Issue 5 (1997), pp. 718–32.

R.R. Miles and C.C. Snow, 'Causes of Failure in Network Organisations', *California Management Review*, 34, Issue 4 (1992), pp. 53–72.

M.R. Millson, S.P. Raj and D. Wilemon, 'Strategic Partnering for Developing New Products', *Research Technology Management*, 39, Issue 3 (1996), pp. 41–9.

D.C. Mowery, 'Firm Structure, Government Policy and the Organisation of Industrial Research: Great Britain and the United States: 1900 to 1950', *Business History Review*, 58 (1980), pp. 504–31.

R. Mullin, 'Managing the Outsourced Enterprise', *Journal of Business Strategy*, 7, Issue 4 (1996), pp. 28–36.

R. Nelson, 'Recent Evolutionary Theorising about Economic Change', *Journal of Economic Literature*, 33, Issue 1 (1995), pp. 48–90.

G.E. Pake, 'Business Payoff from Basic Science at Xerox', *Research Technology Management*, 29, Issue 6 (1986), pp. 35–40.

A. Parkhe, 'Inter-Firm Diversity, Organisational Learning and Longevity in Global Strategic Alliances', *Journal of International Business Studies*, 22, Issue 4, pp. 579–601.

B. Piachaud and F. Moustakis, 'Is there a Valid Case for Mergers within the Defence and Pharmaceutical Industries? A Qualitative Analysis', *Journal of World Affairs and New Technology*, 3, Issue 4 (2000), pp. 1–7.

B. Piachaud and M. Lynas, 'The Biotechnology Revolution: Implications for the Pharmaceutical Industry', *The International Journal of Biotechnology*, 2, Issue 3/4 (2001), pp. 350–61.

B. Piachaud, 'Challenges Facing the Pharmaceutical Industry: Factors Influencing Drug Choice and Strategy', *Contemporary Review*, 280, Issue 1634 (2002), pp. 152–7.

H.E. Post, 'Building a Strategy on Competencies', *The International Journal of Strategic Management: Long Range Planning*, 30, Issue 5 (1997), pp. 733–40.

W.W. Powell, K. Koput and L. Smith-Doerr, 'Inter-organisational Collaboration and the Locus of Innovation: Networks of Learning in Biotechnology', *Administrative Science Quarterly*, 41, Issue 1 (1996), pp. 116–45.

W.W. Powell, 'Learning from Collaboration: Knowledge and Networks in the Biotechnology and Pharmaceutical Industries', *California Management Review*, 40, Issue 3 (1998), pp. 228–40.

C.K. Prahalad, and G. Hamel, 'The Core Competence of the Corporation', *Harvard Business Review*, 68, Issue 3 (1990), pp. 79–91.

J.B. Quinn, T.L. Doorley and P.C. Paquette, 'Beyond Products: Service Based Strategies', *Harvard Business Review*, 68, Issue 2 (1990), pp. 58–67.

J.B. Quinn, T.L. Doorley and P.C. Paquette, 'Technology in Services: Rethinking Strategic Focus', *Sloan Management Review*, 31, Issue 2 (1990), pp. 79–88.

J.B. Quinn and F.G. Hilmer, 'Strategic Outsourcing', *Sloan Management Review*, 35, Issue 4 (1994), pp. 43–55.

P. Ranganath Nayak, 'Should you Outsource Product Development?', *Journal of Business Strategy*, 14, Issue 3 (1993), pp. 44–5.

C.E. Schillaci, 'Designing Successful Joint Ventures', *The Journal of Business Strategy*, 8, Issue 2 (1987), pp. 59–63.

F. Sen and A.H. Rubenstein, 'An Exploration of Factors Affecting the Integration of In-house R&D with External Technology Acquisition Strategies of a Firm', *IEEE Transactions on Engineering Management*, 37, Issue 4 (1990), pp. 246–58.

M. Sharpe, 'Outsourcing, Organisational Competitiveness and Work', *Journal of Labour Research*, 18, Issue 4 (1997), pp. 535–50.

J. Smith, 'Outsourcing as a Strategic Tool', *Competitive Intelligence Review*, 7, Issue 3 (1996), pp. 70–4.

P. Stonham, 'The Future of Strategy: An Interview with Gary Hamel', *European Management Journal*, 11, Issue 2 (1993), pp. 150–7.

J. Stuckey and D. White, 'When and When not to Vertically Integrate', *Sloan Management Review*, 34, Issue 3 (1993), pp. 71–84.

F. Tapon and M. Thong, 'Research Collaborations by Multi-National Orientated Pharmaceutical Firms: 1988–1997', *R&D Management*, 29, Issue 3 (1999), pp. 219–32.

C. Tarabusi and G. Vickery, 'Globalisation in the Pharmaceutical Industry, Part II', *International Journal of Health Services*, 28, Issue 2 (1998), pp. 281–303.

D.J. Teece, G. Pisano and A. Shuen, 'Dynamic Capabilities and Strategic Management', *Strategic Management Journal*, 18, Issue 7 (1997), pp. 509–34.

J. Thompson and B. Richardson, 'Strategic and Competitive Success: Towards a Model of the Comprehensively Competent Organisation', *Management Decision*, 34, Issue 2 (1996), pp. 5–19.

J.R. Vogel and M.I. Linzmayer, 'Achieving Results with Contract Research Organisations: Evaluating and Selecting CROs', *Applied Clinical Trials*, 2, Issue 8 (1993), pp. 36–41.

J.A. Welch and P. Ranganath Nayak, 'Strategic Sourcing: A Progressive Approach to the Make-or-Buy Decision', *The Academy of Management Executive*, 6, Issue 1 (1992), pp. 23–32.

E. Whittaker and J.D. Bower, 'A Shift to External Alliances for Product Development in the Pharmaceutical Industry', *R&D Management*, 24, Issue 3 (1994), pp. 249–61.

L.P. Willcocks, G. Fitzgerald and D.F. Feeny, 'Outsourcing IT: The Strategic Implications', *International Journal of Strategic Management, Long Range Planning*, 28, Issue 5 (1995), pp. 59–69.

H. William, 'Strategic Choices in Technology Management: Lessons from Biotechnology', *Review of Business*, 14, Issue 3 (1993), pp. 14–19.

M.F. Wolff, 'Building Trust in Alliances', *Research Technology Management*, 37, Issue 3 (1994), pp. 12–15.

Books

J. Anderson, R. Fears and B. Taylor (eds), *Managing Technology for Competitive Advantage* (London: Cartermill International & Financial Times Healthcare Publications, 1997).

R. Ballance, J. Pogany and H. Forstner, *The World's Pharmaceutical Industries* (London: Edward Elgar, 1992).

W. Bogner and H. Thomas, *Drugs to Market: Creating Value and Advantage in the Pharmaceutical Industry* (Oxford: Pergamon, 1996).

C. Bowman, and D. Faulkner, *Competitive and Corporate Strategy* (London: Irwin, 1997).

S.M. Bragg, *Outsourcing: A Guide to Selecting the Correct Business Unit, Negotiating the Contract and Maintaining Control of the Process* (New York: John Wiley and Sons Inc., 1998).

D. Cavalla, *Modern Strategy for Pre-Clinical Pharmaceutical R&D: Towards the Virtual Research Company* (Chichester: John Wiley and Sons, 1997).

J. Child, and D. Faulkner, *Strategies of Co-operation: Managing Alliances, Networks and Joint Ventures* (Oxford: Oxford University Press, 1998).

F.J. Contractor and P. Lorange (eds), *Co-operative Strategies in International Business* (New York: Lexington Books, 1988).

J.H. Dunning, *Economic Analysis and the Multinational Enterprise* (London: Allen and Unwin, 1974).

C. Freeman and L. Soete (eds), *New Explorations in the Economics of Technological Change* (London: Pinter Publications, 1990), pp. 3–37.

C. Freeman, M. Sharp and W. Walker (eds), *Technology and the Future of Europe: Global Competition and the Environment in the 1990s* (London: Pinter Publications, 1991).

A. Gambardella, *Science and Innovation: The US Pharmaceutical Industry during the 1980s* (Cambridge: Cambridge University Press, 1995).

C.L. Gay and J. Essinger, *Inside Outsourcing: The Insider's Guide to Managing Strategic Outsourcing* (London: Nicholas Brealey Publishing, 2000).

G. Hamel and A. Heene (eds), *Competence Based Competition: Towards the Roots of Sustainable Competitive Advantage* (Chichester: John Wiley and Sons, 1994).

E. Hoffer, *The Ordeal of Change* (New York: Harper and Row, 1963).

N. Hood and J.E. Vahlne (eds), *Strategies in Global Competition* (London: Routledge, 1988).

E. Hornell and G. Vickery (eds), *Technology and Investment: Crucial Issues for the 1990s* (London: Pinter Publications, 1990).

J. Howells and M. Wood, *The Globalisation of Production and Technology* (London: Belhaven Publishers, 1992).

P. Johnson (ed.), *European Industries: Structure, Conduct and Performance* (London: Edward Elgar, 1993), pp. 75–100.

R.M. Kanter, *When Giants Learn to Dance* (New York: Simon and Schuster, 1989).

J.L. Kay, *Foundations of Corporate Success* (Oxford: Oxford University Press, 1993).

R. Klepper and W. Jones, *Outsourcing Information Technology, Systems and Services* (New York: Prentice Hall, 1997).

D. Leonard-Barton, *Wellsprings of Knowledge: Building and Sustaining the Sources of Innovation* (Cambridge: Harvard University Press, 1995).

A.J. Marcella, *Outsourcing, Downsizing and Re-Engineering: Internal Control Implications* (Florida: The Institute of Internal Auditors, 1995).

K.R. Maromonte, *Corporate Strategic Business Sourcing* (Connecticut: Quorum Books, 1998).

B. Moingeon and A. Edmondson (eds), *Organisational Learning and Competitive Advantage* (London: Sage Publications, 1996).

D.C. Mowery (ed.), *International Collaborative Ventures in US Manufacturing* (New York: Ballinger Publications, 1988).

N. Nohria and E. Eccles (eds), *Networks and Organisations* (Cambridge: Harvard University Press, 1992), pp. 314–47.

J. Pfeffer and G.R. Salancik, *The External Control of Organisations: A Resource Dependence Perspective* (New York: Harper and Row, 1978).

M.E. Porter, *Competitive Strategy: Techniques for Analysing Industries and Competitors* (New York: Free Press, 1980).

M.E. Porter, *Competitive Advantage: Creating and Sustaining Superior Performance* (New York: Free Press, 1985).

M.E. Porter (ed.), *Competition in Global Industries* (Cambridge: Harvard University Press, 1985).

S. Pradhan, *International Pharmaceutical Marketing* (Westport: Quorum Books, 1983).

J.B. Quinn (ed.), *Intelligent Enterprise: A Knowledge and Service Based Paradigm for Industry* (New York: Free Press, 1992).

J. Ronen (ed.), *Entrepreneurship* (London: Lexington Books, 1983).

P.A. Roussel, K.N. Saad, and T.J. Erickson, *Third Generation R&D* (Cambridge: Harvard University Press, 1991).

R. Rumelt, *Strategy, Structure and Economic Performance* (Cambridge: Harvard University Press, 1974).

D. Schwartzmann, *Innovation in the Pharmaceutical Industry* (Baltimore: John Hopkins University Press, 1976).

L. Segil, *Intelligent Business Alliances: How to Profit Using Today's Most Important Strategic Tool* (London: Century Business, 1996).

J. Taggart, *The World Pharmaceutical Industry* (London: Routledge, 1993).

P. Temin, *Taking your Medicine: Drug Regulation in the United States* (Cambridge: Harvard University Press, 1980).

B. Twiss, *Managing Technological Innovation*, Fourth Edition (London: Pitman Publishers, 1992).

H. Walker, *Market Power and Price Levels in the Ethical Drugs Industry* (Indianapolis: Indiana University Press, 1971).

O. Williamson, *Markets and Hierarchies: Analysis and Antitrust Implications* (New York: Free Press, 1975).

Conference proceedings

S. Barabaschi, 'From In-house R&D to a Multi Channel Knowledge Acquisition System', in *European Industrial Research Management Association (EIRMA) Annual Conference*, Mastering the Growth of Scientific and Technological Information, Conference Proceedings, Berlin (1990), pp. 80–8.

A.G. Bodnar, 'Strategic Alliances for Research', in *Financial Times Annual World Pharmaceuticals Conference*, Conference Proceedings, London (1990), pp. 5.1–5.4.

N. Brancaccio, 'Outsourcing in Drug Development: A Strategic Opportunity', in *Outsource '98*, Conference Proceedings, San Francisco (1998), pp. 1–9.

J. Fromson, 'What is Needed from a CRO: Compare and Contrast the Requirements of a Large Multinational with Venture Capitalist Type Companies', in the *6th International Conference on Contract Research Organisations*, Conference Proceedings, Amsterdam (1995), pp. 57–64.

M.E. Gordon, 'Strategic Alliances in the Pharmaceutical Industry: A Qualitative Examination', in *American Marketing Association (AMA) Educators Conference*, Enhancing Knowledge Development in Marketing, Conference Proceedings, Illinois (1995), pp. 553–8.

S. Griggs, 'Why Use Contract Services?', in *Interphase '93*, Conference Proceedings, Utrecht (1993).

G. Haas, 'Increasing Effectiveness in Pharmaceutical R&D', in *European Industrial Research Management Association (EIRMA) Conference*, The Evolution of Industrial R&D, Conference Proceedings, Venice (1997), pp. 85–92.

M. Jawadekar, 'Approach to Managing Strategic Outsourcing of R&D Projects', in *Pharmaceutical Technology Europe Conference*, Conference Proceedings, Düsseldorf (1998).

M. Pilbeam, 'Outsourcing R&D', in *European Industrial Research Management Association (EIRMA) Annual Conference*, The Evolution of Industrial R&D, Conference Proceedings, Venice (1997), pp. 99–104.

W. Schaub, 'Resources and Needs of a Multinational Pharmaceutical Company', in the *6th International Conference on Contract Research Organisations Conference*, Conference Proceedings, Amsterdam (1995).

M. Sharp and P. Patel, 'Europe's Pharmaceutical Industry: An Innovation Profile', in A. Arundel and R. Garrelfs (eds), *Innovation Measurement and Policies*, Conference Proceedings, Luxembourg (1996), pp. 163–8.

Internet sources

Association of the British Pharmaceutical Industry (ABPI), 'Facts and Statistics from the Pharmaceutical Industry: Pharmaceuticals and the UK Economy' (London: ABPI, 2003), *http://www.abpi.org.uk/statistics/section.asp?sect=2*

L. Blumberg, 'How to Engage in a Strategic Sourcing Relationship', The Warren Company (1999), *http://www.outsourcing.com/articles/strategicoutsourcing/main.html*

European Federation of Pharmaceutical Industries and Associations (EFPIA), 'The Pharmaceutical Industry in Figures: 2003 Update' (Brussels: EFPIA, 2003), *http://www.efpia.org/6_publ/Infigures2003.pdf*

European Federation of Pharmaceutical Industries and Associations (EFPIA), 'Did You Know That?' (Brussels: EFPIA, 2003), *http://www.efpia.org/2_industdidyouknow2.htm*

Pharmaceutical Research and Manufacturers of America (PhRMA), 'Pharmaceutical Industry Profile 2003' (Washington, DC: PhRMA, 2003), *http://www.phrma.org/publications/publications/profile02/index.cfm*

The European Patent Office, 'Supplementary Protection Certificates in INPADOC', *http://www.european-patent-office.org/news/epidosnews/source/ epd_2_01/4_2_01_e.htm*

The Outsourcing Institute, 'Managing the Outsourcing Relationship: A Shared Vision Produces Greater Rewards', *http://www.outsourcing.com/content.asp?page=01i/articles/process/tarsh_managing_outsourcing.html&nonav=true*

D.E. Wierenga and C.E. Eaton, 'The Drug Development and Approval Process', Office of Research and Development, Pharmaceutical Research Association (1999), *http:www.allp.com*

Magazines and industry publications

'Why the Tough need Acquisitions to Keep Going', *Mergers & Acquisitions*, 28, Issue 6 (1994), pp. 11–19.

'Pharmaceutical Companies Confront High Costs of Drug Development', *R&D*, 38, Issue 11 (1996), pp. 17.
'Reducing Time to Drug Discovery', *Combinatorial Chemistry*, 77, Issue 10 (1999), pp. 33–48.
'The Sequence of the Human Genome', *Science Magazine*, 291, Issue 5507 (2001), pp. 1304–51.
R. Arnold and J. Grindley, 'Matchmaking: Identifying and Evaluating Drug Discovery Partners', *Drug Discovery Today*, 1, Issue 79 (1996).
D. Boath, P. Hess and C. Munch, 'Virtual R&D: A Core Competency Approach to Outsourcing', *Pharmaceutical Executive*, 16, Issue 6 (1996), pp. 72–8.
J. Drews, 'Pharmaceutical Industry in Transition', *Drug News and Perspectives*, 5, Issue 3 (1992), pp. 133–8.
M. Dodgson, 'Learning, Trust and Technological Collaboration', *Human Relations*, 46, Issue 1 (1993), pp. 77–95.
H. Graham and G. Hunter, 'Its All in the Contract', *Human Resources Magazine*, 33 (1997), pp. 73–6.
P. Van Arnum, 'The R&D Race is on', *Chemical Market Reporter*, 256, Issue 7 (1999), pp. 1–7.
M.E. Watanabe, 'Research-for-Hire Companies Proliferate', *The Scientist*, 9, Issue 24 (1995), pp. 4–5.

Newspapers

'Consolidation Enters a More Frantic Phase: Pharmaceutical Companies Face Increasing Pressures to Merge', *Financial Times*, 15 March 1999.
C. Cookson, 'Research and Development: Industry is Aiming for Harder Target', *Financial Times*, 24 April 1997.

Research reports and occasional reports

International Federation of Pharmaceutical Manufacturers Association (IFPMA), *The Question of Patents: The Key to Medical Progress and Industrial Development* (Geneva, IFPMA, 1998).
Lehman Brothers Report, *Pharma Pipelines* (London: Lehman Brothers, 1996).
Management Today Report, *Outsourcing Strategies: The UK Outsourcing Report* (London: Management Today, 2000).
National Institute for Health Care Management (NIHCM), *A Primer: Generic Drugs, Patents and the Pharmaceutical Industry* (Washington DC: NICHAM, 2002).
PriceWaterhouse Coopers Report, *Pharmaceutical Sector Global Market and Deal Survey* (London: PriceWaterhouse Coopers, 1997).
PriceWaterhouse Coopers Healthcare Report, *Pharma 2005: An Industrial Revolution in R&D* (London: PriceWaterhouse Coopers Healthcare Publishing, 1998).
Scrip Report, *Strategic Management of R&D in the Pharmaceutical Industry* (London: PJB Publications Limited, 1995).
United Nations Centre on Transnational Corporations (UNCTC), *Transnational Corporations and the Pharmaceutical Industry: Introduction and Summary of Findings* (New York: United Nations, 1979).

P.S. Briggs, *Major Mergers in the Pharmaceutical Industry,* Scrip Reports (London: PJB Publications Limited, 1993).

M.L. Burstall, *Research on the Costs of Non-Europe: Basic Findings* (Brussels: Economists Advisory Group, 1992).

M.L. Burstall, *1992 and the Regulation of the Pharmaceutical Industry* (London: The IEA Health and Welfare Unit, 1990).

R. Caines (ed.), *Keynote Market Review: The UK Pharmaceutical Industry,* Second Edition (London, 1995).

D. Harnden and D. MacArthur, *The Management of Pharmaceutical R&D: The Keys to Success,* Scrip Reports (London: PJB Publications Limited, 1990).

R. Hughes and C.E. Lumley (eds) *Current Strategies and Future Prospects in Pharmaceutical Outsourcing* (London: Technomark Consulting Services Limited and the Centre for Medicines Research International, 1999).

B.G. James, *The Pharmaceutical Industry in 2000: Reinventing the Pharmaceutical Company* (London: The Economic Intelligence Unit, 1994).

T. Jones, *The Chances of Market Success in Pharmaceutical Research and Development* (London: Office of Health Economics, 1999).

E. Konecny, C.P. Quinn, K. Sachs and D.P. Thompson, *Universities and Industrial Research* (Cambridge: The Royal Society of Chemistry, 1995).

F. Leverick and D.A. Littler, *The Risks and Rewards of Collaboration: A Survey of Collaborative Product Development in UK Companies',* Manchester School of Management, Manchester University, Manchester (1993).

D. MacArthur, *Optimising the Use of Contract Services by the Pharmaceutical Industry,* Scrip Reports (London: PJB Publications Limited, 1994).

R. McNeil, *Pharmaceutical Strategies: Class Acts* (London: Financial Times Health and Healthcare Publishing, 1996).

P. Taafe, *Outsourcing in the Pharmaceutical Industry* (London: Financial Times Health and Healthcare Publishing, 1996).

Working papers and occasional papers

A. Arora, and A. Gambardella, 'New Trends in Technological Change: Towards an Innovative Division of Labour', *Working Paper No: 92–37,* John Heinz III, School of Public Policy and Management, Carnegie Mellon University, Pittsburgh (1992), pp. 259–77.

M. Brannback, J. Nasi and M. Renko 'Technological, Structural and Strategic Change in the Global Pharmaceutical Industry: The Finnish Biotechnology Industry', *Unpublished Papers,* Turku School of Economics and Business Administration, Tampere University of Technology and Industrial Management, Tampere (2001), pp. 1–26.

H. Buhariwala and J. Hassard, 'Strategic Research and Development: Towards Co-operative Agreements in the Pharmaceutical Industry', *Working Paper No: 91–21,* Department of Economics and Management Science, University of Keel, Staffordshire (1991), pp. 1–23.

T. Corley, 'The British Pharmaceutical Industry Since 1851', *Discussion Paper,* XII, Series A, Centre for International Business History, University of Reading, Reading (2000), pp. 1–33.

P. Ramirez and A. Tylecote, 'Technological Change in the Pharmaceutical Industry: A Literature Review from the Point of View of Corporate Governance', *Unpublished Papers*, Sheffield University Management School, University of Sheffield, Sheffield (1999), pp. 1–35.

M. Sharp, 'The New Biotechnology: European Governments in Search of a Strategy', *Working Paper No: 15*, Science Policy Research Unit, University of Sussex, Sussex (1985).

M. Sharp, 'Collaboration and the Pharmaceutical Industry: Is it the Way Forward?', *Unpublished Papers*, Science Policy Research Unit, University of Sussex, Sussex (1989), pp. 1–33.

F. Tapon and M. Thong, 'Outsourcing of Research by Pharmaceutical and Biotechnology Firms: 1988–1996', *Working Paper No: 1997–2*, Department of Economics, University of Guelph, Ontario (1997), pp. 1–52.

F. Todtling, 'Firm Strategies and Restructuring in a Globalising Economy', *IIR Discussion Paper No: 53* (1995), pp. 1–15.

Index